Health, Wealth and Housing

Aspects of Social Policy
General editor: J. P. Martin
Professor of Sociology and Social Administration,
University of Southampton

The Poverty Business: Britain and America
JOAN HIGGINS

Provision for the Disabled
EDA TOPLISS

Efficiency in the Social Services
ALAN WILLIAMS *and* ROBERT ANDERSON

Capitalism and Social Welfare: A Comparative Study
ROGER LAWSON

Alternative Strategies for Coping with Crime
edited by NORMAN TUTT

Reorganizing the National Health Service
A Case Study of Administrative Change
R. G. S. BROWN

The Social Context of Health Care
PAUL BREARLEY, AGNES MILES, EDA TOPLISS,
GRAHAM WOODS, JANE GIBBONS

Understanding Social Policy
MICHAEL HILL

The Sociology of Welfare
Social Policy, Stratification and Political Order
GRAHAM ROOM

Reserved for the Poor
The Means Test in British Social Policy
ERIC BRIGGS *and* ALAN DEACON

The Family, the State and the Labour Market
HILARY LAND

Planning for Welfare
Social Policy and the Expenditure Process
edited by TIMOTHY A. BOOTH

Comparing Social Policies
JOAN HIGGINS

Health, Wealth and Housing

Edited by

R. A. B. LEAPER

BASIL BLACKWELL · OXFORD
MARTIN ROBERTSON · OXFORD

© Basil Blackwell 1980

First published in the United Kingdom by
Basil Blackwell Publisher Ltd
and by Martin Robertson and Co. Ltd

British Library Cataloguing in Publication Data

Health, wealth and housing. – (Aspects of social policy).
   1.   Great Britain – Social policy
   2.   Great Britain – Social conditions – 1945 –
I. Leaper, Robert Anthony Bernard   II. Series
300′.941   HN383.5

ISBN 0–631–10391–0
ISBN 0–631–12241–9 Pbk

Set in Great Britain by Vantage Photosetting Co. Ltd,
Southampton and London,
and printed by Billing and Sons Ltd,
London, Guildford and Worcester

Contents

Introduction

R. A. B. LEAPER

The substance of most of the chapters of this book has appeared as articles in recent issues of the journal *Social Policy and Administration* (formerly *Social and Economic Administration*). They have been up-dated and revised. Their raw material is the 'social services', and their coverage is health, housing, social security, and what are now known as the 'personal social services'. By the latter we refer here to the services provided since the 1970 Act by local authority social services departments in England and Wales ànd the social work departments in Scotland since 1968. The 'social services' cover a great deal more than social work. They may be defined as all collective provisions whose primary and immediate objective is to meet needs or solve problems which society recognizes as impossible or undesirable for individuals to meet adequately from their own resources or those of their immediate kin. The services are supported by collective funds, administered by designated institutionalized arrangements, and mostly staffed by professional and full-time workers. The study and critical assessment of their development and of the parallel services provided by independent initiative is the subject matter of social administration. Since social policy and administration emerged as a separately recognized subject of academic study about thirty years ago, we have moved beyond the rather simplistic description of the linear development of provisions to meet social needs. Recent literature in social administration has been much concerned with the inter-play of economic, social and political forces and the influence of professionals in social services.[1] This book is a contribution to the analysis of such processes and their outcomes.

The definition of 'social policy' has proved difficult for the authors of several books which bear the title.[2] There is a readiness to describe influences, to trace evolution, to advance ideological explanations of discerned tendencies, but a reluctance to define the essence of social policy. In this book we refer to social policy as a framework of generally acceptable social objectives often made explicit through social legislation and translated into a network of services. The services are intended to be of more than temporary duration and to have a fair measure of internal coherence. Apparent inconsistencies or illogicalities, either between one service and another or between services and declared objectives, are held to be justifiably subject to adverse criticism. There is, of course, disagreement about what the objectives of social policy ought to be, and their formulation will always be subject to debate and change in a democratic society. Underlying policy will not always be apparent or explicit from reviews of practice. Social analysts may claim to discern motives or undisclosed objectives implicit in policymakers' choice of priorities among competing claims for resource allocation. The diagnosis (still more the prescription) will depend upon the ideological stance of the investigator, whether declared or disguised. The study of social policy, therefore, involves the study of its determinants – political, social, economic and organizational. However, an apparently logical sequence model of setting objectives, deciding policy and organizing consequent services is unsatisfactory. The inter-play of policy and administration is complex and kaleidoscopic.[3]

In the opening chapters on social security ideological questions come immediately to the fore. Indeed, they run through almost all the chapters and in this book are not treated systematically or separately. Unfortunately, recent literature in this field is both assertive and unsatisfactory. 'Highly seductive have been the calls to join the hunt for a grand theory of social policy.'[4] Those who have the comfort of a total explanation need do no more than use the evidence of continuing human need and social provision as an introduction to a re-statement of their grand theme. But even those who are not satisfied with a blinkered analysis tend to impose upon social policy and administration macro-categories of explanation. These in turn fashion the evidence into shapes in the ideological potter's hands, ignoring the complex nature of the material in the effort to produce an intellectually satisfying symmetry. Tentative models of social policy are first advanced as useful means of analysing data, but are in danger of becoming fixed reference points against which social policy and provision must be measured and judged.[5] In a pluralistic society such as ours the classic theorists – Marx, Durkheim, Weber, Spencer are usually quoted – may provide intellectual stimulus (or total explanation for disciples) but are otherwise unsatisfactory as analytical tools of British social policy and administration. The complexity of social reality in our field may be more accurately analysed – and better prescriptions for meeting future social need worked out – by reference to what I may call middle-range social policy theorists. Reading R. H. Tawney and Richard Titmuss is far more relevant to the understanding of social policy since the war than is a study of Marx or Weber. A critical review of Hayek and Seldon is more productive, it can be argued, tha intellectual immersion in Spencer or the classical economists. Few recent writers seem inclined to enter the debate at this level of empirical thought and action, though Kathleen Jones' recent intro-ductory text[6] and Forder's framework for analysis in social administration[7] are hopeful steps in this direction. The student of ideological influences upon social policy may thus do better with a review of political ideas in modern Britain than with ambitious attempts to relate grand theories to social policy objectives and practice.

A study of the recent growth of our physical environment, and in particular of our housing policies, will illustrate in stark terms the problems of choice in social policy and administration. After Don-nison's broad over-view of urban development, Cooper and Staf-ford examine aspects of housing provision on which both of them have written widely as social economists. Probably in no other area of services is it more difficult to relate general statistics of provision and distribution to local situations and to the perception of workers in allied services. It is possible, for example, for a standard text on social work in Britain to affirm,

> The rate of house building fell every year from 1968 and private tenancies declined.... Social Services departments could do no more than relieve problems of homelessness: the only answer was more housing where it was most needed.... The provision of new housing, the demolition of outworn accommodation and abatement of overcrowding all failed to keep pace with the growth of population between 1950 and 1975.[8]

This may be compared with,

> Since the early 1960s, there has been a very substantial improvement in the overall supply of housing compared to demand . . . not only has the number of households sharing dwellings fallen substantially, but the number living in bad housing is also very much lower.[9]

There is qualification later in the same article from which the quotation comes, that

> A crude surplus of dwellings over households does not, of course, necessarily imply that there are too many houses.[10]

The contradiction between the assertions of the two writers is, however, striking: it is even more perplexing when one realizes that by the manipulation of data both writers may be partly correct in their analysis. Cooper and Stafford seek to bring some rationality into the controversies about housing in British society, where 54 per cent of the population are owner-occupiers (and where even more would like to be), and yet where homelessness (however defined) remains a social problem.

The chapters on the health services open with an assessment of the concerns and possible outcomes of the ambitious review of the National Health Service by the Royal Commission, whose report was published in July 1979 and has been widely discussed. The regulation of an old and key profession in any society involves disparate notions of the role and rights of individuals, professional groups, and society – which may have some unintended outcomes, as both Maynard and Jones show. Cooper raises a related question of the variable perception of need and its relationship to the use of services: an issue which brings into the field of play the element of personal choice and the many influences upon it. Some prescriptions for social provision lay great stress upon this element, whilst others minimize it or claim that it can be a cover for inadequate social provision, from which the most needy will suffer most.

We are left with the operational engineering. It used to be said that with the end of ideology that was all there is left to do. That view is no longer widely held, but the engineering remains to be done. Bebbington relates such considerations to a careful analysis of the changing needs of the elderly in society since 1965. Scrivens' contribution is to bring together some of the attempts that have been made to deal with the process of rationing in services where demand seems infinite and resources are bound to be limited, except at a stage of rapid economic expansion and increased disposable surplus. She invites us to move 'Towards a theory of rationing' if more legitimacy and logic are to be brought to social administration.

In social policy and administration policies and practices change quickly: the reference point of this book is the beginning of 1980.

Notes and References

1. For example, Hall, Land, Parker and Webb, *Change, Choice and Conflict in Social Policy*, Heinemann, 1975. Helmut Heisler (ed.), *Foundations of Social Administration*, Macmillan, 1977.
2. See Joyce Warham, *Social Policy in Context*, Batsford, 1970.
   Robert Pinker, *Social Theory and Social Policy*, Heinemann, 1971.
   T. H. Marshall, *Social Policy*, Hutchinson, 1970.
   Peter Townsend, *Sociology and Social Policy*, Allen Lane, 1975. In fairness it must be said that Townsend devotes several pages to reviewing possible definitions of social policy.
3. This discussion is carried further in R. A. B. Leaper, 'The British

Welfare State in its International Context' in *Human Well-being*, I.C.S.W. Vienna, 1978.

4. R. A. B. Leaper, *The Determinants of Social Policy*, University of Exeter Press, 1971.
5. Cf. Julia Parker, *Social Policy and Citizenship*, Macmillan, 1975.
   Ramesh Mishra, *Society and Social Policy*, Macmillan, 1977.
6. Kathleen Jones, *Issues in Social Policy*, R.K.P., 1978.
7. Anthony Forder, *Concepts in Social Administration*, R.K.P., 1974.
8. Eileen Younghusband, *Social Work in Britain 1950–75*, Allen and Unwin, 1978.
9. *Social Trends*, No. 9, Chapter on housing, H.M.S.O., 1979.
10. Ibid.
11. Report of the Royal Commission on the National Health Service. CMND. 7615. H.M.S.O. 1979.
    Also the shortened version – A Service for Patients. H.M.S.O., 1979.

PART I

Social Security

CHAPTER ONE

Social Assistance: A Watershed?

R. A. B. LEAPER

(1) It is thirty years since the passing of an Act of Parliament '. . . to terminate the existing poor law and to provide in lieu thereof for the assistance of persons in need by the National Assistance Board and by the local authorities'. The Act ensured that 'The existing poor law shall cease to have effect and shall be replaced by the provisions of Part II of this Act as to the rendering, out of moneys provided by Parliament, of assistance to persons in need. . . .'[1] The Board was 'to assist persons in Great Britain who are without resources to meet their requirements, or whose resources (including benefits received under the National Insurance Acts 1946) must be supplemented in order to meet their requirements.'[2] The Minister was to regulate the computation of requirements and resources, which were to be aggregated for the applicant and dependant members of the same household. Assistance grants were not to be paid to those in full-time work, and applicants could be required to register for employment if they were out of work and below retirement age. 'A man shall be liable to maintain his wife and his children, and a woman shall be liable to maintain her husband and her children.'[3] These essentials of the 1948 National Assistance Act have ever since characterized our national provisions for those whose income is maintained out of public funds by test of need and of means. The Ministry of Social Security Act of 1966, which co-ordinated the

3

policy for all social security and made a single government department responsible for it, also appointed the Supplementary Benefits
Commission whose title recalled the phraseology of Section 4 of the
1948 Act. The 1966 Act merged the administration of insurance
and assistance benefits and used a new terminology stressing rights
and claims rather than assistance and applications, but the scheme
remained essentially as laid down in the 1948 Act.[4] The purposes
and scope of that Act have been grossly distorted, its provisions
have been subjected to disjointed incrementalism, and the review
and reform of income maintenance provisions are overdue.

Four randomly-chosen examples of distortion of the purposes of
the 1948 and 1966 Acts may be quoted: (i) by November 1977
almost three million claimants were receiving Supplementary
Benefit as regular weekly payments (about 58 per cent pensioners
and about 22 per cent unemployed), and the claimants had
1,768,000 dependants,[5] which means that a scheme intended to
provide for only a limited number of cases which could not be
covered by National Insurance or by supplementary voluntary
effort is now supporting about four and three-quarter million
persons compared with one and a quarter million in 1948 and to the
tune of £1,950 million a year; (ii) *exceptional* circumstances additions (which are intended for the purpose stated) are now added to
the basic benefits received by 54 per cent of the beneficiaries, and
1,144,000 exceptional needs payments were made in 1977;[5] (iii) a
large number of local authority social service departments as well as
independent social agencies employ full-time workers and issue a
variety of publications to explain peoples' rights to the '60 ways you
can get cash help' (to quote the D.H.S.S. pamphlet)[6] and to guide
them through a maze of complicated conditions, although a small
proportion of needy people are still given financial help by local
authorities and charitable agencies; (iv) almost every British university now has a full-time welfare worker, who is paid ultimately
out of local authority funds, and is required as one of his tasks to
help those receiving grants as full-time students to get more money
from supplementary benefits during university vacations.

After a great deal of internal discussion of the operation of social
security, a team of civil servants from the D.H.S.S. was appointed in
1976 'with a general remit to conduct a comprehensive review of

the supplementary benefits scheme'. It produced its report in July 1978,[7] and there then followed a series of conferences and seminars, many of them addressed by Alan Palmer and members of the team which produced the Report. Following all this David Donnison, chairman of the Supplementary Benefits Commission, made their own commentary on the report.[8] 'Social Assistance' has been given wide publicity and a number of organizations concerned with social security benefits have sent their views, as requested, to the D.H.S.S. team who published them. The majority appear to be critical of, and a number are hostile to, the recommendations in the review, suggesting that, if implemented, the review would worsen the situation of supplementary benefits claimants.[9] The report therefore, could mark a watershed in British social security provisions, or it could – for a variety of political and administrative reasons – merely result in minor changes in some aspects of supplementary benefit payments. If the latter happens, an opportunity will have been lost to overhaul drastically a system of income maintenance out of public funds which has strayed far from its original purpose, has become complex and variable in its operation, and increasingly expensive to administer.

(2) A number of the commentaries on the review have referred to the Beveridge report and have reproached successive Governments with failing to implement the proposals therein for a level of benefit 'sufficient without further resources to provide the minimum income needed for subsistence in all normal cases'.[10] If insurance benefits in case of sickness, retirement and unemployment, it is argued, had from the outset been at the levels envisaged by the Beveridge report, there would be far less dependance upon means-tested benefits. Considered in isolation from the rest of the report, this thesis is obviously true. However, four comments must be made.

(i) The general tenor of the Beveridge Report was certainly not favourable to large-scale dependance upon generous state benefits financed out of taxation and used as a major means of redressing income distribution in British society. The very title of the report stressed the importance of the insurance principle – that entitlement to benefit (and the size of the benefit) must be related to the number of contributions paid. The 'fundamental principle' of flat-rate contributions for flat-rate benefits was justified, partly because it stressed the universality of the new scheme and partly because 'it gives room and a basis for additional voluntary provision' although 'it should not leave either to National Assistance or to voluntary insurance any risk so general and so uniform that social insurance can be justified. For National Assistance involves a means test which may discourage voluntary insurance or personal saving'.[11] Emphasis, therefore, has to be placed on the level of contributions as well as the level of benefits. 'The plan for social security is designed to meet this need; to establish a national minimum above which prosperity can grow, with want abolished'.[12]

(ii) On the other hand, the reality of the insurance principle in social security is very questionable. As McClements comments, 'Unlike private insurance, National Insurance Benefits are unfunded, there is no relationship between benefit levels and the risk involved, benefits are not paid out of accumulated assets, and the return on premium varies enormously'.[13] Contributions to social security are, therefore, more an earmarked tax. Accounting for them separately from other taxes may emphasize to workers the significance of paying for social security, but may mislead us into thinking of a direct actuarial relationship between contributions and benefits. The latter, of course, are paid for out of other money which workers have to contribute from income tax and from indirect taxation. It would, therefore, be more accurate to refer (in Britain at any rate) to the *contribution* principle in social security rather than to the *insurance* principle. This also implies that all branches of social security have to be thought of as parts of the same tree.

(iii) As has often been remarked, the post-war Labour Government introduced retirement pensions from the start of the provisions of the 1946 National Insurance Act, and did not wait for the period required to see if the 'insurance' principle had been maintained, thereby entitling pensioners to benefits justified by their contributions. This made clear the 'pay-as-you-go' nature of the scheme. It was popular in its political appeal inasmuch as the 'insurance' entitlement was set aside and the benefits came immediately to a group of people about whose eligibility there was least public controversy.[14] Interestingly enough, a later Labour Government introduced its new Pensions Plan by the Act of 1975, which stipulated a lapse of twenty years before the plan can come to full maturity, thus showing itself closer to Beveridge's insistence on the contributory principle than its predecessors had been.[15] Under this Act the number of retirement pensioners needing a supplementary pension to reach the D.H.S.S. minimum income level will gradually decrease, but not for at least twenty years will the need disappear.

(iv) The National Insurance Act 1959 introduced an important change in the social security scheme whereby pensions were henceforth related to a variable rate of contributions based on earnings. These earnings-related contributions and benefits were extended to unemployment, sickness and industrial injuries benefits in 1966. An interestingly varied combination of pressures converged to cause this departure from the universality view of social security, ranging from the criticism by Richard Titmuss[16] of the extent of private supplementary insurance whose premiums were exempt from income tax to the desire of the Conservative Government (which introduced the 1959 legislation) for a better relationship between occupational pensions schemes and the state scheme. This principle of earnings-related contributions and benefits has been carried still further in 1978 by the deduction of a variable percentage of income through the P.A.Y.E. system as contributions towards all Social Security Benefits. This means the end of the flat-rate principle; it also brings a further complication into the system of benefits, including the computation of means for Supplementary Benefits' purposes.

This long digression from examining the Review of Supplementary Benefits has been necessary to emphasize some points in the framework within which the Supplementary Benefits scheme has to operate, and to stress that the scheme cannot be examined in isolation from the total context of all forms of social security, taxation, wages and employment.

(3) As a preamble to the Review, a few comments are justified on the Supplementary Benefits Commission and its work record. Created by the 1966 Act, the Commission replaced the National Assistance Board, but did not inherit from the Board its own field staff or the power to fix or amend benefit scale rates; both of these were now merged into the Ministry of Social Security with a Minister at its head. The chairman and members of the Commission were appointed by the Minister, were responsible for seeing that the scheme ran according to the Act, and were given certain powers to vary assessment for benefit. They also had their own small Supplementary Benefits Inspectorate and a number of advisers and headquarters administrative staff. The first two chairmen were trade unionists, and the members of the Commission came to include academics concerned with the study of social policy and the operation of social services,[17] as well as representatives of local authorities and health administrations. The succession of David Donnison in 1975 to the chairmanship, previously held by Lord Collison, was accompanied by important changes, both in the composition of the Commission, in its public relationships, and Barbara Castle's permission[18] for the Commission to publish its own annual report (instead of having a section in the D.H.S.S. report), to increase its other publications and to 'be free to comment on developments and express views about priorities'. Its three annual reports in 1975, 1976 and 1977 have gone, at some depth, into the history and development of social security and have reviewed critically future options in income maintenance and related questions in employment, housing finance, rehabilitation, low wages and personal social services. It has made considerable efforts to publicize Supplementary Benefits in simple and more intelligible leaflets. Eventually the new Conservative Secretary of State for the Social Services decided at the end of 1979, that changes in the administration of the supplementary benefits system should include the abolition of the Commission, its functions being merged into a new Social Security Advisory Committee.[19]

(4) The review report (and its forty background papers) had a

wide circulation, being distributed free of charge on written request, with a resulting demand which temporarily overwhelmed available supplies. It was the first time that a public review of social assistance with such full (and free) documentation had been undertaken. The wide public discussion of the review led to a great deal of polemic in the press and in pamphlet form, so that the original contents may have become obscured. It is worth summarizing here the main points of the review before commenting on them.

(i) The joint foreword by the Secretary of State for the Social Services and the Minister for Social Security makes clear that this 127-page report by a team of officials was for public discussion with no commitment by Government or Commission to its contents. The two Ministers, however, stated: 'There is a strong case for a simpler and clearer scheme, so that both claimants and officials can know where they stand'.

(ii) The team's interpretation of its remit may be summarized thus:

(a) to analyse the operation of the scheme in all its relationships,

(b) to produce a simpler scheme,

(c) to deploy future finances more effectively,

(d) to contain rising demands on staff,

(e) to work out a more effective appeals system in the light of the Bell Report,[20]

(f) to examine the role of the Commission in all its aspects.

(iii) After wide consultations the review team tried to work out how the scheme can best be managed *within its present resources.* Six main areas are considered:

(a) simplification of the main structure,

(b) phasing out most exceptional needs payments and concentrating on regular lump sums,

(c) a clearer legal structure, with a less formal (and published) code, and a better appeals system,

(d) dealing separately with housing costs,

(e) greater equality in treatment of married women,

(f) clearer definition of the scheme's relationship to other benefits and services,

(g) dealing separately with fuel costs.

(iv) Future trends which will affect the scheme's operations included:
  (a) a slow decline in number and an increase in age, of retired people,
  (b) the rise in unemployment with long-term unemployed being more dependant on the scheme,
  (c) the increase in the number of lone parents,
  (d) a slow but real rise in sick and handicapped people,
  (e) more working women and wives,
  (f) greater emphasis on rights, explanations, challenges and appeals,
  (g) more devolution of management.

(v) The issues, of a general nature, each examined in detail, were given thus:
  We see the most important issues as: a simpler and clearer legal structure; a short-term scheme for new claimants under pension age; simplifying the rules for calculating claimants' resources; the treatment of housing costs, and the replacement of additional discretionary payments with benefits as of right as far as possible, with special attention given to claimants with unusual and continuing difficulties, in close co-operation with other services (para. 1.34).

(vi) In discussing the 'most important issues' thus identified several proposals were mooted:
  (a) Pensioners, unemployed, lone parents and the congenitally sick will continue to depend on the scheme and there is no scope for reducing these main demands. The only possible candidates for elimination are immigrants, school-leavers and students. You cannot do much about the first except to be vigilant, the second should receive benefit only at the end of the holiday after they have left school, and parents should get child benefit meanwhile, while students should continue in much the same position as now.
  (b) Housing costs have always been treated as an additional and variable payment to benefits now amounting to £600 million a year. 'This reflects an average allowance of £5 a week to over 2.25 million householders, about

half of whom are Council tenants' (para. 7.1). Rent and rate rebate systems overlap with Supplementary Benefits and it is tempting to suggest that local housing authorities deal with housing costs; the whole question is now being studied by another group.

(c) The assessment of capital resources has become complicated and needs to be simplified, a simple cut-off upper point would be best as this would save money. Disregard of earnings is a more difficult question, but a single disregard of £4 for all adults is best, single parents being left with an option.

(d) Expenses to be covered by the scale rates should be identified and published in understandable form. Increasingly there have been differential scale rates since 1966, and long-term rates are intended for those dependant on Supplementary Benefits for a long time. The latter really should cover all needs without 'exceptional' additions, and making this change would save staff and money payments. There is also a case for extending the long-term rates to the unemployed as for other long-term claimants, but it would be expensive. The possibility should be considered of making 'adult scale-rates, both ordinary and long-term, the same as the corresponding National Insurance rates' (para. 5.25). Assessment of initial claims could be simplified and short-term rates could be paid for the first eight weeks with assessment for long-term rates after six weeks if still on benefit. This would simplify matters for claimants and save staff time which could then be used to help with more difficult and complex claims. If housing costs could be dealt with differently, the short-term rates could last for 13 weeks.

(e) Discretionary additions to the basic scale have been numerous and various, mainly exceptional circumstances' additions (which a majority of claimants get) and lump-sum payments for exceptional needs about which there is a great deal of anxiety and inequity, and which go more to working-age claimants (especially lone parents) whereas most exceptional circumstances' benefits (E.C.A.s) go to pensioners. Heating additions account for the bulk of E.C.A.s, which could be reduced by consolidating these into the long-term benefit rate or, at least, doing so for pensioners and families with children. As the increased cost of heating affects all people on low incomes the Minister ought to study separately the question of fuel costs. Dietary additions should be phased out and laundry additions reduced. Long-term rates ought to meet exceptional needs, and only expenses not covered by scale rates should be met, probably best by periodic lump-sum payments.

(f) You need to retain some discretionary power in a Supplementary Benefit Scheme, including a power to withhold or reduce benefit, but it should be exceptional, 'its present uses being given specific, legislative force wherever possible' (para. 9.53 [10]).

(g) Things have changed since the 1940s when National Assistance started and when the husband in a family was assumed to be the 'breadwinner'. 'By 1975, 61 per cent of husbands under pension age had working wives' (para. 11.2), and other pieces of legislation have ensured equal treatment for women, including the 1975 Social Security Pensions Act. There ought to be equal treatment in Supplementary Benefits, but to deal with cohabiting couples as individuals and not as a family unit (possibly with dependant children) would be inequitable and unworkable. The review considers a number of possible alternatives here, and concludes that it is best to allow a couple to decide on a 'nominated breadwinner' for Supplementary Benefits, though it would mean employing some extra staff. For supplementary pensions 'we conclude that the best course would be to enable a couple to qualify for a supplementary pension when either spouse reached the age of 65' (para. 11.28).

(h) A lot has recently been done to improve communications, publish pamphlets written in clearer and simpler language (and also in minority languages used in Britain), and studies of practices such as giving written notice of assessment, simplifying forms, and having regular consultations with pressure groups and with groups representative of claimants. More needs to be done in all these directions, but it would be greatly helped by a simpler, more codified system of benefits. The A Code is being re-written, and policy statements in it are to be transferred to the published Handbook. Some experiments in computer use for assessment have been studied.

(i) Appeals' Tribunals should remain, with the improvements in composition and in legal skills now in train, but appeals about the use of discretion (for example over E.N.P.s) should be reduced as this merely involves someone else using their discretion – 'in fact a second claim rather than an appeal as normally understood' (para. 9.51). Tribunals will be greatly helped by being able to refer to a published Code of Practice, as suggested in the Review Report.

(5) The review concluded that many issues remain for further study and report, and it listed seventeen of these, saying that the discussion of the review may well add some more. These are in addition to the major questions of housing and heating costs for supplementary beneficiaries (and other people). As illustrations of the need to provide statutory backing for discretionary rules, the review dealt with young people at school, students at universities, and people in full-time work. The requirement for those of working age and capability to register for work ought to be made a statutory condition, with any exceptions stated in the proposed code. In an annexe the review deals with the relationship between benefits and incomes at work. After a full and well-documented study of this question the review concludes with the words:

There are real problems in this area, but they have not been caused by over-generous benefit levels, but by the falling real levels of low wages and child benefits in recent years. The Government are already embarked on measures to improve the position of those in work. High priority is being given to the Child Benefit Scheme and to increasing the level of this benefit in real terms, and also to changes in taxation which will raise the real standard of living of the low to medium wage earner. The various means-tested benefits have been improved as has access to them.

(6) Despite the care and the length at which present policies and practices are examined, the conclusions of the document are disappointing. Some of the really major issues (housing costs and – quite separately – financial aid to strikers, for example) are left aside for study by some other body.

The fundamental question of the total provision for income in society would involve a study of wages, the whole of social security provisions – insurance, needs-tested assistance and general grants – and taxation. As Titmuss[21] long ago asserted, the problems of distribution of income in society must also deal with occupational welfare. To this must be added income tax refunds and redundancy payments, two sources of income only very briefly mentioned in the section on disregards (paras 8.32 to 8.34). The authors of the review report accept this by referring to their limited remit and stating that 'there is no prospect of finding the massive sums for National Insurance Benefits or other services that would be needed to reduce the number of Supplementary Benefit claimants to a low enough level to permit a largely discretionary system to operate', which is why they have not dealt with reforms of national insurance or the tax system.[13] But the conclusion is reached much too hastily that 'the most realistic aim is to fit the scheme to its mass role of coping with millions of claimants in known and readily-defined categories for the foreseeable future' (para. 1.14). Since 'it is doubtful whether in any other urban industrial society such large and easily definable groups have their social security cover underpinned to such an extent by means-tested social assistance' (para. 1.7), one must ask why Britain should be so different from other countries, and one can hardly avoid the conclusion that to have such a 'mass role' for means-tested social assistance is a misguided and obsolete system for dealing with income maintenance.

The first and major criticism of the review must, therefore, be that it did not go far enough, and that the opportunity must not be lost of studying again the merits of the many schemes already well documented and widely discussed of linking social insurance, assistance, taxation, employment and wages.[22]

It is by no means established that the more ambitious and thorough-going schemes for social security reform are 'vastly more expensive', nor indeed, even if they did cost more, that there would be total public resistance to them in Britain, whose expenditure on tax and social security is by no means the highest in Europe. Such reforms, indeed, might be more acceptable to workers and taxpayers (as well as being better for claimants) than the present Supplementary Benefits (S.B.) system. If the basic premise is accepted that a 'mass role' for social assistance is to persist 'for the foreseeable future', it is a timorous and incompetent conclusion. We need a new overall policy for income maintenance and distribution, of which the new pension plan and the new system of child benefits are only minor instalments. To this end social scientists and political parties should now address themselves.

(7) However, if we do accept that : (a) until more thorough and comprehensive reforms of social security are brought about, we must make the best of the Supplementary Benefits Scheme, and (b) even when we have reduced its scope there will still be need for some discretionary income maintenance scheme (rather as Beveridge anticipated), there are comments to be made on some of the more important points made in the review. All its detailed analyses and recommendations are subject to a basic question – namely, is more, the same, or less money to be spent on Supplementary Benefits than at present if the recommendations in the review are accepted? Critics of the Report's recommendations who have written in the specialist press, and almost everybody at the N.C.S.S. seminar,[23] asserted that more money must be spent on Supplementary Benefits and that any future simplification of the system, as proposed, must not result in lower benefits anywhere. This seems to me an easy evasion of the strongly felt public view that an increase of expenditure on Supplementary Benefits is unacceptable and that probably the majority of the population would like to see it reduced. This is clearly shown in the thorough public opinion survey whose results appear as one of the many annexes to the review entitled

Report on Research on Public Attitudes towards the Supplementary Benefit System, January 1978. The interested groups, therefore, C.P.A.G., Claimants Union, Age Concern and the rest, are manifestly out of line with expressed public opinion if they claim that more should be spent on Supplementary Benefits. The 1979 Conservative government clearly believed they were assured of enough public support in stating: 'Additional resources are not now available, but some important changes can be made within the present costs of the scheme and as a first stage in its reform.'[18] Attention has, therefore, been given first to those parts of the review which reduce reliance on S.B. for certain categories of people. While we are waiting for 1998 and the maturation of the Pension Plan, it should be possible to give income maintenance at least at the S.B. level and without the formality of a means-test to most retired people. The 1979 White Paper asserts, however, 'It would now cost £2.2 billion to raise retirement pensions to a level at which half the people receiving supplementary pension would no longer need it.'[19] The treatment of resources which are disregarded in assessment has become too complex. The White Paper follows the reviews in proposing new rules about capital earnings, occupational pensions and sick pay.[19] On the whole they seem sensible, but it remains to be seen what happens to pension up-ratings. Since a high percentage of exceptional circumstances additions (E.C.A.s) are paid to pensioners and since about 66 per cent of supplementary pensioners get E.C.A.s, it would surely be much better to consolidate the additional amount into the basic pension rate. This would not be unjust in view of the almost universal needs of pensioners and the increase proposed above from the first basic retirement pension rate. On the age of retirement the considerations mentioned by Michael Fogarty in his recent study of pensions are to be commended.[24]

(8) Persistent demands have come from various quarters of quite different political and ideological tendencies for (a) simplification of the over-complex system, and (b) greater publicity for an understandable system. To this extent the review was an honest attempt to meet an oft-expressed demand. The White Paper followed its general line. It is hard to forsee the effects of simplification upon the exercise of discretion, upon the comprehensibility of the system to the average claimant, and upon the now strong movement of

various bodies involved in 'welfare rights'. The latter will naturally be resistant to simplification, since it makes them superfluous. This is not to say that 'welfare rights' groups are parasitical. They have pressed for and obtained improvements in benefits (both in cash and in services) for their particular constituencies, and inevitably they take a view that is partial and advocatory. Hence, politicians may in answer to their pleas make disjointed additions to benefits until a review becomes unavoidable. By this time the sectional interests will have become more demanding, and cover narrower and more specialized areas of need or deeply felt grievance, leaving elected authorities and Governments in the permanently unenviable position of denial, defence of the *status quo*, and of having to make choices between demands on inelastic resources.

As information agencies, groups such as C.P.A.G., C.A.Bx., Community Associations, Tenants' Associations and some trade unions play a large part in making better known the details of a complex system, and also act as advocates or representatives of claimants. Indeed, some groups have received money from other government departments to employ people to do this work.[25] Local authority social service departments also employ welfare rights' workers in many cases.[26] While independent advice, and sometimes representation, of claimants is clearly useful, it seems an odd expenditure of public funds to build up a system so complicated and with so many discretionary elements in it that specialists (part-time or full-time) have to work and train to understand it and so become indispensable interpreters to the consumers of the service. It would seem more logical, and far better for claimants to benefits as rights, to set as priorities simplification of the system, full and clearly-expressed publicized information about it, more and better-trained staff in the agency to deal with its clients. The S.B. Commission commented in 1977,

> The overall picture then is of a service trying to cope with a very large and growing number of claimants and beneficiaries and coming under increased strain. . . . We are making unreasonable demands on the system and we are not going to be able to reverse the faults and improve the service by having more staff, undertaking more training, or placing less reliance on the use of

casual staff or overtime. We need to change the basic structure
of the scheme.[27]

(9) It is important to stress the need to continue the periodic
updating and re-issue of the *Supplementary Benefits Handbook*
as the major authoritative statement of rights, obligations and
benefits. The White Paper promises that the simplified rules for
S.B. will be publicized in full. The vexed question of the use of the
'A' code – the code of departmental instructions to officers on the
S.B. scheme – has been the subject of complaint by pressure groups.
Many sensational press articles have suggested that the 'A' code is
evidence of secret codes of behaviour not revealed in publications
like the Handbook.[28] The code, as I have seen it, is a large, bulky
departmental guidance code, such as is used in many government
departments, quite unsuitable for publication. What is needed is, as
the White Paper proposes, a simplification of the scheme, and the
issue of a code of practice with a re-written code for departmental
use.[29] Nevertheless, the Commission and the D.H.S.S. were ill-
advised to have appeared for so long to have been reluctant to state
what was in the 'A' code, as this gave an impression of mystery and
secrecy which puzzled clients, impeded good-will towards staff, and
gave joy only to those who wanted to discredit the whole Social
Security Scheme.

(10) The perception of the role of Supplementary Benefits and
one's attitude towards the institutions of social security will naturally be affected by one's ideological interpretations of British
society and of its social provisions. Some academic commentators
have seen social security simply as a device to mollify the poor in an
unjust society. George[30] writes: 'Social security services have
developed into a complex administrative maze which openly rein-
forces the inequalities of the wage system and helps to accommo-
date the working class to its inferior position in the social structure.'
Important in this respect is Simpson's description of the activities of
local authority welfare rights' workers: 'Their ideologies stressed
support for radical solutions, suspicion of consensus and belief in an
oppositional function, which was realised in some forms of advocacy work, such as pre-occupation with tribunal work.'[26] Writing of
Welfare Rights advocacy in Batley, Taylor-Gooby states, 'The

ultimate goal of these activities are to enforce existing rights and to extort new rights',[25] and this led to a number of clashes with S.B. staff, not only over particular claims to E.N.P.s, but about the whole objectives of the scheme.

Whether one agrees or disagrees with these analyses of the functions of Supplementary Benefits, it is clear that such perceptions of the nature of society will lead intermediaries and advocate workers to stress the conflict model of contacts with social security officers and to be pre-occupied with argument about complexities and obscurities and obtaining more from the system. The system, of course, provides for contestation by its very complexity. It also provides, through its tribunals, for appeal against decision: to win a case at a tribunal is not to have beaten the system, but to have used it.[32]

(11) The review was remarkably reticent about S.B. payments to full-time students. Clearly, the Social Security system was never intended to provide supplementary income for claimants who receive grants from education authorities. These grants should be adequate to cover all needs of a full-time student, including his vacation periods when he is required to work at his studies or field work connected with them. If grants are inadequate, they should be raised, and indeed, there is a strong case for indexing student grants to costs of living and (many would say) for abolishing discriminatory parental income differentiation in grant awards. The increasing use made by students of S.B. is wrong. It is remarkable that the Department of Education and Science has remained mute on the topic, unless it is a case of a rather undignified passing of the buck between departments. Full-time grants should be adequate for total maintenance (including that of dependants) and not reliant on claims for means-tested supplementation. Students' timetables allow for holidays, and if they wish to do other work than their studies to gain extra money, this should not involve registering for work to obtain S.B. The White Paper proposes to disqualify school-leavers from S.B. and to continue child benefit for them until the end of the summer vacation, but students over 19 years remain so far untouched during that period.

This group of people should, therefore, cease to be a charge on the scheme, except in circumstances of exceptional need, where their rights are those of any other citizen. This would not, of course, affect their rights under social insurance provisions which may, for example, give entitlements from previous working situations.[31]

(12) The treatment of housing costs has always been a problematic element in the scheme. The suggestion in the review that there might be a co-ordinated approach to dealing with all housing costs for people on low incomes through the housing authorities was welcome.[33] The results of the study of means-tested housing benefits are awaited with interest: it is to be hoped that further studies will deal with the treatment of the homeless and of people discharged from hospital or institutions who need re-settlement facilities.

(13) The treatment of discretionary heating additions in the review raises the whole question of fuel policy, which was the subject of campaigns during 1976–9. The proposal to simplify the scheme by reducing E.C.A.s would also involve the possible incorporation of heating additions within an improved scale rate, certainly for retired pensioners and families with children. As a general principle, however, it is surely better and more dignified for claimants to receive a scale payment which covers heating costs, rather than to be subjected to patronizing questions on their needs for heating – or indeed for other items commonly found in any household budget.

(14) Most important, there are the sections of the review which deal with the rate of benefits and their comparison with wages. The scale rate has come to be called the 'poverty-line', a most misleading appellation. As the review stated (Chapter 5), the controversy about rates of benefit really revolves around ideas about relationships, either to costs of living or to average wages (or both).

Some confusion has been introduced into the debate by the use of the word 'poverty' not in the 'subsistence' sense, but in the comparative sense. What the S.B. scheme has come to expect, therefore, is that there shall be some relationship between the standard of living of an S.B. claimant and any other citizen. That relationship has to take account of two conflicting constraints – not to let S.B. standards slip very much below wage rates (allowing for wider differences in the short term), and yet not to exceed working wages because benefits allow additions for dependant children and market wages do not. By far the most important intervention here, of course, is the institution of tax-free child benefits to all children, with the simultaneous phasing out of income tax child allowances. This is a more radical approach to the whole problem and re-asserts parental responsibility as well as rights.

Further study of the effect of more ambitious and more generous family allowance systems in France and Belgium, for example, and of their cost being borne by employers, should be carefully made and not simply dismissed because they are products of a very different administrative system. If unemployment does not affect a smaller percentage of the employed population over the next five years (structural unemployment makes this unlikely), the treatment of long-term rates for the unemployed becomes a priority. The other strategy suggested above, however, may not make this so necessary for as many people as at present. There has been much doubt cast upon the credibility of the 'work ethic' in British society. Evidence from surveys are hard to interpret, although my own impression from the attitudes of young unemployed people towards temporary work schemes under the Job Creation Programmes and the new Youth Opportunities Programmes is that the 'work ethic' is strongly felt.[34]

This is generally supported by the sections in the 1977 Supplementary Benefits Commission report dealing with the possible disincentive effects of benefits on work. Most of those whose cases are reviewed preferred to be back at work, except in a few marginal cases.[35] Nor is the press campaign that is sometimes conducted against alleged 'scroungers' really justified by the facts, as a House of Commons committee report made clear.[36] Nevertheless, fraud and abuse of the system serve only to discredit rightful claimants, and can no more be condoned than income tax falsification or fiddling of expenses.[37] What is really important is to maintain a reasonable relativity between benefits, average standard of living and wages. Table 1 (see p. 22) in the annexe to the review illustrates this point clearly. The review report adds this comment:

> The poverty trap stems not from poverty itself but from the means to relieve it. Means-tested benefits such as FIS have been substantially improved and extended in recent years. This

TABLE 1   *National Assistance and Supplementary Benefit scale rates as percentages of the average net [a] earnings of male manual workers[b]*

| | Percentages | | | |
| | Ordinary scale rates | | Long-term scale rates | |
Date	Single householder	Married couple	Single householder	Married couple
July 1948	22.9	36.1		
June 1950	22.3	35.9		
September 1951	23.4	37.1		
June 1952	24.9	40.0		
September 1954	25.2	40.3		
July 1955	22.5	35.7		
January 1956	22.9	35.8		
January 1958	24.1	38.2		
April 1961	24.9	39.3		
September 1962	25.9	40.4		
May 1963	26.5	41.7		
March 1965	29.4	46.5		
November 1966	30.0	47.1	33.3	50.3
October 1967	30.8	48.5	34.0	51.6
October 1968	30.5	48.1	33.8	51.3
November 1969	30.1	47.6	33.2	50.6
November 1970	28.7	45.3	31.5	47.9
September 1971	29.8	47.2	32.3	49.7
October 1972	27.8	44.3	30.3	46.8
October 1973	27.2	42.6	31.0	47.0
July 1974	28.8	45.4	35.7	54.4
April 1975		unchanged		
November 1975	29.9	47.7	37.5	57.9
November 1976	31.6	50.2	39.1	60.4
November 1977[c]	32.0	50.0	39.5	60.2

Notes:

[a] Net earnings for this purpose are taken as gross earnings less income tax, national insurance contributions and average rent and rates. The rent estimates are based on the rent increase for all unemployed householders in receipt of supplementary benefit.

[b] From July 1948 to November 1969 the average earnings relate to full-time male manual workers (ages 21 and over) in manufacturing and some of the principal non-manufacturing industries in the United Kingdom taken from the enquiry conducted by the Department of Employment in October of each year. From November 1970 onwards the figures relate to the gross earnings of full-time male manual workers (aged 21 and over) in all industries and services in Great Britain when absence has not affected their pay. The estimate for April 1975 was obtained from the New Earnings Survey (N.E.S.). Estimates for other

months are less reliable and were derived by interpolation between (or extrapolation from) N.E.S. estimates, assuming that movements of average earnings of full-time male manual workers were similar to the movements in the seasonally adjusted monthly index of average earnings published in the Department of Employment Gazette (Table 127).
ᶜEstimated.

has undoubtedly helped to relieve poverty but, in conjunction with tax thresholds that have declined in real terms, it has also considerably increased the numbers affected by the 'poverty trap'. The more means-tested help that is given, and the higher up the income scale that it extends, the less people gain in total income support from increases in their earnings, and the wider the range of earnings over which this result of withdrawing means-tested benefits applies.

This problem area raises, of course, the question of low wages. The improvement of the latter can be helped by two devices in our social security system – Family Income Supplement and Child Benefit, the latter being potentially far more effective. There is also a range of means-tested benefits for those in work, on which the review comments 'there is much ignorance about them and reluctance to claim them (paras A.15.16[d]). The effect of these on people in work makes it hard simply to suppress services in kind and give claimants more consumer choice by increasing benefits, and letting them buy services at present given free on the 'passport'. This whole area needs to be looked at more thoroughly. But within the market wage system, low wages may demand not just an increase all round to cope with inflation. At a time of low productivity and no surplus this will involve a substantial re-adjustment of differentials within industry, commerce and the professions, which very few better-paid workers have the courage to accept.[38] Within the scale rates the present system seems about right, with the important relationship to wages and living standards being maintained, and with the sensible proposal in the review to retain variable age rates and to up-rate them in line with earnings rather than prices. Reducing children's scale rates to three only has some attractions, and this the White Paper proposes, with the claim that 'About ½ million children will be affected . . .'.[19]

TABLE 2   *Comparison of total income support when working and when in receipt of Supplementary Benefit*

(1) Family unit	(2) Gross earnings	(3) T.I.S. in work	(4) T.I.S. on supplementary benefit, also as a % of (3). 'Incentive' in brackets	
	£	£	%	£
Married couple	45	31.09	£23.55=76	(07.54)
no children	55	34.81	68	(11.26)
(Rent and rates	65	40.87	58	(17.32)
=£7.25)	75	46.92	50	(23.37)
	85	52.96	44	(29.41)
	95	59.01	40	(35.46)
Married couple	45	35.32	£28.53=81	(06.79)
and 1 child age	55	38.25	75	(09.72)
3 years	65	42.80	67	(14.29)
(Rent and rates	75	48.85	59	(20.32)
=£8.25)	85	54.89	52	(26.36)
	95	60.94	47	(32.41)
Married couple	45	41.15	£34.73=84	(06.42)
and 2 children	55	43.14	81	(08.41)
aged 4 and 6	65	45.47	76	(10.74)
(Rent and rates	75	51.38	68	(16.65)
=£8.65)	85	57.42	60	(22.69)
	95	63.47	55	(28.74)
Married couple	45	47.76	£42.08=88	(05.68)
and 3 children	55	49.31	85	(07.23)
aged, 3, 8 and 12	65	52.19	81	(10.11)
(Rent and rates	75	54.54	77	(12.46)
=£8.65)	85	6058	69	(18.50)
	95	66.63	63	(24.55)
Married couple	45	54.11	£52.19=97	(01.88)
and 4 children	55	54.59	96	(02.36)
aged 3, 8, 11	65	58.09	90	(05.82)
and 16	75	60.92	86	(08.69)
(Rent and rates	85	62.68	83	(10.45)
=£9.90)	95	68.73	76	(16.50)

Notes:
1. Column (3) is the figure resulting after deduction of income tax and national insurance from gross earnings in Column (2), payment of rent/rates and assumes work expenses of £2.10; but including full assumed take-up of all available

benefits such as family income supplement, child benefit, rate rebate, rent rebate/allowance, free school dinners, welfare milk and the like, as appropriate.
2. The bracketed 'incentive' figure in Column (4) is the actual cash amount to be gained by a claimant taking up work at the gross figure corresponding in Column (1) and, of course, pre-supposing full take-up of other benefits as indicated in Note 1 above.

(15) It is clear that at least until a thorough overhaul of the system, such as I have advocated, is undertaken, the Commission and local D.H.S.S. officers paying S.B. must be the major sources of income for those who categorically qualify for benefit. There is also the question which has only once occurred in the discussions I have described, but which may be of particular interest and concern to voluntary bodies and should therefore be taken up by the N.C.S.S.: What is the effect of supplementary benefits upon charitable bodies? We know their role is declining, but how far and in what ways? A critical review of the activities of the Society of St Vincent de Paul in Ireland three years ago has not, to my knowledge, been matched by any similar review in this country. Has the Charity Commission or any other body carried out such an exercise? If not, it ought to be undertaken.

More attention and documentation has been given to the operation of the 1963 Act under which social workers in local authorities, in order to prevent children coming into care, 'may, if the local authority think fit, include provisions for giving assistance in kind, or in exceptional circumstances, in cash'.[39] It appears that the use of powers under this Act are still confined to a very small number of families, but that half of the recipients are also on S.B.[40] Clearly, there is an unresolved boundary problem here, involving a good deal of overlap. Some of the controversy centres on the role of the social worker, who may feel strongly that getting material help to the client's family is at least as important as his casework help to them. It is difficult to see, however, why this cannot be better achieved by the social worker acting as adviser and advocate to a family in difficulty, and helping to obtain its S.B. rights. Some fears have been expressed that S.B.C. officers were neglecting claimants, and that their tasks of income maintenance were being taken over by local authority social workers, whose relationship was thus compromised.[41]

It seems very doubtful if this is at all an accurate picture, but it also seems clear that the kind of emergency payments made by social workers cannot really prevent children coming into care. The study of American social workers' identification with material assistance has led to a revulsion at the practice here among social work writers.[42] However, there is close connection between social workers and social assistance officers in France and in Belgium, for example. In the newly-reformed Belgian system of 'Centres d'Aide Sociale', and in France with the Family Allowance Agencies, the alliance of social work and social assistance seems to work well, and is not regarded as compromising the social worker's role. However, the far higher rate of family allowances, the much greater role of social insurance, and the comparatively residual role of social assistance in France and Belgium must be remembered.[43] In the circumstances of British S.B. there seems to be no valid case for continuing the operation of cash grants by local authority social service departments, and I would advocate that they be discontinued forthwith. However, if this is done, there must be available a full emergency service through the S.B. local office to deal with crisis situations. There have been frequent complaints that this is not the case, and that a needy person could be stranded without money from Friday night till Monday morning. This must clearly be provided for by the local social security office, and staff consultation on the question should ensure a speedy conclusion.

(16) The White Paper has been followed by a bill introduced into the House for the reform of the S.B. system. It seems sure that a new Supplementary Benefits Act will be on the statute book in 1980. The general simplification of the complex scheme, its greater publicity, the awareness of the narrow margins between benefits and low wages – all these are welcome developments. They will demand redeployed and better trained staff. Improvements in relative values of benefits may have to wait. The review may well be a watershed in our income maintenance provisions. Really important changes will now be possible, involving a thorough overhaul of benefits, contributions, low wages and taxes, all of which are closely inter-related. The 1980 Act will be just 'an important first step in the simplification of the scheme'[44] – which is to everyone's benefit.

Notes and References

1. National Assistance Act, 1948.
2. Ibid., Section 4.
3. Ibid., Section 42.
4. Strictly speaking the work of the Commission and of D.H.S.S. officers was governed by the Supplementary Benefits (Amendment) Act, 1976, and – to some extent – by the Social Security Benefits Act, 1975, which deal *inter alia* with the treatment of resources of claimants. Neither of these Acts, however, altered fundamentally the essentials of the system, but it has been argued that the 1966 Act 'can be seen as extending significantly the statutory basis of social assistance, even for claimants under pension age, and correspondingly reducing the discretionary element'. (Supplementary Benefits Commission Annual Report, 1976 – Appendix A on the legislative history of supplementary benefits, para. A.37.)
5. Supplementary Benefits Commission Annual Report for 1977 (published 1978).
6. D.H.S.S. Pamphlet F.B.2, 'Which benefit?', November 1978.
7. 'Social Assistance – a Review of the Supplementary Benefits Scheme in Great Britain', D.H.S.S., July 1978.
8. Response of S.B.C. to 'Social Assistance', H.M.S.O., 1979.
9. See, for example, the column 'Dear Claimant' by Bill Jordan in *New Society*, 1978; 'Social Assistance – the Real Challenge' by Ruth Lister, C.P.A.G., 1978, and the views of F.S.U. and others reported in *Community Care*, December 1978 and January 1979.
10. Report of Inter-departmental Committee on Social Insurance and Allied Services, Cmnd. 6464, H.M.S.O., 1942, para. 307.
11. Ibid., paras 304–308.
12. Ibid., para. 450.
13. Leslie McClements, *The Economics of Social Security*, Heinemann, 1978.
14. See, for example, Victor George, *Social Security: Beveridge and After*, Routledge and Kegan Paul, 1968. A. K. Maynard, 'A Survey of Social Security in the U.K.', *Social and Economic Administration*, Vol. 7, No. 1.
15. 'Better Pensions', Cmnd. 5713, H.M.S.O., 5713.
16. R. M. Titmuss, *Essays on the Welfare State*, Allen and Unwin, 1963.
17. These included Richard Titmuss, David Marsh, Barbara Rodgers and David Donnison, who later became chairman.

18. Barbara Castle (then Secretary of State for Social Services) in Hansard, 2 May 1975, Vol. 891, col. 262.
19. Reform of the Supplementary Benefits Scheme. Cmnd. 7773, H.M.S.O., 1979.
20. Kathleen Bell, 'Report of research study on Supplementary Benefits Appeals Tribunals', H.M.S.O., 1975.
21. Richard Titmuss, *Essays on the Welfare State*, Allen and Unwin, 1962, *Social Policy*, Allen and Unwin, 1977.
22. See, for example, the comprehensive report by Institute for fiscal studies, edited by Professor J. E. Meade, *The Structure and Reform of Direct Taxation*, Allen and Unwin, 1978 (especially the chapters on social security). Also: Green Paper, 'Proposal for a tax credit system', Cmnd. 5116, H.M.S.O., 1972. 'Report of Select Committee on Tax Credit proposals', House of Commons paper, H.M.S.O., 1973. G. Polanyi, 'Tax Credits' in *Westminster Bank Review*, 1973; M. H. Cooper, 'Tax Credits' in *Social & Economic Administration*, 1973; J. F. Abbott, 'Unemployment, benefits and incentives', *Social Policy and Administration*, 1979.
23. This was one of a series addressed by Alan Palmer of the review team and by Bill Jordan and R. A. B. Leaper and organized by the National Council of Social Service in London, November 1978.
24. Michael Fogarty, 'Pensions – where next?' Centre for Studies in Social Policy, 1976.
25. One interesting development here was money given under the Job Creation Programme of the Manpower Services Commission to 'welfare-rights' groups' of many kinds. Another is the 'welfare rights' work done under government community development projects, of which one example is reported in P. Taylor-Gooby, *Welfare Benefits Advocacy in Batley*, University of York, 1977.
26. See Tony Simpson,[9] *Advocacy and Social Change – a Study of Welfare Rights Workers*, National Institute for Social Work, 1978.
27. Supplementary Benefits Commission Annual Report, 1976, H.M.S.O., 1977.
28. See, for example, Melanie Phillips in *The Guardian*, 4 January 1979, and Andrew Brown in *Community Care*, 11 January 1979.
29. Mr Patrick Jenkin promised in 1979 that this would be done (*Community Care*, November 1979).
30. V. George, *Social Security and Society*, Routledge and Kegan Paul, 1973.
31. This question is dealt with in 'Unemployment Benefit for Students', Cmnd. 7613, H.M.S.O., 1979.

32. Supplementary Benefit Appeals Tribunals, H.M.S.O., 1970. A review of the whole area is given by R. A. B. Leaper, 'The British Welfare State in its international context' in *Human Well-being*, I.C.S.W., 1978.
33. See D. C. Stafford, *The Economics of Housing*, Croom Helm, 1978.
34. The author has been chairman of the area board for South-west England of the Manpower Services Commission special programmes for the unemployed.
35. Supplementary Benefits Commission Annual Report for 1977, H.M.S.O., 1978, pp. 44–48.
36. Report of the Official Co-ordinating committee on Abuse, House of Commons, 1977.
37. See Stuart Henry, *The Hidden Economy*, Martin Robertson, 1978.
38. See the publications of the Low Pay Unit.
39. Children & Young Persons Act, 1963, Section 1.
40. The study referred to is: Michael Hill and Peter Laing, *Social Work and Money*, Allen & Unwin, 1979.
41. Bill Jordan, *Poor Parents*, Routledge & Kegan Paul, 1974.
42. Z. T. Butrym, *The Nature of Social Work*, Macmillan, 1976.
43. See Jean-Marie Berger, *Le défi des Centres Publics d'aide sociale*, Editions Labor, 1978.
44. These words are in the last paragraph of the White Paper (Cmnd. 7773) forecasting the introduction of the new legislation in 1980.
45. Government proposals for the use of powers to make regulations under the new 1980 legislation were made available from the D.H.S.S. in February, 1980. Local benefit officers will have guidance from a new Chief Supplementary Benefits Officer.

CHAPTER TWO

Benefits, Disincentives and Unemployment[1]

BRIAN SHOWLER

One of the most important areas of overlap between economic theory and the provision of social security lies in the question of work incentives. Not only is the issue of importance to the economist and social administrationist, but it is frequently at the centre of political and popular debate concerning the appropriate size of unemployment and/or supplementary benefit payments to the unemployed. The nature and extent of public concern over the issue can be clearly seen in two recent surveys of attitudes towards the unemployed and the benefit system in Nichols and Benyon and in a report by the Schlackman Research Organization.[2]

The economist's contribution at the theoretical level is limited to establishing an analytical framework. There is clearly a possible trade-off or substitution effect between the supply of work effort (determining income and consumption) and leisure. The theory cannot, however, predict what will happen in practice if (i) an increase in real wages occurs that enables an individual to have both more goods and more leisure; (ii) an increase in taxation reduces real income from a given unit of work effort; or (iii) an increase in social security payments occurs thereby narrowing the differential between work and non-work income. The outcome will depend upon a whole set of socio-economic variables, including for example the perceived social status of work itself, which will determine the degree of substitution between work and leisure in response to any such changes in the exogenous environment. Thus, only empirical research can provide policy makers with the means of predicting the likely consequences of a decision to change any of the above parameters.

The literature on the effects of taxation and social security payments upon work incentives is relatively limited, but is, nevertheless, beyond the scope of this Chapter.[3] Here, the aim is to examine first research concerning the effect of two major changes in British social security legislation, namely, the start of a national scheme for redundancy payments in 1965, and the provision of earnings-related unemployment benefit in 1966, which for an increased number of workers narrowed the work/non-work pay differential. The second objective is to examine the possible effects of such changes in social security provision upon the duration of registered unemployment, and the relationship between the level of unemployment and the level of vacancies. And third, to discuss the effects of the changed labour market situation and changes in the nature and characteristics of social security payments for the unemployed in the late 1970s with particular reference to the issue of work incentives.

It appears necessary to separate the effects of 'lump sum' redundancy payments from the effects of the 'on-going' increases in income associated with earnings-related benefits. The evidence on redundancy payments tends to suggest that such payments do not have a significant effect upon incentives if patterns of job search behaviour and length of unemployment following redundancy are taken as surrogate measures of the potential disincentives. A case study[4] in the United States in 1961 provided some early evidence that the size of severance pay was not correlated with the length of the post-redundancy adjustment period.

British research into the effects of the Redundancy Payments Act tends to confirm this American finding. Parker and others[5] in their report for the Department of Employment found that their respondents receiving redundancy pay spent on average no longer in unemployment than those who did not receive payments, and indeed 25 per cent of the paid redundants as opposed to 17 per cent of the unpaid redundants started a new job immediately. Among those who did receive payment, however, the larger the payment, the longer the period of unemployment; but, when the data were standardized by age, it became clear that the difficulty or slowness in finding new work was, in fact, accounted for by the lower employability of older workers, who because of generally longer service also received higher redundancy payments.

Mackay and Reid[6] in their study of redundancy in the Midlands engineering industry 1966–8, concluded that, ... there is no evidence of a significant relationship between the amount of redundancy pay a man receives and the length of time before he finds another job, provided that one allows for the other factors which affect that period, such as the man's age.

Daniel,[7] in his survey of a large-scale redundancy in south-east London in 1968, tested the effects of the size of redundancy payments upon a number of possible labour market behaviour patterns, and found that the size of payment did not affect the timing of job search, nor willingness to turn down suitable jobs because of lack of economic incentive, and there was no tendency for unemployment to increase with size of payment. Age was again shown as the most important variable affecting length of unemployment, rather than the existence or size of redundancy payments, a point further supported by Martin and Fryer.[8]

Hill's study[9] of unemployment in three English towns found that the unemployed in receipt of redundancy pay did spend longer periods in joblessness, but once again when the results were adjusted by age the relationship disappeared. In fact, this study found, once age had been taken into account, that the supposed disincentive effects were negative, with the recipients of redundancy pay experiencing shorter unemployment than non-recipients. This the authors ascribe to the fact that re-employment is often highly dependent upon a good employment record in terms of long service and other factors, which are also important in determining of the size of the redundancy payment.

It is also necessary to consider in this context the proportion of the unemployed who actually receive redundancy payments. The impression created by many analysts is that a large number of the unemployed do. This is not the case. In 1975, for example, 340,000 employees were entitled to benefits under the scheme, and received an average payment of £524. In that year 4,400,000 people registered a claim for unemployment benefit, and therefore only 7 per cent of the unemployed received any redundancy payment.[10]

Thus, the empirical results, as far as the disincentive effects of redundancy payments are concerned, indicate no such disadvantageous economic consequences. But it may well be that lump-sum payments of this kind are viewed as 'once and for all' payments or 'windfall' capital gains which are not regarded as income, whereas an increase in unemployment benefit via the earnings-related supplement tends to narrow the gap between unemployment income compared with employment income for those unemployed workers who receive it, and may, therefore, have more significant effects upon work incentives than do lump-sum payments. It is, therefore, also necessary to examine the case studies in order to attempt to throw some light on the potential disincentive effects of the earnings-related supplement introduced in 1966. One is here, of course, concerned with the differential effect of the supplement, and not with any absolute disincentive effect as previously associated with flat-rate unemployment benefit.

The evidence is, however, conflicting, with three studies indicating some possible disincentive effects, and one indicating either no effect or a negative disincentive effect.

Daniel[11] found that, 'there was a steady and consistent trend for men to have been more likely to have refused job offers, the higher the level of their weekly benefits'. Nevertheless, a number of qualifications were made. About half of those involved in the particular redundancy found work within a month, and Daniel concluded that the effect was negligible for a substantial number of workers. It was also the case that the observed effect was not solely due to the state-provided earnings-related benefit, as in Woolwich the employer provided a further supplement for those who remained jobless for some time, and in fact some 41 per cent received such additional supplementation. It is not, therefore, possible to conclude with certainty that the higher rate of job refusal among the larger benefit receivers was associated with the national earnings-related scheme. In any case, Daniel argued that the payment of enhanced benefits improved the job selection process and had an economic spin-off in enabling men to turn down inferior, low status and low-paid jobs, and to find more satisfactory and productive employment.

Parker's study[12] found that unemployment benefit levels varied, with older redundant men being more likely to receive benefit and to receive it for longer periods, but that the highest rates of benefit went to men aged between thirty and thirty-nine. It was also found that this age group experienced the greatest difficulty in finding work offering pay greater than unemployment benefit income. However, only 16 per cent of the paid redundant in the study expressed difficulty in finding such jobs, while a further 24 per cent expressed difficulty in getting any job at all. This emphasizes the importance of the general economic situation in job finding, and is, no doubt, also an important influence upon the level of pay offered in the case of the first 16 per cent. The study then went on to examine the job finding behaviour of those who had expressed difficulty in finding jobs paying more than unemployment benefit levels. Over half (54 per cent) turned down no jobs for this reason, which tends to point to the existence of a strong work orientation amongst the majority. However, 13 per cent turned down one job, 7 per cent two jobs, and 26 per cent three jobs or more, because of the low wage offered compared to benefit levels payable. It must be remembered, of course, that the percentages relate only to the group expressing difficulty in finding jobs on this score. Thus, only 65 out of the 912 paid redundant men in the sample turned down any jobs where the influence of benefit levels was apparent. But, nevertheless, there was evidence of some disincentive effect among this minority.

Mackay and Reid[13] concluded: 'Our evidence is, therefore, that an increase in unemployment benefit does have some disincentive effect.' They considered that an increase in unemployment benefit of £1 per week tended to increase the length of unemployment by almost one half of a week. Nevertheless, the relationship was a weak one, and indicated no tendency for those in receipt of the earnings-related supplement to spend very long in unemployment for this reason. For the average wage earner with two children the effect might have been an extension of under one and a half weeks in the duration of joblessness, while, of course, the supplement is potentially payable for up to six months. The authors comment that the slight increase in unemployment length is not too high a price to pay in order to provide some measure of compensation for those suffering the effects of adjustments in the labour market.

Against these three case studies of redundancy, Hill's more general study of unemployment[14] in three 'typical' towns looked at the length of unemployment, and found no evidence to support the hypothesis that earnings-related benefits deterred workers from getting work quickly. In fact, in one of the three towns, it was found that there was a 'statistically significant tendency for those without an earnings-related supplement to remain unemployed the longest'.

It must, however, be acknowledged that the weight of the case study evidence indicates that some disincentive effect, although weak, seems to be associated with earnings-related unemployment benefits. But none of the case studies support the suggestion that redundancy payments have such disincentive effects. Thus, it seems somewhat sweeping to claim, as some writers have,[15] that it is the *combined* effect of these two pieces of social security legislation that explains the changed relationship between unemployment and vacancy rates that began in the fourth quarter of 1966. Before that quarter, for virtually the entire post-war period, the inverse relationship between registered unemployment and notified vacancies was remarkably stable, and, therefore, meant that one could predict the other with reasonable accuracy. This was no longer the case after 1966, with unemployment in 1967 some 90,000 above the level 'expected', given the number of vacancies notified, and some 130,000 higher in 1968. It has proved tempting to associate this change with a change in job seeking behaviour, as a consequence of a shift in the ratio of employment pay to unemployment benefit. However, it is unlikely on the case study evidence presented above that such a dramatic shift could be explained by the changes in social security legislation in 1965–6.

Apart from using case studies to attempt to assess the possible disincentive effects of increases in relative benefit levels, it is also possible to analyse various time series data to establish whether any relevant associations are revealed. Some studies have endeavoured to co-relate changes in the ratio of net benefits to net average income against changes in the level of unemployment (referred to below). It is also of interest to examine the possible effects of social security changes upon the duration characteristics of the unemployed. There is, of course, always some danger in suggesting a monocausal explanation for what is clearly a highly complex and multi-causal situation. Nevertheless, it could be expected, if the disincentive hypothesis holds, that the duration of unemployment would increase in response to a relative increase in benefit levels, thus encouraging more voluntary and longer-term unemployment. The important period during which such a change could have been expected was between 1966 and 1968. There are various ways in which unemployment duration can be expressed, but first, the percentage distribution of unemployment in various duration categories in July 1966 and July 1969[16] set out in Table 1 will be considered.

TABLE 1   *Percentage in duration category*

Duration category (weeks)	July 1966		July 1969	
	Males	*Females*	*Males*	*Females*
Up to 4	32.2	36.2	28.0	36.9
Over 4 up to 8	12.0	14.7	12.9	14.6
Over 8 up to 26	22.4	26.0	24.3	24.9
Over 26 up to 52	13.1	11.1	14.9	11.7
Over 52	20.4	12.0	20.0	11.9

The table shows that there was in fact an upward shift in the representation of the higher duration categories for males, with a particularly large increase in the eight-to-fifty-two-week categories, although the share of very long-term unemployed declined slightly. Thus, some support for the disincentive hypothesis can be gained from these figures, especially as no change in the distribution of female employment by duration groups took place. It is to be expected that changes in social security legislation would exert much less influence upon female labour market behaviour, as relatively few pay full National Insurance contributions, and their generally lower pay and shorter job tenure would tend to greatly reduce the size of any earnings-related or redundancy payment.

The increase in the unemployment duration is also confirmed by using the acturial method of duration calculation developed by Fowler.[17] This method involves examining the expected stay on the register of a given cohort of new registrants, and involves a 'steady state' assumption concerning unemployment flows through the register. Calculations for the period 1961–5 (when the mean unemployment rate was 1.7 per cent) and for 1967–70 (mean unemployment rate 2.4 per cent) are shown in Table 2.

TABLE 2 *Unemployment duration – actuarial method*

	Percentage remaining on register after stated week	
Week	1961–5	1967–70
1	73	78
2	54	52
4	32	40
8	20	25
12	13	17
16	10	12
26	5	7
52	2	3

Source: Department of Employment Gazette (February 1973).

Thus, any given cohort entering the unemployment register between 1967 and 1970 would expect to remain unemployed for a longer period than if he or she had been registered between 1961 and 1965. Again, a result generally supportive of a disincentive hypothesis, although it is of interest to note that duration lengthened throughout the scale, including the 'over six months' groups who would, of course, have exhausted any rights to earnings-related benefit. It is highly unlikely that job search behaviour among these long-term groups would have been affected by the 1965–6 social security changes.

These methods of estimating changes in the pattern of unemployment duration, therefore, tend to give some measure of support to the hypothesis that the changes in social security legislation may have affected job search behaviour and lengthened average unemployment periods. But these measures do not take adequate account of the significance of cyclical changes in the level of unemployment upon its duration characteristics. In order to examine this relationship, correlation coefficients were calculated for the seasonally adjusted quarterly unemployment rate for males and females in Great Britain, and the seasonally adjusted median duration of unemployment for the period 1949–71. Because of the inevitable time lag in any duration series when related to unemployment levels, the relationship was lagged, and it was found that lagging the median duration series by a period of three quarters yielded the highest correlation coefficient. For the period 1949 I to 1971 IV, R^2 on the data so lagged was +0.78 (significant at the 0.1 per cent level). Taking 1966 as a watershed, R^2 for the two variables 1949 I–1966 II (again the three quarter duration time-lag giving the best results) was +0.67 (significant at the 0.1 per cent level); and for 1966 III–1971 IV R^2 was +0.86 (this latter series showed that a two quarter time-lag in the median duration series gave the best result, again significant at the 0.1 per cent level).

There is, therefore, evidence to suggest that the cyclical level of unemployment is the most important determinant of unemployment duration. It is clear that the rise in the median duration level after 1966 was in no way exceptional, as a rise of virtually the same dimensions was apparent in both the 1958–9 and 1963 recessions. Indeed, it could be expected, given the much longer period of relatively high unemployment since 1966 compared with the relatively short earlier recessions, that the median duration of unemployment could have been somewhat higher than the actual level achieved. It is also clear that the relationship between the level and the duration of unemployment was stronger after 1966 than before, and if anything, a change in the level of unemployment led to an earlier influence upon the median duration of unemployment.

The emphasis that this analysis puts upon the general level of demand for labour as perhaps the most important determinant of job finding and unemployment duration behaviour is given some support by the results of most of the above mentioned case studies, although Mackay and Reid[6] did not find employment conditions to be very important in explaining unemployment experience. It seems, therefore, that any change in the overall duration characteristics of the unemployed is, in most cases, far more significantly influenced by the buoyancy of the general economic climate than by changes in social security legislation. Thus, at aggregate level, the change in the duration of unemployment is entirely consistent with the cyclical level of unemployment. Apparently any disincentive effects associated with social security changes are counter-balanced by opposite effects among other unemployed workers, such that the median unemployment duration can be predicted with a reasonable degree of accuracy by the level of unemployment, at least from the late 1950s down to 1972.

Other studies[18] have regressed male unemployment or unemployment duration on the benefit/income ratio. Maki and Spindler suggest that the introduction of earnings-related benefit had a pronounced effect upon the level of male unemployment, increasing it by some 33 per cent, although they point out that for the period 1967–72 male unemployment was still some 54 per cent higher *after* the effect of earnings-related benefit was taken into account. There is, however, a fundamental weakness in their measurement of the benefit / income ratio, in that it relates to a purely notional 'average' man, and not to the actual level of benefit paid. This leads to a considerable over-estimate of the benefit / income ratio, as only a minority of the unemployed receive any earning-related supplement at all. Table 3 sets out the information currently available from Hansard and other sources on the

TABLE 3 *Percentage of registered unemployed*

Year	(a) Receiving earnings-related supplement (%)	(b) Affected by the 85 per cent earnings ceiling (%)
1968	N.A.	0.75
1969	N.A.	0.53
1970	19.0	1.02
1971	19.6	0.73
1972	19.0	1.64
1973	15.8	2.52
1974	17.5	3.53
1975	21.1	8.54
1976	20.4	11.00
1977	16.0	N.A.

Sources: House of Lords and House of Commons Hansards and D.H.S.S.

proportion of the registered unemployed receiving the earnings-related supplement, and the proportion receiving unemployment benefit whose benefit entitlement is affected by the 85 per cent earnings ceiling.

The table shows that rarely have more than 20 per cent of the unemployed received any earnings-related supplement in any of the last ten years, and that this proportion had fallen to 16 per cent in 1977. It is also clear that an increasing proportion in receipt of the supplement have had their entitlement reduced by the ruling that total benefit, including the supplement, shall not exceed 85 per cent of previous earnings. This proportion was negligible in the early 1970s, but 11 per cent were affected by 1976. It is further the case that the supplement is not always even sufficient to lift total benefit income above the 'poverty line', as 12.6 per cent of those receiving the supplement in May 1977 were also claiming Supplementary Benefit.

Thus, any disincentive effects associated with the introduction of earnings-related benefit in the mid-1960s can be applied only to a relatively small minority of the registered unemployed, and even within this category the amount of additional benefit payable can be quite small.

Nickell,[19] using a model which includes a value for the probability of obtaining work for the average unemployed man, and using more realistic estimates of actual benefits payable, suggests that the likely impact of unemployment level and duration of the earnings-related supplement is of the order of 11 per cent, that is, about one-third of the impact estimated by Maki and Spindler. The evidence in a report of a Department of Employment working party[20] on the changed relationship between unemployment and vacancies suggests that Nickell's estimate of an 11 per cent impact on unemployment levels is itself the maximum likely effect. The report, comparing *inter alia* the effect on unemployment in 1967–8 with the level in 1962–3, shows that it would require an assumption that the receipt of the earnings-related supplement doubled the length of an individual's spell out of work for an increase of 50,000 in unemployment to occur (that is about 10 per cent of total registered unemployment in 1967–8). There is little evidence that an assumption of this order is realistic. The report also shows, by looking at the increase in those unemployed for two to twenty-six weeks (the relevant duration category for those in receipt of the supplement), that it would require an assumption that virtually the whole of that increase was associated with the effects of the earnings-related supplement for unemployment in the period to be increased by about 10 per cent. This is an assumption that is again unrealistic, given the fact that the unemployment in most duration categories increased generally in the period (see Tables 1 and 2 above).

The discussion has focused upon the effect on unemployment of changes in the benefit/income ratio following the introduction of new types of Social Security Provision in the mid-1960s, and has compared reasonably enough the situation in the early 1960s with the early 1970s. The upward trend in unemployment has also continued throughout the 1970s, and it is interesting to note that this has occurred while the benefit / income ratio appears to have fallen somewhat from the levels applying in 1968–70. The National Institute of Economic and Social Research[21] have calculated the benefit / income ratio using short-term unemployment benefit entitlement, including the earnings-related supplement, expressed as a percentage of net disposable income for a married couple with two children on average male manual earnings. This is again a notional calculation and, given the restricted entitlement to the earnings-related supplement noted above, is likely to over-estimate the actual ratio. Nevertheless, the results show that the benefit / income ratio reached a peak of 71 per cent in 1968, and was 70 per cent in 1970, but in all subsequent years to 1976 it was between only 65 per cent and 67 per cent. If the above studies were, therefore, to include data from the mid- and late 1970s the values obtained for the effects of social security changes on unemployment levels are likely to be considerably reduced.

Before drawing a conclusion from the analysis of the possible disincentive effects of the two major changes in social security provision dating from the mid-1960s, it is necessary to consider the other changes that have taken place in the social security position of the unemployed during the 1970s. A substantial part of this change is associated with the rapid growth of long-term unemployment. Table 4 shows this change for selected years since 1950.

It is clear from Table 4 that the trend towards increased duration

TABLE 4   *Unemployment by duration selected years since 1950* (in thousands)

Month/year	Up to 8 weeks		Over 8 weeks to 26 weeks		Over 26 weeks to 52 weeks		Over 52 weeks		
	No.	%	No.	%	No.	%	No.	%	Total
Sept. 1950	159.4	58.2	52.3	19.1	26.3	9.6	35.9	13.1	273.9
Sept. 1955	113.9	63.0	29.4	16.2	15.7	8.7	21.9	12.1	180.9
Sept. 1960	142.8	48.9	58.5	20.0	35.6	12.2	55.3	18.9	292.2
Oct. 1965	158.8	52.0	64.6	21.1	31.2	10.2	51.5	16.8	305.7
Oct. 1970	259.0	45.1	143.1	24.9	70.2	12.2	101.7	17.7	574.0
Oct. 1975	425.3	38.7	357.6	32.6	154.5	14.1	161.2	14.7	1098.2
Oct. 1976	416.7	31.5	414.3	31.4	225.3	17.1	264.6	20.0	1320.9
Oct. 1977	429.7	29.5	469.8	32.2	232.8	16.0	324.3	22.3	1456.6
July 1978	580.3	38.4	360.7	23.8	243.0	16.1	328.4	21.7	1512.5

Sources: Department of Employment Gazette and F. Field (ed.), *The Conscript Army*, Routledge, 1977.

of unemployment has continued into the late 1970s. In July 1978, 243,000 of the unemployed had been unemployed for over six months, and a further 328,400 had been unemployed continuously for over a year. The latter category alone are now more numerous than was the *total* of unemployment in the 1950s and early 1960s. Both of these long-term unemployed categories will have exhausted any entitlement they may have had to the earnings-related supplement, and the over-fifty-two-week category will have also exhausted their rights to basic Unemployment Benefit. This situation, with an increased number in shorter duration categories, who because of deficiencies in their National Insurance contribution records (largely attributable to previous repeated spells of unemployment or sickness and previous full-time education or self-employment), has meant a rapid increase in dependency of the unemployed on means-tested Supplementary Benefit, which will be further examined below.

For the 571,000 in long-term unemployment the problem is less a lack of incentive to find work, and much more a lack of opportunity to do so. Employers, faced with an excess supply of applicants, are likely to screen out those with a long record of unemployment, on the grounds that they have had less recent experience of employment, and any skills they may have had will be of little current value.

This pattern is reinforced by the referral practices of the employment service, which leads to many more referrals for the recently unemployed than for the long-term unemployed. Thus, a ratchet effect on future levels of unemployment is likely to occur as more and more of the long-term unemployed are written-off as unemployable, making their chances of re-employment weaker, even if a major fall in the general level of unemployment occurs. Harrison[22] has pointed to the severe social and psychological ill-effects of long-term unemployment; the jobless often develop a depressing and fatalistic acceptance of their situation. Yet the evidence suggests that, even among this group, work is seen as infinitely preferable for the majority. Marsden and Duff concluded:

We found that so strong are the pressures and informal sanctions supporting work in our society that some of the workless cling to the desire to work to a much greater degree than our society has a right to expect. . . . For those we interviewed, talk about the 'opportunity' or 'leisure' afforded by unemployment seems decidedly premature.[23]

Returning specifically to the growing number and proportion of the unemployed who are partially or wholly dependent on Supplementary Benefit, Table 5 shows the benefit position in May 1977.

TABLE 5   *Registered unemployed analysed by benefit entitlement, May 1977*

Unemployment Benefit only	Unemployment Benefit and Supplementary Benefit	Supplementary Benefit	Other	Total
426,000	117,000	528,000	254,000	1,325,000

Source: Department of Employment Gazette, September 1978.

The table shows that there are now far more partially or wholly dependent on Supplementary Benefit (S.B.) than on Unemployment Benefit alone. The latter group among the unemployed have been a falling proportion of the total for most of the post-war period. The proportion of unemployed claimants drawing National Insurance benefits has fallen from over 70 per cent in 1948 to under 40 per cent in 1977.

Given this situation it is arguably more important to examine any disincentive effects associated with Supplementary Benefits levels on unemployment than Unemployment Benefits with or without the earnings-related supplement. The Department of Health and Social Security review[24] of the Supplementary Benefit Scheme in Great Britain has examined aspects of this problem. The review shows that the ordinary scale rate plus average rent increases for both single and married couples, as a percentage of average net earnings of male manual workers, has not increased significantly since 1967. The percentages in October 1967 were 30.8 per cent (single householder) and 48.6 per cent (married couple), falling somewhat during the early 1970s, recovering after October 1973, and by November 1977 were 32 per cent and 50 per cent respectively.

Such averages, of course, suffer from the same disadvantages as the notional unemployment benefit work income ratios referred to earlier, taking no account of differences in family circumstances and actual family income received in employment. Accordingly, the review provides a more detailed comparison of total income support when working and when in receipt of S.B. for various income levels and family circumstances.[25] The income-in-work estimates include a deduction for work expenses, but assume the full take-up of all available benefits. The analysis shows, for example, that total income support on S.B. for a married couple with previous gross earnings of £75 per week was 50 per cent of total income support in work, increasing to 68 per cent for a couple with two children, and to 86 per cent to one with four children. The corresponding percentages for those with very low gross earnings of £45 per week were 76 per cent, 84 per cent and 97 per cent respectively. The review concludes that it is only where there are four or more children in the household that total income support can exceed 90 per cent of that applying when employed. It is the combination of low earnings and a large family that can give rise to S.B. income close to that in work. Such a situation applies in only a small number of cases, with less than 5 per cent of men in work with gross earnings below £45 per week, and only 4 per cent of S.B. beneficiaries below pension age have families with four or more children.

Some support for the view that any disincentive effects are likely to be associated with differences in family circumstances can be found in Daniel and Stilgoe's follow-up study[26] of the earlier P.E.P. National Survey of the Unemployed. They show that over a three-year period their sample of unemployed men with full-time working wives spent 83 per cent of that time in employment, compared with only 44 per cent for men with wives with no paid work. Men with one child were employed for 69 per cent of time in the three years, compared with only 33 per cent of time for men with four or more children. The study concludes that it is likely that differences in dependants' allowances may affect benefit levels in such a way as to influence some men's willingness to accept jobs, but that this effect was concentrated among low-skilled, low-paid men.

Surveys by the D.H.S.S. of actual cases, however, disclose that few of those with relatively high S.B. income have refused to return to work when it was available, particularly when the availability of means-tested benefits for those in work were explained, although the surveys also showed widespread ignorance, misunderstanding and a reluctance to claim these benefits.

A summary of the discussion above suggests that the introduction of Redundancy Payments has had little or no effect upon the level and duration of unemployment, and in any case eligibility for such payments among the unemployed is restricted to a very small minority (7 per cent in 1975). It also seems likely that several studies have greatly over-estimated the possible disincentive effects of the introduction of earnings-related benefit by using unrealistic notional estimates of the benefit / income ratio, and by over-estimating the proportion of the unemployed entitled to such supplementation (less than 20 per cent). The above analysis of unemployment duration has shown that the changing duration characteristics are quite consistent with the general upward trend in total unemployment. It is also apparent that no significant change in general benefit / income ratios has occurred during the 1970s, in respect of either National Insurance Benefits or S.B. The growing dependency of the unemployed on the latter benefit has been outlined, and in this respect any potential disincentive effect is likely to be concentrated upon the low-skilled, low-paid with large families, a group whose employment potential has been most adversely affected by changes in the pattern of demand in the labour market.

In conclusion, given the marginal impact upon estimates of voluntary unemployment of changes in social security provision, it is not inappropriate to suggest that the present discrimination in benefit provision for the vast majority of the unemployed and particularly the long-term unemployed should be corrected. There appears to be no strong economic argument against the restoration of the real value of the earnings-related supplement, for the extension of entitlement to adequate National Insurance Unemployment Benefit for a longer period, and for the long-term unemployed to be entitled to the long-term rate of Supplementary Benefit from which they are presently excluded. Any possible further disincentive effects from such changes could be avoided by the provision of adequate income support for those in low-paid employment and increased Child Benefit provision.

Notes and References

1. First appeared as an article in *Social and Economic Administration*, Vol. 9, No. 2, Summer 1975.
2. T. Nichols and Benyon, *Living with Capitalism*, Routledge and Kegan Paul, 1977.
   Schlackman Research Organisation, *Report on Research on public attitudes towards the Supplementary Benefit System* for the Supplementary Benefits Commission Review, mimeo, January 1978.
3. David Macarov, *Incentives to Work*, Jossey-Bass, San Francisco, 1970.
4. J. W. Dorsey, 'The Mack Case: A Study in Unemployment' in O. Eckstein, *Studies in the Economics of Income Maintenance*, Brookings Institute, Washington, 1967.
5. S. R. Parker, *et al.*, *Effects of the Redundancy Payments Act*, Office of Population Censuses and Surveys, H.M.S.O., 1971, p. 108.
6. D. I. Mackay and G. L. Reid, 'Redundancy, Unemployment and Manpower Policy', *Economic Journal*, Vol. 81, No. 328, 1972, pp. 1270–1.

7. W. W. Daniel, *Whatever happened to the workers in Woolwich?*, P.E.P. Broadsheet 537, 1972, pp. 99–102.
8. R. Martin and R. H. Fryer, *Redundancy and Paternalist Capitalism*, Allen and Unwin, 1973, pp. 125–6.
9. Hill, M. J., *et al.*, *Men out of Work*, Cambridge University Press, 1973, pp. 130–1.
10. F. Field (ed.), *The Conscript Army*, Routledge, 1977, p. 39.
11. W. W. Daniel, *op. cit.*, pp. 42–5.
12. S. R. Parker, *op. cit.*, p. 11.
13. D. I. Mackay and G. L. Reid, *op. cit.*, p. 1268.
14. M. J. Hill, *et al.*, *op cit.*, p. 82.
15. D. Gujarati, 'The behaviour of unemployment and unfilled vacancies: Great Britain 1968–71', *Economic Journal*, Vol. 81, No. 321, 1971, pp. 195–204.
16. Detailed duration analyses are published in the Department of Employment Gazette quarterly, hence July 1966 was chosen as representative of the relevant month under which the 'old' unemployment: vacancies relationship could be expected to hold. The 'new' relationship appears to have stablilized in July 1968, but in order to take account of the fact that it will take twelve months before the new accessions to the unemployment register in 1968 reach the relevant duration category, July 1969 was chosen for comparison.
17. R. F. Fowler, *Duration of Unemployment on the Register of Wholly Unemployed*, H.M.S.O., 1968.
18. See for example, D. Maki and Z. A. Spindler, 'The effect of unemployment compensation on the rate of unemployment in Britain', *Oxford Economic Papers*, Vol. 27, No. 3, 1975, pp. 440–454; and J. S. Cubbin and K. Foley, 'The Extent of Benefit-Induced Unemployment in Great Britain: Some New Evidence', *Oxford Economic Papers*, Vol. 29, No. 2, 1977, pp. 128–140.
19. S. J. Nickell, *The Effect of Unemployment and Related Benefits on the Duration of Unemployment*, Centre for Labour Economics, L.S.E., Discussion Paper No. 8, November 1977.
20. Department of Employment, 'The Changed Relationship between Unemployment and Vacancies', *Department of Employment Gazette*, Vol. 84, October 1976, pp. 1093–1099.
21. N.I.E.S.R., *National Institute Review*, No. 79, February 1977, p. 15.
22. R. Harrison, 'The demoralising experience of prolonged unemployment', *Department of Employment Gazette*, Vol. 84, April 1976, pp. 339–348.

23. D. Marsden and E. Duff, *Workless – Some Unemployed Men and their Families*, Penguin, 1975, p. 264.
24. D.H.S.S., *Social Assistance: A Review of the Supplementary Benefits Scheme in Great Britain*, D.H.S.S., July 1978, pp. 112–121.
25. D.H.S.S., *op. cit.*, Table A5.1, p. 1118.
26. W. W. Daniel and E. Stilgoe, *Where are they now?* P.E.P., October 1977.

PART II

Housing and
Urban Development

CHAPTER THREE

Urban Development and Social Policies[1]

DAVID DONNISON

Although its roots run much further back,[2] town planning in Britain
was founded on a series of measures[3] formulated during the Second
World War and enacted soon after. With hindsight we can see that
town planning was built upon a consensus amongst a coalition
of diverse interests. New town visionaries, liberal economists interested in problems of compensation and betterment, country
gentlemen and commuters anxious to conserve rural England and
the country's architectural heritage, the public health movement
concerned about squalor, disease and disorder, the labour movement speaking for cities and regions in which hunger marchers had
assembled during the depression years, and even the Ministry of
Defence, disturbed by the growing concentration of productive
capacity in the exposed south-eastern corner of the country – all
supported the new legislation, and their expectations helped to
shape the profession it created. Mr Silkin, the Minister who introduced the great Act of 1947, began his two-hour speech[4] with an
exposition of 'the objects of town and country planning' which
amounted to a roll call of these interests.

The town planners and their colleagues in central and local
government went far to clear the slums, to contain the spreading
cities and ring them with green belts, to protect cherished buildings
and pull down the advertising hoardings, to reduce oppressively

51

high densities and raise wastefully low ones, and to impose a reasonably humane imprint on British patterns of urban development. But the assumptions and the vision which informed the consensus founded on this coalition were in many respects feudal, anti-urban, economically illiterate, élitist and politically naïve. The surprising thing is not that the consensus eventually broke up but that it lasted so long. It survived because the coalition was real: its main priorities – the reduction of the highest densities, the containment of the great conurbations, and the dispersal of population to middle-sized and smaller towns on the periphery of the major urban regions – suited powerful interests (manufacturers, house buyers, car drivers and so on). With or without British-style planning, similar patterns of urban development took shape in most of the world's more highly developed urban economies.

For reasons which I shall explore later, that cosy, rather paternalistic consensus has broken up. By the mid-1960s it was becoming increasingly clear that town planning was not just about land use, transport, the design of townscapes, and the management of things which can be inscribed on maps. It was also about access to opportunities, the distribution of limited resources among people competing for a share of the good things an urban society should afford them, and the politics of urban development.

In 1948 the first examination paper in one of the country's most prestigious town planning diplomas, set by Holford and Forshaw – two of the most revered exponents of the profession's 1947 vision of its functions – began thus:

What are the main building uses which you would expect to find in the central area of a town with a population of a quarter of a million? Give your opinion as to which of these can be satisfactorily combined in one building, one street block, or one zone; and mention the disadvantages in convenience and amenity that result from indiscriminately mixed uses.

This picture of the planner as estate manager to the urban community would have been perfectly familiar to the men who designed the squares of London and Dublin two hundred years ago. The first question in the equivalent examination in 1976 was:

Critically evalute the contribution, actual and potential, made by empirical studies of local communities or of particular sections of the population in helping planners to do their job more effectively.[5]

The titles of the books on the reading lists of the students who answered that question breathe the new tone – *Race, Community and Conflict*,[6] *Whose City?*,[7] *Social Justice and the City*,[8] *Citizens in Conflict*,[9] are among those which appear most often.

Social policy 'goes spatial'

At about the same time students of social policy, social workers, educationists and much of what Vice-President Agnew once called 'the radical liberal establishment' came increasingly to recognize that they were dealing not merely with individual clients, patients, pupils, delinquents and their families, but with people in the setting of a local community and the neighbourhoods in which they lived. That was not a new idea: it would have been entirely familiar to the reverend Thomas Chalmers at the start of the nineteenth century and to Charles Booth at the end of it. But in Britain the 'welfare state' had been designed to assure national minimum standards in place of the services hitherto provided by local government, local friendly societies, and local charities. It was created as a reaction against all the variations, confusions and injustices which reliance on the local community had previously entailed. The reaction, it was now felt, had gone too far.

The literature which records these changes includes: the Plowden Report[10] on primary schools, calling for educational priority areas in which extra educational resources of all kinds would be concentrated on deprived communities; the Seebohm Report,[11] calling for the concentration of extra resources in 'designated areas of special need', and the unification of social services hitherto provided by different departments of local government, and henceforth to be deployed in area teams, which were to include community workers; and the Milner Holland Report[12] on Housing in London, which called for a more comprehensive attack on bad housing conditions in 'areas of special control'. In 1968 the government's Urban Aid Programme was launched to provide larger resources for housing, health and welfare services, day nurseries, education and other services in 'areas of special social need'.[13]

Voluntary organizations were thinking on similar lines. A report,[14] sponsored by the Gulbenkian Foundation, called for the recruitment and training of many more community workers. The Child Poverty Action Group, Shelter, Gingerbread, the Claimants' Unions and other new pressure groups, which together constituted a formidable poverty lobby, set up local branches and action groups in many parts of the country. The older National Council for Civil Liberties did likewise. Lawyers have been recruited to law centres, supported by statutory and voluntary funds, to provide a free legal service for people in the more deprived neighbourhoods. There they have come to recognize that free legal services offered to individuals (to secure a divorce for a deserted wife, for example) will generally be conservative in their ultimate effect, however beneficial to the client concerned. To bring about more fundamental changes, lawyers must act for collectively organized groups (tenants' associations, trade unions and neighbourhood action groups, for example) and seek strategic judgments which will extend their rights and modify the balances of power between them and their employers, creditors, landlords and governments.[15]

'Neighbourhood', 'priority area', and 'community' have become well worn in the vocabulary of debate about social policies. Thus it was that town planners (who had been talking about neighbourhoods and communities since the days of their founding fathers who had tried to build Utopias in the eighteenth and early nineteenth centuries) met the social policy makers coming from the opposite direction (people now rediscovering the community and the spatial aspects of the problems they had so long contended with in aspatial fashion).

Some of the forces at work

These developments were not due simply to changes in intellectual fashion. Similar things were taking shape, initially in a quite unco-ordinated way, in different fields of public service, in different academic disciplines, and in different countries throughout the world. Why? To answer that question fully would call for a major work of contemporary history, but we may be able to throw some light upon it more briefly.

The post-Beveridge, 'Butskellite' coalition of interests served by the slowly evolving institutions of the 'welfare state' did not share as complete a consensus as the coalition supporting the movement for town planning. Battles over pension schemes, housing policies and the reorganization of secondary education were real. Yet in both fields most people probably shared four fundamental assumptions. These were, first, the belief that the community should 'level up' the distributions of income and realized opportunities by bringing those at the bottom of these distributions closer to their averages; secondly, the belief that the state was the natural and principal instrument for achieving that; and, thirdly, the belief that constant inquiry, analysis, and publication, monitoring social conditions and reporting on the plight of those at the bottom of the heap, would gain the support of public opinion and democratic governments for the action required. Fourthly, and most important of all, was the belief that, although governments would regulate the processes of economic development, succour the casualties of economic growth, and stimulate the economy or steer it in particular directions, the economic motor itself could be relied on to keep turning – and so, too, would the motor of demographic growth which assured a constantly expanding demand for the economy's products.

These tend to be the assumptions of liberal democracies of a peaceful, homogeneous kind after many years of full employment; and for most purposes they have been justified. Even if differences between the attainments of different social classes remained obstinately difficult to change, the life expectations, housing conditions, academic achievements and other important features of each class in Britain showed striking improvements during the post-war years. Here, as in many other countries, the 1950s seemed a period of such peaceful domestic progress that some foresaw an end to ideological conflict. Demonstrations of political passion, when they occurred, often dealt with foreign affairs, nuclear disarmament, and other issues not felt to be directly related to the old class conflicts of urban, industrial societies.

Gradually these assumptions were eroded. In Britain the town planners had for a decade and a half after the Second World War devoted most of their attention to new developments on blitzed sites or in green fields outside the cities. Since few people were displaced, and those who would later use the new houses, work in the new factories (or deplore the tardy appearance of local services there) could not be identified at the time when decisions to develop were taken, planning could proceed between officials, developers, land-owners, lenders and their solicitors in bureaucracy's backrooms without the public knowing or caring much about the outcome. But from the early 1960s the bulldozers began to bite into the inner cities: slum clearance in Britain rose from less than 35,000 houses a year in 1955 to a steady 70,000 a year from 1960. In that year 135,000 houses were improved with the help of government grants: in 1955 there had been too little improvement to record in official statistics. City centre redevelopment, the boom in office building, the expansion of universities, polytechnics and hospitals, and the urban motorways that carved through Glasgow, Birmingham and other great cities posed similar problems. Planning could no longer proceed in a private, non-partisan, élitist fashion: it was increasingly clear who gained and who lost in the course of these developments, and who was taking the planning decisions.

The dispersal of people to increasingly distant suburbs and the growing concentrations of service industries in city centres were bound to lead to a re-invasion by young professionals and executives of inner areas long abandoned to the working class. The Rent Act of 1957 made it much easier to sell them housing, which had previously been rented, and the massive boom in the stock markets, coupled with the generous provision of improvement grants, helped them to buy. 'Gentrification', a term coined by Ruth Glass for this process, entered the vocabulary of planning debate. Competition for space, often in nearby areas, was dramatized by the arrival of unexpectedly large numbers of immigrants seeking to enter the country before the barriers imposed by the 1962 Commonwealth Immigrants Act and subsequent legislation were lowered. The long-established, local working class were rehoused on a massive scale, but many were stacked in tower blocks: the numbers of Council flats in England and Wales built fifteen or more storeys from the ground rose from 8 in 1955 to 17,351 in 1965. There began to take shape a social division, long widespread on the continent, between middle-class people living in houses and workers living in flats – 'people silos' as they were called in Sweden. Even before one of them collapsed in a gas explosion at Ronan Point in London, the tower block became a focus of special hatred. Meanwhile the rediscovery of poverty and deep-rooted social inequalities in the 1960s led contributors to debates about social policy to concentrate increasingly on problems such as racial discrimination, the plight of the homeless, the more extreme hardships still to be found in an affluent society and the social conflicts associated with them.

Britain's political response to this rougher weather was at first a hopeful one. In the mid-1960s, under a government which had promised in the election of 1964 to achieve sustained economic growth and put an end to the 'stop-go-stop' style of economic management, Royal Commissions and public inquiries were set on foot, asking radical questions about many hallowed institutions (local government, the marriage laws, the public schools, the jury system and Parliament itself were among those examined), and a major effort was made to shake labour out of stagnant industries and equip workers with more productive skills.

But the continuing decline in industrial investment, and the increasingly disastrous weakness of the economy and its balance of payments with other countries led to the July measures of 1966, the abandonment of the National Plan, recurring cuts in public expenditure, and deepening disillusionment with social democracy, with Westminster politics and with government itself. At the scale of the big city these trends and problems were sharpened by what amounted to the collapse of the inner city economy. Docks, warehousing and manufacturing industry closed, or moved out to smaller towns and suburbs. Although the growth of service industries in city centres maintained the total numbers of jobs for a while, the growth sectors of the urban economy relied heavily on women working in routine administrative and service occupations – no replacement for the lost earnings and self-confidence of the older skilled men who were being displaced.

Meanwhile the demographic motor was faltering too: the rise in the birthrate, which constantly surpassed official forecasts from

1956 to 1965, was succeeded by an equally constant and unforeseen decline. These changes had a crippling effect on professions which proceed largely by steering and regulating development pressed onward by economic and demographic growth. The South East Study of 1964[16] and other major initiatives in urban and regional planning were prompted by the need to find space for forthcoming, unforeseen growth; but today planners in many parts of Britain have zoned enough land for housing, undustry and other uses to last them until the end of the century. Similar things are happening for similar reasons to those responsible for planning the country's housing, education and health services.

Thus the loss of confidence in government and the public service professions, the pluralism, the localism, the populism and the more abrasive conflicts appearing in debates about social and planning policies during the late 1960s and early 1970s were a response to more profound changes in a country no longer able to assume that the economic motor would keep turning to generate the resources for policy makers to redistribute, or to assume that democratically elected governments could confidently.speak with one voice on behalf of the majority of their citizens when dealing with the biggest social questions of the day.

These generalizations must not be too highly coloured: compared with most countries in the world, Britain (but not the United Kingdom) is still an exceedingly wealthy, peaceful, consensual society. Nevertheless, it is clear that the country's economic situation and the political climate within which policy makers have to operate have changed profoundly. Like other professions, town planners and social policy makers, to whom I now return, have been making their groping response to these changes.

Community development projects: the rise and fall of an experiment

There were many points at which the two movements came together to grapple with these dilemmas; but their most interesting encounter took place in the twelve Community Development Projects (C.D.P.s), staffed by young people drawn from social work, social research, planning, local government and political action, set up by the Home Office in collaboration with local authorities in deprived neighbourhoods of different kinds – and particularly in the inner parts of the great conurbations. Their original aim was to study the needs of these areas, to help the public services working in them to formulate more effective and more closely co-ordinated programmes, to focus public attention locally and nationally upon these needs, and to give the people living in these areas a voice in the debate and opportunities for doing things for themselves.

In many neglected communities remarkable things have been achieved by the C.D.P.s and the local authorities which responded to their sometimes unorthodox and disturbing interventions. Nursery schools, welfare rights offices, hostels for the homeless and other projects have been set up; programmes of urban renewal and house building have been reshaped in significant ways; links have been forged with tenants' associations, claimants' unions, trade unions and other bodies. Yet most people, and certainly the leaders of the projects themselves, would say that the C.D.P.s have failed. Why?

Those who worked on these projects were not content with local, small-scale, amelioration. They wanted to improve the living conditions and enlarge the opportunities and the self-confidence of the people who lived in their areas, and to set in train a programme which would achieve similar things in many other places. Their pursuit of these more ambitious objectives led them to two depressing conclusions.

They saw the neighbourhoods in which they worked as an integral part of a larger industrial society, their problems caused by the decay of that society and its economy. They were 'hard pressed working-class communities suffering progressive under-development in terms of industrial decline and the changing composition of the local labour force'. Three of these areas 'suffer the effects of decline in port-related industries', two 'the decline of textile industries', two 'the closure of mining enterprises' and three 'the decline of manufacturing industries'.[17] The decay of these local economies had been brought about over many years by the run-down and withdrawal of capital re-invested by its owners in other parts of Britain and in other countries. The decline of earnings and employment in the Chrysler plant in Coventry, they argued, could not be understood without looking at the policies adopted by Chrysler in plants all over the world.

The C.D.P.s' second sombre conclusion dealt with government. After trying fruitlessly – too briefly and ineptly, some would say – to gain from central and local authorities the massive resources they were convinced they needed, they rejected the liberal-democratic assumptions on which their projects had been founded. Government, they argued, was ultimately the servant of the interests and classes which dominate the society in which we live. Notwithstanding their concern for social welfare – a very natural concern for rulers who must avoid scandal and prevent serious disorder if they are to survive – governments will do nothing to disturb the basic structure of society and the economic order on which it is based. If you are seeking not just some extra nursery school places, but a transformation of opportunities throughout the neighbourhood, then government is your problem rather than the solution.

'Experience', said the C.D.P. teams, 'has led them largely to discount the value of attempting to influence policy and promote technical strategies for change in isolation from the development of working class action.' They 'do not have strong expectations of the national policy effect of their documents, and consider their main importance as generating a debate within local political networks and local administrative systems.' Further, they maintained that: 'Instead of feeding local evidence about local people to the decision makers in the perhaps naïve hope that they will do something about their problem, we will concentrate more on feeding facts and figures about the cause of a problem to local people so that they can create the pressure for change.'[18]

I find much of this analysis convincing. (Indeed, somewhat similar accounts of the large-scale economic causes of urban deprivation and the ineffectiveness of local, small-scale government interventions in such areas have come from analysts approaching the subject from the Right rather than the Left, who emerge with conclusions – about the need to give entrepreneurs greater freedom and monetary incentives – very different from those of the C.D.P. teams.) Thus, rather than argue about the fine print here, I shall press on and ask: what follows from this analysis? For it was when the C.D.P.s prescribed strategies for action that they became less cogent.

First, we need to know what economic strategies to follow. Re-interpreting the question for the town planner, he needs to know what kind of city we want. Suppose fundamental changes in the country's social structure are achieved; suppose 'the commanding heights of the economy' are captured – suppose the revolution itself. What then? If we do not have a convincing and widely understood answer to offer, governments, anxious to survive, will tend to prop up the lame ducks in order to retain as many as possible of the jobs in declining industries and declining communities. That encourages over-manning, low pay and continuing decline. The outcome, even under a supposedly revolutionary régime, may be destructively conservative.

Secondly, as spokesmen of the deprived become clearer about their objectives, they must next consider how the people for whom they speak can gain influence. As their analysis of the problems afflicting the neighbourhoods in which they work has grown larger, looking to the city, the nation and ultimately the world for an explanation of the economic crisis of capitalism in which we find ourselves, the arenas in which they have chosen to act have grown smaller and smaller. Deliberately cutting themselves off from central and local government, some of the teams concentrated on working with shop stewards in particular factories, tenants' associations on particular estates, and mothers who may be enabled to run a play group or a youth club. How will they rebuild their links with power upon a scale that matches the scale of the problems they have identified? Where, in particular, will those for whom they speak find the workers and the funds for a movement of this kind? During the concluding agonies of the C.D.P. movement its leaders turned successively to the Home Office, the Social Science Research Council, and the Gulbenkian, Rowntree, Nuffield, Cadbury and Sainsbury Foundations – virtually a roll call of power within the society which the C.D.P.s intend to overturn. It is not surprising the projects are coming to an end: there is no subsidized revolution.

The answer given to these difficult questions by the most articulate spokesmen of the movement has been that they are building their links from the bottom of the political system with groups which represent the indigenous, local working class. Their aim is not to advise governments, but to arm these groups with the information they need in order to do battle for themselves in the political arenas of the nation. Coolly examined – and shorn of a certain romanticism about shop stewards and tenants' leaders – that answer suggests to me that the C.D.P.s may be laboriously re-inventing the wheel – or, to be more precise, re-inventing the Labour Party. For that is how and why the party was originally created, and it is a party which still dominates all the areas in which the C.D.P.s operate. If it has failed, what went wrong? And how do those, now so laboriously re-inventing it, avoid re-enacting the same story, or (worse still) dividing and destroying the fallible instrument they already have?

Closer study of the deprived areas and groups among which the C.D.P.s work suggests to me that it is no accident that they tend to be neglected – under any régime. The political movements set up to articulate the social conflicts of urban, industrial society and the institutions they create to resolve conflicts and ameliorate conditions have, over the years, gone a long way to secure greater justice for organized workers and their families. Social democratic and Christian democratic parties in many parts of the world have achieved greater security of employment for the working man, notably a pensioned retirement, an income when his work is interrupted by sickness or redundancy, virtually free medical care and education, a secure home in housing that is a reasonably satisfactory version of the kind of dwelling that used to be available only to the bourgeoisie, and effective spokesmen to defend them when in conflict with employers, governments and other authorities. Across most of the English speaking world and much of Europe, East and West, that is now the situation of most well-organized and long established working-class men and their families.

I am not complacent about these achievements. Major differences in life-chances still distinguish the different social classes – differences reflected in the heights and weights of school children, in morbidity and mortality rates and life expectations, in educational attainment and much else. The point I am making is not that all is now well for the working class, but that some of the most deprived people in an urban industrial society suffer from handicaps which can neither be wholly explained nor completely resolved in traditional, vulgar-Marxist terms of class conflict.

It is no accident that those who live on the margins of the welfare state are excluded from the benefits which many working people receive. They are not well represented by the trade unions (who are naturally less enthusiastic about them than they are about their own dues-paying members). They may also be forgotten by political parties (who naturally listen first to the well-established local people who provide their funds, do their leg work and turn out to vote). They are too diverse and ill-defined an array of people to form an identifiable, representable interest. The services the community does provide for the most deprived of them – means-tested supplementary benefit, not contributory benefits; special housing for the homeless, not conventional council houses; prisons, not mental hospitals – may then meet their needs in stigmatizing ways which expose them to hostility and make it harder for them to gain a foothold in the secure and central areas of the labour market, the housing market, the education system and other spheres of urban society.

The problem is a very old one. Charles Booth understood it more than eighty years ago: 'To the rich the very poor are a sentimental interest: to the poor they are a crushing load. The poverty of the poor is mainly the result of the competition of the very poor'.[19] Such news as we get today from the centrally-planned countries of eastern Europe suggests that revolutions do not necessarily change these relationships or resolve the conflicts they provoke.

All this may sound like an attack on the C.D.P.s. On the contrary, anyone who explores the formidable problems they have tackled will encounter the same dilemmas, and since they have been among the boldest explorers, the dilemmas have been posed more starkly in their work than elsewhere. I cannot resolve them, but I will try to throw a little more light on them in the rest of this chapter, dealing first with urban structure and planning policies, and then with social policies.

Priorities for urban development

Research I am doing at the Centre for Environmental Studies with Paul Soto suggests that manual workers in general, and the least skilled of them in particular, tend to do best in comparison with similar workers elsewhere in the country in towns where there has been a good deal of new investment over the last generation or more, where new industries prosper and new skills are in demand. By 'doing best' I particularly mean that they are less likely to be unemployed, more likely to own a car and drive it to work, and more likely to live in a town with a plentiful supply of council housing.

There is some evidence to suggest that other 'marginal' citizens may do better in these places too. If I am right in guessing that a woman with two children under school age who works full-time is often reluctantly compelled by economic circumstances to do this, then it is significant that in our more prosperous, growing towns women with children under the age of five are more likely to work for eight hours a week or less, and less likely to work for thirty hours or more, than they are elsewhere in the country, and part-time work for women in general is more plentiful.

The non-manual workers in general, and the most skilled professional, executive and managerial staff in particular tend to do best by comparison with others of their own kind elsewhere in the same relatively prosperous towns. By 'doing best' I again mean that they are less likely to be unemployed, more likely to own a car and drive it to work, and more likely to live in a town with a plentiful supply of owner-occupied housing. But these 'top people' are not so much better off in these more prosperous places as the manual workers and the least skilled are. Although they tend to do worse in the older and more stagnant industrial areas than similar people elsewhere, their condition is not so much worse as that of the manual workers and the least skilled, who appear to suffer more from economic stagnation and decay.

Thus, economic prosperity and urban growth generally benefit all classes, but tend to benefit manual workers and the less skilled most of all. Growth, greater prosperity for vulnerable people, and a movement towards greater equality can, therefore, be achieved together.

We believe there are several reasons for this pattern. One may be the differences between the mobility of the most skilled and the least skilled. Because the most skilled, the richer people and the younger workers, are more likely than others to move house, more likely to move long distances, and more likely to travel long distances from their homes to work, they are more likely to gain access to the richer opportunities of the expanding urban labour markets; but there they will compete with more of their own kind who travel to the same prosperous centres. The less skilled, being also less mobile, are less likely to gain access to these growth centres; but those who do get there reap greater advantages because they have to compete with fewer of their own kind than they would find in the more stagnant towns.

More important, however, may be structural changes going on in the British economy. The declining industries – certain kinds of heavy engineering, mining, port-related industries and so on – tend to be concentrated in the old industrial towns and in the centres of conurbations, particularly in the North, and they employ a lot of male manual workers. Their decline impoverishes these people and makes these places more unequal in various ways.

If factors such as these are the main causes of the patterns we observe, then the outlook for those who care about their country as well as their home town is bleak. The different kinds of cities in Britain – and we have been working with thirteen different clusters or categories of towns, distinguished by the character of their industries and labour markets, and related factors such as housing, transport, education and demographic structure – are not independent of each other. They are parts of the same urban system. What happens in the more prosperous places such as the new towns and the most rapidly growing industrial and residential suburbs – concentrated mainly in the southern half of England – has an impact on converse places, such as the central cores of the old conurbations, the mining towns of South Wales, the textile towns of Lancashire and Yorkshire and the Scottish industrial cities – concentrated mainly in the north. For every town borne along by economic success towards greater prosperity and equality, there must be other more stagnant places which tend to grow relatively less prosperous and more unequal – the places which house disproportionate numbers of the less skilled, the less mobile, the older workers and the marginal citizens, and offer them fewer and less generous opportunities.

However, we believe there may be other factors at work besides these. They may include – and here I am speculating, not presenting proven findings – the growth of more diverse opportunities concentrated in the central reaches of the labour market, demanding adaptable and reasonably skilled manual workers and offering middle-range incomes. Where these opportunities are well matched with an equivalent range of opportunities in a housing market offering reasonably good, middle-priced houses both for purchase and for renting, and the whole system is sustained by a reasonably good education system, serving workers as well as youngsters still in school, and by adequate transport and communications, then a city may grow more prosperous and distribute its opportunities rather more equally than most, despite the fact that it houses at least its fair share of the more vulnerable citizens – the less skilled, larger families and one-parent families, immigrants from the new Commonwealth countries, and so on.

One of our clusters seems to fit this description. Its thirteen towns are of all kinds: some free standing (like Peterborough and Gloucester), some suburban appendages to major conurbations (like Ormskirk and Thurrock). They appear in the north as well as the south (from Teesside to Gosport). Some (like Swindon) were probably not in this category twenty years earlier, before their leaders set about turning stagnation into growth. They may also fall out of this category again (we do not know what the troubles of the motor industry have done to Luton and Coventry since 1971). I believe these places may have other interesting social and political characteristics. Although the Labour Party often holds a majority of their councils' seats it does not always do so – they are not monopolized by any one party. Most of them are accustomed to accepting a considerable flow of newcomers, and a considerable proportion of their people leave them too: they are open communities. They are more likely than most to have reorganized their secondary schools on comprehensive lines, and they generally have large public housing programmes. They have, one feels, few sacred cows – few 'listed buildings' to be preserved, for example – and no dominant local aristocracy of birth or status. Only two of some thousand entries in the 1976 *Good Food Guide* appear in these towns, and none of their hotels or restaurants got the 'rosettes' awarded to over 200 hotels and restaurants by the Automobile Association's Guide. There is only a single university among them, although they have several excellent technical colleges. I am tempted to draw the rather depressing conclusion that Britain is unlikely to create many places of this kind because our ruling classes neither love them nor live in them. John Betjeman, writing about one of them during the Second World War, expressed the attitude of the gentry to such places: 'Come friendly bombs and fall on Slough . . .'.[20]

Priorities for social development

Turning back to social policies, I shall note a few points which may interest those who share the renewed concern for communities, urban problems and spatial aspects of social policy. These will be presented in order of spatial scale, starting with the urban neighbourhood, and continuing through city and local authority to national scales of action.

At the scale of the small urban neighbourhood, it is clear that community action has a limited but potentially important part to play. By itself, community development work will not change the world. But it can be a valuable learning process (helping people to understand the complex inter-relations between different human capacities, needs and problems – the relations between jobs, incomes, housing and politics, for example) and it can identify needs which are apt to be neglected by conventional political institutions operating on a larger scale (for example, the needs of ethnic minorities, one-parent families and others who may be concen-trated in particular neighbourhoods). It is the community worker's job to work with people as members of communities, not only as employees, pupils, patients, or in other more limited capacities. But major social changes are unlikely to be brought about by people operating only on this scale.

Programmes and policies operating at city, region, or local authority scales will often be most effective in providing the 'infrastructure' of communications, education and training, housing and health services, and in relating these services more effectively to each other in the light of some general pattern of priorities.

It is at the national scale that the major redistributions of re-sources have to be brought about. In 1974, the poorest fifth of households in Britain drew 49 per cent of their incomes from social security payments provided through central government: only 40 per cent came from earnings. For the whole population, only 10 per cent of income came from social security payments and 79 per cent came from earnings.[21] It is the central government too which must be mainly responsible for regional policies, and for subsidies to particular industries such as agriculture and fishing, which create opportunities for work and earnings, and redistribute resources between regions on a large scale.

Conclusion

In conclusion I will draw together the main threads of my argument. For manual workers, and particularly for the less skilled and the less mobile among them, sustained economic growth is a vital prerequisite for better opportunities. It can provide not only the resources for raising the living standards of the deprived, but also the more confident political climate which makes it easier for the electorate and its rulers to be generous to those who would in more depressed times be seen as threatening the standards of those who are slightly better off.

But economic growth will not automatically achieve those results. At the scale of the urban labour market – the city and its surrounding 'commutershed' from which it draws workers – we must study the social and distributional implications of different patterns of development; and the impact which apparently benign patterns may have on other cities, bearing in mind that we are dealing with a national system of settlements, not one city at a time.

To achieve the patterns of development we want – indeed, to achieve any development at all – central and local authorities must devote more attention to the economy than hitherto: if the economic motor is not to run down, governments will have to provide much of the risk capital required to keep it going. This means they must learn to assume the rights of a collective shareholder, concerned with opportunities, earnings and living conditions in national and local communities, not only with the profitability of multi-national enterprise.

For those concerned with marginal members of society who are likely to be neglected by powerful interests on the Left and the Right, it may be tempting to conclude that more selective policies are needed to help those who might otherwise be discriminated against. But although positive discrimination, as in the educational priority areas, may indeed be needed, politicians and administrators can only help marginal and potentially stigmatized groups of people if they are providing more universal services for the whole population on a scale sufficiently generous to enable them to help the poorest without repeatedly threatening the position of slightly richer people – those described in the United States as 'middle America'. (People are more likely to accept the rehousing of homeless families or recently arrived newcomers if they do not themselves have to wait ten years for a house.)

For similar reasons community workers and others should enable marginal groups – one-parent families and ethnic minorities, for example – to gain a hearing, but in ways which eventually bring trade unions, political parties and other more broadly based formations to recognise the needs of minorities and incorporate them in their programmes. Those seeking to do that should beware of calling for 'poverty' programmes for people who are thereby identified as marginal to the rest of the community. We may do better to talk about 'families', 'pensioners', 'jobs', 'housing' and 'education' instead – needs and programmes with which all can identify themselves.

We cannot rely on that strategy to succeed. Meanwhile, therefore, governments must monitor and regularly report on social conditions and the distribution of earnings, opportunities and resources of various kinds, distinguishing potentially vulnerable groups, and showing the social composition of the most deprived groups and neighbourhoods, and the extent of their divergence from society's constantly evolving average standards of living.

Notes and References

1. First appeared as an article in *Social and Economic Administration*, Vol. 11, No. 3, Autumn 1977. A fuller report – 'The Good City' by

David Donnison and Paul Soto – is to be published by Heinemann Educational Books in 1980.

2. See W. Ashworth, *The Genesis of Modern British Town Planning*, Routledge and Kegan Paul, 1954, and J. B. Cullingworth, *Environmental Planning*, Vol. 1, *Reconstruction and Land Use Planning, 1939–1947*, H.M.S.O., 1975.

3. Distribution of Industry Act 1945; New Towns Act 1946; Town and Country Planning Act 1947; National Parks and Access to the Countryside Act 1949; Town Development Act 1952.

4. Hansard Official Report, 1946–47, Vol. 432, Col. 947 *et seq.*

5. Advanced Practice and Civic Design', Academic Diplomas in Town Planning, etc., 1948; and 'Planning Studies I', M.Phil. in Town Planning, 1976; University College, London.

6. J. Rex and R. Moore, Oxford University Press, 1967.

7. R. E. Pahl, Longmans, 1970.

8. David Harvey, Arnold, 1973.

9. James Simmie, Hutchinson Educational, 1974.

10. *Children and Their Primary Schools*, Report of the Central Advisory Council for Education (England), H.M.S.O., 1967.

11. Report of the Committee on Local Authority and Allied Personal Social Services, Cmnd. 3703., H.M.S.O., 1968.

12. Housing in Greater London, *Cmnd. 2605*, 1965.

13. *Home Office, Urban Programme, Circular No. 1*, October 1968.

14. *Community work and Social change*, Longmans, 1968.

15. Richard White, 'Lawyers and the Enforcement of Rights' in Pauline Morris *et al.*, *Social Needs and Legal Action*, Martin Robertson, 1973.

16. 'Ministry of Housing and Local Government', *The South East Study*, H.M.S.O., 1964.

17. 'The National Community Development Project', *Forward Plan, 1975–76*, C.D.P. Information and Intelligence Unit, 1975, p. 2.

18. *Forward Plan, 1975–76*; pp. 1, 6, 16.

19. Charles Booth, *Life and Labour of the People of London*, Macmillan, 1892, Vol. I, Chap. 5, p. 154.

20. *Continual Dew*, Murray, 1937.

21. Family Expenditure Survey, 1974.

CHAPTER FOUR

Housing Policy: Objectives and Strategies

DAVID C. STAFFORD

The housing debate

Two years ago, the Labour Government published a Green Paper[1] on housing policy, the outcome of a comprehensive review of the economic and social issues of housing which began in 1975. The initiative was taken by the then Minister, the late Mr. Anthony Crosland, who echoed the sentiments of many when he sought a new housing system that was 'more efficient and more equitable than the present dog's breakfast'. Throughout the postwar period, the United Kingdom housing policy had been remarkable for its paucity of informed and comprehensive information on the one hand, and the sheer complexity of legislation and rapid growth of public expenditure on the other.

Government housing expenditure had grown considerably in the early 1970s. Between 1972 and 1974, total public expenditure on housing had risen from £2,477 million to £3,466 million, representing an 11 per cent increase in 'volume' terms and 119 per cent in 'cost' terms, whereas total public expenditure had increased by 14 per cent in 'volume' terms and 20 per cent in 'cost' terms.[2] At the time the housing finance review was initiated in 1975, total expenditure on housing had risen to £4,300 million. There can be little doubt that a major review was timely, particularly as expenditure was being incurred through a system that had developed piecemeal in a profusion of post-war Housing Acts, *ad hoc* and distorting taxation measures and a proliferation of subsidies generally regarded as inequitable and inefficient; and administered by various Government departments and agencies.

Since 1945, there has been at least one new Housing Act each year, and during the last decade there have been three Acts 'reforming' local authority housing finance, and every one of them has been based on inherently faulty principles. The Housing Act 1967 underestimated the effects of modest inflation and high interest rates. The rising costs of local authority house building prompted the Housing Finance Act 1972 which, instead of adopting economic rents in the public sector, implemented the nebulous concept of 'fair rents' which had already been introduced in the private rented sector in 1965. This Act, in turn, was repealed and replaced by a hastily conceived but generous subsidy system under the Housing Act 1975. Housing has in recent times been a political football, a battleground for ideological initiatives, and susceptible to populist bids by politicians ever eager to solve the 'housing problem' by the imposition of yet another 'solution'.[3]

The Green Paper was published as a consultative document and the three technical volumes include a great deal of new and comprehensive information on the state of housing and households in England and Wales. It recognized that there is no longer an absolute shortage of dwellings and that the quantity and quality of homes have shown a consistent improvement, to the extent that British people today are better housed than people are in many other industrial countries with higher per capita domestic products. The Green Paper also acknowledged that there are many paradoxical features of the housing scene – such as the increase in homelessness, the increase in local authority house waiting lists and the decrease in household mobility. Notwithstanding these adverse developments, the Green Paper proposed only modest reforms on the grounds that housing objectives can be achieved through existing strategies. The validity of this belief would have been strengthened had the Green Paper explored the causes of persistent housing problems and the broad costs and benefits to be derived from more radical reforms. In the event, the Labour Government appeared to believe that a new 'flexibility' could be achieved within the present policy without recourse to any reform of legislation relating to private and public sector rent determination and the subsidy and taxation system applied to the housing tenures. In short, the Labour Government was clearly not convinced that many of the existing housing problems and inconsistencies are an inevitable result of the present system or that they will never be satisfactorily overcome until fundamental reform, rather than periodic tinkering, is made. Such reform requires that all aspects of present government intervention, particularly rents, subsidies and taxation, are placed within a framework that does apply principles of equity and efficiency geared effectively towards those in need, and not administered, as at present, under a system where the recipients' inability to pay is not the general rule.

The reaction of the Labour Government to any fundamental reforms was perhaps inevitable, albeit on rather tenuous grounds, in that it might impose increased costs for those who had budgeted on the basis of existing arrangements. Certainly some would gain and not a few would lose if major reform were implemented. This proved to be politically unacceptable for the past Government, particularly as it took the view that the problems in housing finance arose at the margin only. On the other hand, the inherent inequalities and inefficiencies do remain, and if the new Government intends to pursue the existing main strategies of policy with all their ramifications into the 1980s, then the consequence for the growth of housing expenditure may be such that the Government will be forced into applying far more draconian changes in policy than any structural reform initiated now would imply. Moreover, the perpetuation of existing policy is likely to prove counterproductive in view of the continuous undesired consequences of policy.

Before these general and specific effects of present policy are examined, it is important first to examine the special characteristics of housing together with the economic and social case for government intervention in the housing market to establish its relationship with the present social and economic objectives of government.

The characteristics of housing

Housing has always been considered something special to a family. Indeed, a constant theme and justification for successive housing policies has been that the price mechanism is not an appropriate method of allocation and distribution of housing. Housing is a durable good, producing both necessary and luxury flows of consumption services as well as representing a capital asset to its owner. Houses are heterogeneous, immobile and expensive in relation to income. The services they provide depend on the type, structure and size of house and on the amenity in which they are located. These services are numerous and diverse, and the inherent durability of houses, subject to maintenance, is such that the services they provide may become obsolete or disturbed. The market is dominated by the exchange of second-hand houses and new house construction takes time to plan, is labour-intensive, requires significant inputs of materials and land and is highly susceptible to the economic business cycle. Since the market is highly fragmented, the process of price adjustment may be slow in relation to changing economic circumstances, leading to a local shortage/excess of certain types of housing. Finally, housing is not only regarded as a necessity per se, but a certain minimum of housing services is socially demanded, enforced by building and planning controls and public health legislation. These social conditions, within the framework of a complicated market structure, may mean that people have great difficulty in actually acquiring *a decent home at a price within their means.*

These difficulties in the separation of the consumption and investment elements of housing and the very substantial costs involved may well give rise to problems of allocation and distribution such that the market mechanism may be imperfect and would justify government intervention. The economic rationale for intervention may take a number of forms: natural monopoly, the existence of externalities, income distribution and consumer rationality, including uncertainty and imperfect capital markets. These merit investigation, and while one may conclude that certain inefficiencies and inequities may exist, it is by no means certain that present policy is successful in overcoming any particular element of market failure.[4]

Natural monopoly

Any market dominated by a small number of large producers may give rise to market inefficiency. Evidence of any tendency towards natural monopoly in the housing market for new or second-hand houses is scant. The largest national building firm accounts for only 6 per cent of total output and the large number of competing small builders suggests that producers cannot act monopolistically. Even if local monopolies did exist, it still does not follow that the public housing sector should be called on to supplement or replace them or even to compete locally. Thus, the arguments surrounding local authorities' building for sale or the sale of council houses should be examined within the context of whether local authority housing costs the community less than private housing.

Externalities

The 'external' economic effects arising from the housing market may be divided into two broad forms. The first arises from the belief that it is necessary to legislate in order to maintain the 'right' type, quality, design and location of houses and to protect the adjacent environment and prospective occupier. The Town and Country Planning Acts and building control regulations provide the legislative framework. The other form of externality, frequently analysed within a theory of blight, results from the assertion that substantial detrimental social and economic spill-over effects can be transmitted to neighbouring properties if the tenure, state or use of a property changes. A typical example is the fall in the demand for inner city housing by middle income groups who have moved to suburbs seeking improved transport facilities, decentralization of employment location and preferred environmental and residential facilities. As these older inner city houses are vacated they are purchased by lower income householders whose limited purchasing power does not permit them to maintain the houses at the same level. Deterioration continues as more houses are under-maintained and divided for multiple accommodation, leading to overcrowding and reduced facilities. Once this process has begun, there is unlikely to be a reversal unless the cost disparities between inner and outer city areas become so marked that 'gentrification' takes place. More usually, no improvement in the quality of the stock of houses will take place. First, the costs are likely to be extremely high not only because the houses are old, but because they were not originally built to modern building standards. Second, there is little financial incentive for any one owner to invest in his property because of the risks associated with recovering his outlay. This is because house prices are considerably influenced by the quality of adjacent properties and an individual owner will only receive a full economic return if other property owners are also prepared to undertake investment. The growth of General Improvement Areas and Housing Action Areas and their accompanying improvement and environmental grants owe much to the lead and financial backing given by local authorities to encourage owners to invest in their property. Such public policy may, however, be counter-productive in the face of conflicting policies: two conspicuous cases are the effects of the present Rent Acts on the maintenance of property, and planning and highway decisions which may create dilapidation and planning blight.

Distribution of income and wealth

Inequalities in the distribution of income and wealth may justify government intervention. The poor will always find themselves in difficulty in paying rent or in securing finance for house purchase. This has led to the introduction of a number of policies intended to benefit low income householders – rent control, Exchequer subsidies, rent rebates, rent allowances, option mortgage schemes. There is little real evidence, however, that these subsidies have actually improved the distribution of housing resources. In the privately rented sector, the major subsidy is borne by the private landlord. In the local authority sector, where rents are based on the pooled average historic costs of housebuilding, repairs and maintenance, authorities have at best only been allowed to balance their housing revenue account by rate support and have not been permitted to generate funds from that account for net increases in their housing stocks. The present rent rebates and allowances bear a haphazard and indiscriminate connection to equity, for the determining criteria are related to sub-market (subsidized) rents in both rented sectors as well as to family circumstances. Later, it will be shown that the present subsidy system neither stimulates the economic use of available accommodation nor helps prospective tenants to find or acquire housing.

Local authorities have also been ecouraged to lend to low income households for the purchase of older property. Much of alleged attractiveness of these 'social' mortgages has been eliminated by the level of mortgage interest rates offered by local authorities, which have usually been higher than the basic building societies. This is because a local authority's borrowing, irrespective of purpose, is pooled and an average (historic) rate of interest applied. The interest rate charged for private house purchase cannot legally be less than one-quarter per cent above the pooled or average rate, and any scheme must not operate in deficit. Local authority lending volume has been significant only when long-term market interest rates have been temporarily high.

Consumer rationality

For a market mechanism to be an efficient allocator of housing resources, rational decision-making requires householders to have sufficient information to calculate cost and benefits. As with the purchase of any good, specialists exist to provide information and expertise on house construction, and risks can be reduced through house insurance and life assurance. Although housing is especially expensive in relation to income, in neither of these situations in which the market may fail to provide full information to individuals to make choices is there an a priori case for directly providing subsidies. However, there may be a case for government intervention to prescribe minimum housing standards and building and advisory services.

Although these economic criteria for government intervention in the housing and mortgage field are by no means exhaustive, they are not as conclusive as frequently assumed. There is no a priori evidence for the supremacy of government housing provision, and the rationale for intervention through controls, incentives and deterrents requires individual scrutiny, analysis and assessment. A case for government intervention must be able to prove not only that the market breaks down in the provision of housing, but that the government can do better and does do better than the market.

Government housing objectives

An examination of successive governments' policy documents reveals a remarkable similarity of housing objectives and even broad strategies in spite of their respective criticisms of government policy when in opposition. In the 1973 White Paper *Widening the Choice: The Next Steps in Housing,*[5] the Conservative Government stated that 'the ultimate aim of housing policy is that everyone should have a decent home with a reasonable choice of owning or renting the sort of home they want'. While the incoming Government in 1974 was quick to rescind the Housing Finance Act 1972, it was not until the publication of the Green Paper in 1977 that the Labour Government proposed the following objectives for housing over the next decade:

(i) The traditional aim of a decent home for all families at a price within their means.

(ii) A better balance between investment in new houses and the improvement and repair of older houses, with regard to the needs of the individual and the community, as well as to cost.

(iii) Housing costs should be a reasonably stable element in family finance.

(iv) The housing needs of groups such as frail elderly people, the disabled and the handicapped should be met.

(v) A reasonable degree of priority in access to public rented sector housing and home ownership for people in housing need for people who, in the past, have found themselves at the end of the queue.

(vi) Increased scope for mobility in housing.

(vii) Greater ease for people to obtain the tenure they want.

(viii) The independence of tenants must be safeguarded.

The new Conservative Government has not repudiated these

objectives, possibly less because of any disagreement than because they may be very broadly interpreted.

In the years 1978–80, the pursuit of a housing strategy that will achieve the objective of an increase in the supply and use of housing has led to a marked divergence between Labour and Conservative policy. To the Labour Government, an emphasis on supply involved strategies directed towards local and flexible policies but within a national framework, while improved use of housing meant helping people acquire the kind of tenure they want and encouraging the development of those types of tenure that are preferred. Given the decision of the Labour Government to maintain, almost intact, the housing system that had developed up to 1977, it is difficult to see how the supply and use of housing could have been improved. By contrast, the new Conservative Government has announced council house building finance cuts and controls over muncipalization, and launched a major council house sales policy with higher discounts than ever before. There is, however, little evidence to conclude that sales, in aggregate, at least, will be any more significant both in terms of total numbers involved and the proportion of sales to the total local authority housing stock than they were in the period 1971–3, when they never achieved more than 0.5 per cent of total local authority stock in any one year. While there has been a major controversy over the merits and demerits of selling council houses,[6] the simple deterrent to large and sustained sales lies in the fact that the average council tenant who purchases his house with a discount between 30 and 50 per cent, will find that his initial housing costs in the form of mortgage interest (after tax relief), capital repayments and maintenance will be approximately four times greater than if he were to continue to rent the same house. Neither the Labour nor the Conservative Government appears to have interpreted their own objectives of increasing the supply and use of housing with strategies that will improve the effective access of households to and between tenures of their choice through the development of an efficient and equitable taxation and subsidy system.

The general effects of policy

While housing objectives may be economic, social and political, the mechanics are always economic and a disregard of the elementary points of economic theory can have serious repercussions on the mutual compatibility and attainment of objectives.[7] The problems of the British housing market during the post-war period, and particularly during the last decade, provide an excellent illustration of the failure of successive governments to recognize the economic implications of policy. In particular, policy makers have paid insufficient attention to the fact that both the demand and supply of housing are related to price. In an attempt to regulate the housing market, governments have introduced legislation to affect the condition of tenure without full consideration of the effects on demand and supply.

A social objective of decent housing implies the provision of substantial subsidies to bring adequate housing within the means of most families. It also implies substantial capital expenditure on construction and renovation in order to build up a sufficient stock of housing. Throughout the post-war period, successive British governments have attempted to allocate housing resources in the rented housing sectors, not in accordance with each individual's ability and willingness to pay, but in accordance with each individual's relative need. Those in 'need' are considered to require attention by experts or elected representatives – for the most part housing managers, rent officers and local councillors' action under greater or lesser direction from central government. Thus need is technically, but elusively, defined by reference to the contemporary social priorities of central and local government. In the case of the public housing sector, allocation according to 'need' has taken a number of forms, especially that of subsidies in money and in kind, in an attempt to keep rents low, despite growing waiting lists. Unfortunately, the control of rents has generally resulted in the inconsistent and inequitable subsidization of housing units, rather than in aid to needy tenants. This arises from the nature and form of government subsidies and the calculation of rents by reference to the historic costs of house building. In the case of the private rented sector, regulated rents (or 'fair' rents), together with security of tenure provision, have led to bureaucratic control of private rented housing since 1965, with dire consequences for the provision and stock quality of such housing for prospective and existing tenants.

Housing and household trends

The dominant feature of housing tenure shares has been the persi-
tent trend towards owner-occupation through new housebuilding
and sale of privately rented housing for owner-occupation. At the
end of 1978, 54 per cent of dwellings were owner-occupied, 31 per
cent were rented from public authorities and 15 per cent were
privately rented. The post-war crude shortage of dwellings (dwellings less households) was remedied in the early 1960s, and even in
1966 there were 100,000 more dwellings than households. During
the last decade, not only has the share of the privately rented sector
in the total stock fallen, but the actual number of privately rented
dwellings has also fallen at an annual rate of 3 per cent. The effect
has been an annual net rate of growth of aggregate housing stock of
1.4 per cent between 1967 and 1977, which has exceeded, over the
same period, the annual growth of households of 1.0 per cent and of
the population, 0.4 per cent. Thus, in crude aggregate terms, there
has been an increase in the amount of housing per head.[8]

It is not surprising that the crude surplus of housing rose to
800,000 at the end of 1976, or that now the average density of
occupation at 2.7 persons per dwelling is better than the figure for
most other industrial countries. It is important to emphazise that
this crude measure makes no allowance for the age, structure or
distribution of the population or the location, type and size distribution of dwellings, since a major failing of policy discussion on
housing is the implicit assumption that it is an homogeneous com-
modity. Nevertheless, it can be inferred that the overall or absolute
availability of housing has not diminished.

Although the quality of many houses is not up to modern
standards, the overall possession of amenities has improved year by
year. In 1951, there were about ten million households living in
unfit or sub-standard houses, in overcrowded conditions or sharing.
By 1976, this figure had fallen to about 2.7 million, representing a
fall in the proportion of those households badly housed from about
70 per cent in 1951 to about 15 per cent in 1976. This dramatic
improvement was recognized in the Green Paper: 'We have more
and better houses in relation to the number of households than ever
before.'

The Green Paper recognized this improvement and was realistic in the projections for future housebuilding. The 'maximization' policies of the 1960s led to unrealistic targets of 500,000 houses per annum with all the social and economic ramifications of capacity strain in the building industry, the building of tower blocks and vast bleak estates, and the enthusiastic wave of determined urban clearance and renewal. These policies, pursued irrespective of people's wishes or economic and social implications, fostered a legacy of disrupted communities and urban blight and decay. The recent introduction of Housing Investment Programmes for local authority housebuilding and the recent White Paper on the Inner City problem owe much to the failures of past policies.

The Green Paper concluded that during the next five years housing completions in the private sector would approximate to 200,000 units p.a., while public sector completions would decline to just over 100,000 units p.a. The Labour Government also intended to direct greater investment towards inner area renovation and improvement of the existing stock. It was surprising, therefore, that this major change of policy did not appear to justify any major reform of housing finance, particularly as the present system encourages new investment through a national and uniform subsidy scheme. In the event, the Labour Government's commitment led to a modest £100 million of public expenditure towards 'inner city areas'. If the problem of housing is more a matter of distribution than of production,[9] then it is valid to question the justification for the perpetuation of past strategies. For while there has been improvement in both the quantity and quality of housing, this achievement has not been without heavy costs in the recent past which are likely to increase progressively in the future.

Table 1 shows that housing costs have increased considerably in real terms during the 1970s. There have been a number of contributory factors. In particular, the balance between level of subsidies and tax allowances, compared with new investment, has changed considerably. Between 1970 and 1975, financial assistance in the form of tax relief and subsidies rose by 122 per cent, compared with 35 per cent for investment. An implication of this trend is that existing tenants in particular, and owner-occupiers, have been benefiting increasingly compared with prospective tenants and owner-occupiers, and this owes much to the way present rents are determined in the public sector.

TABLE 1 *Public expenditure on housing: actual and planned*[a]

	Great Britain		£ million and indices			
	£ million at current prices		Indices (1975–6=100) at constant prices			
	1975–6	1976–7[b]	1971–2	1975–6	1977–8	1978–9
Public sector housing:						
Subsidies	1,060	1,359	51	100	123	122
Rent rebates	254	322	—	100	119	134
Investment:						
Local authorities:						
land purchases	161	122	30	100	53	56
new dwellings	1,294	1,497	105	100	88	84
acquisitions	184	104	35	100	38	54
improvements	440	439	54	100	87	90
other	93	86	78	100	71	71
New towns[c] investment	251	261	69	100	76	75
Sales[d]	73	81	413	100	165	368
Private sector housing:						
Improvement grants	76	79	107	100	99	143
Lending to private persons:						
Gross	415	208	59	100	21	23
Repayments	204	227	89	100	89	87
Option mortgage subsidy	109	140	28	100	111	120
Rent allowances to private tenants	43	68	—	100	156	156
Loans and capital grants to housing associations (net)	356	483	33	100	109	107
Other lending (net)	117	13	37	100	—	—
Administration	34	41	57	100	113	118
Total	4,376	4,913	59	100	93	92

[a] See *Social Trends* 1977 introductory text to Resources and Expenditure section, page 121.
[b] Provisional.
[c] Including Scottish Special Housing Association.
[d] Local authorities, new towns and Scottish Special Housing Association.

Source: H.M. Treasury and *Social Trends* 1977.

The wider issue of attempts to reconcile supply with demand has had important economic and social repercussions within the owner-occupied and rented sectors, reflected in sustained price increases in the former and waiting lists and homelessness in the latter. Specifically, successive policies have attempted to impose solutions on the housing markets, mainly by legal controls and housing subsidies, which have militated against household mobility, access to rented housing, and restricted choice, opportunity and independence all in direct opposition to past governments' housing objectives as enunciated in the successive policy documents.

A recurring theme of successive housing policies, be it in the context of rent control of 'cheap' mortgages, is the belief that lower prices, through subsidies, reduce scarcity. In fact, they simply increase demand, encourage under-occupation and increase household formation. For the poor, massive public subsidies for new house building have not been a sufficient condition for the reduction of homelessness. Instead, successive governments have made access to rented housing more difficult for the young, the newly married, single parent families, the poor and those wishing to retain mobility. If the price of meeting a social need had caused moderate distortions and imperfections in other housing markets in the process, then the policy might be condoned. Unfortunately, attempts to meet social need in these instances have not been successful, either in terms of policy objectives or realization. For, if policies had indeed been directed at those deemed to be in social need, it remains a bitter irony that these very households have been forced into a smaller and smaller 'free market' rental sector, noted for the absence of legal controls and public subsidies or tax relief. As a result of the 1965 Rent Act, these households were forced into the furnished sector and received no rent allowance until 1972 and no security of tenure until the Rent Act 1974. Since 1974, those in social need are often still without security of tenure, rent control or allowance, for they belong to the latest of the exceptions to government protection as tenants of resident landlords. For prospective tenants, the situation remains gloomy with increasing homelessness and record waiting lists in a period of record under-utilization and empty property.

Owner-occupation

The trend towards increasing owner-occupation may be regarded as one objective that has achieved relative success. This is not primarily due to the efforts of government, but to the strong desire for ownership, particularly among the young, reflected in successive surveys. Policies directed towards the private rented sector have encouraged sales to sitting tenants, although the scope for this decreases as this sector declines. However, the scope for increasing owner-occupation is likely to be constrained, since very large scales of local authority housing would be implied. Average unrebated council house rents are only a quarter of the cost of a mortgage on new properties of similar capital value and thus the financial incentives for sitting council tenants to purchase is weak and the corresponding extent of public subsidies enormous. Instead, local authorities have been urged to keep building more new houses to meet waiting lists and existing tenants are cushioned from the real costs of such housing by subsidies and rent regulation. For the moment, therefore, there remain very considerable limitations to greater owner-occupation from the existing stock. In the case of new building for owner-occupation, all proposals by government to make housing 'cheap' have been to subsidize demand. Such proposals include low cost mortgages[10] and subsidized interest rates which simply increase demand and, at least in the short run, drive up house prices. In recent years, government has sought simultaneously to limit the volume of lending by building societies and to control their mortgage rates at levels below market rates. Any such attempt to reduce rates below market levels can only lead to excess demand for funds and instability in the mortgage and housing markets.[11] Moreover, such attempts benefit only existing owner-occupiers and do little for the aspirations of prospective owner-occupiers. If the government wishes to increase the supply of owner-occupied housing, capital subsidies to builders may be more effective and efficient.

The extent to which owner-occupiers are 'subsidized' is a perennial controversy. Three different concepts of housing benefit are relevant to owner-occupiers:

(a)   mortgage interest tax relief

   (b) lack of a tax on imputed net rental income (Schedule A tax abolished in 1963)

   (c) freedom from capital gains tax, net of capital expenditure (owner-occupied housing was excluded in the capital gains tax legislation in 1965).

These three concepts are not mutually exclusive and are discussed at length elsewhere.[12] If owner-occupied housing is regarded as an investment good, then the sum of (b) and (c) may be regarded as the benefits. This is because an individual who purchases a business asset is taxed on the stream of income yielded by the asset and also the capital gain. However, he may set this against depreciation allowances and interest costs on the original loan. Moreover, capital gains tax would be charged only if the proceeds from the scale of the asset were not 'rolled over' into the purchase of a further business asset. Similarly, a house can be seen as an asset yielding a stream of services (in kind) and offering a potential capital gain. Thus any depreciation and interest payments on house loans would be an allowable expense against a tax on imputed rental income, and 'roll-over' relief would be allowed in the assessment of capital gains. On the other hand, if owner-occupied housing is regarded as a consumer durable then mortgage tax relief on its own would be the appropriate concept of benefit. This is because a consumer good is neither subject to tax on the services (imputed income in kind) it provides, or capital gains. Since 1974, an individual has not been able to set interest payments on loans against earned income. Therefore, if housing is treated as a pure consumption good, the only benefit is tax relief relative to other consumption goods. However, the issue is not quite as straightforward as this implies, since there is an important relationship between such tax relief on mortgage interest and tax paid on building society shares and deposits. Increases in tax relief and the 'composite' tax rate go hand in hand, and Revell[13] has argued that it is a taxation subsidy from those savers whose incomes are too low to pay tax to those whose marginal rate is the basic rate.

Although owner-occupied housing is frequently regarded as a consumer durable with a very long life, there appears to be a stronger case for regarding it as an investment good due to its characteristics discussed earlier in the chapter.[14] If the principle of tax neutrality between different investment goods is to be upheld, then the benefits of untaxed imputed rental income and capital gains tax exemption should be withdrawn, but income tax relief would remain admissible. The effects on income distribution would be that all owner-occupiers would be worse off, but those in relatively more expensive houses would be more seriously affected than those in cheaper houses. On the other hand, if owner-occupied housing is treated as a consumption good with a long life, then the income distribution effects of withdrawing income tax relief on mortgages would be that all mortgagors would be affected, with those at the beginning of their repayment period affected much more than those nearing the end of repayments.

Local authority housing

An important policy strategy since the introduction of local authority houses has been to keep rents as low as possible, and a number of policies have been pursued – average historic cost basis, 'fair' rents between 1972 and 1974, and more recently, 'reasonable' rents. Their common characteristic is that they subsidize the dwelling rather than directly benefiting the tenant. As a result they have brought about serious injustices, since rents are a function of a local authority's total housing stock, distribution, age, and local politics, rather than the financial and personal circumstances of tenants. Since rents tend to be determined by reference to the average historic cost of provision with subsidies to enable low income earners to afford adequate housing, the result has been significant cross subsidization between tenants, with taxpayers and ratepayers subsidizing all council tenants, irrespective of income. As the Family Expenditure Survey shows each year, it is by no means true that low income earners are concentrated in the public sector or that all those in the public housing sector are low income earners. Some of the subsidy is thus misapplied and it is evident that it is also insufficient, for many low income families receive additional subsidies, through rent and rate rebates.

During the last decade, governments have been loath to increase the rents of local authority tenants, and today average rents represent 7.2 per cent of average household income. This may be illustrated by the fact that average weekly rents of council tenants have risen from £3.70 in 1968 to £5.95 in 1977, in spite of rapid price inflation. In consequence, public sector rents contributed only 40 per cent to public sector housing revenue accounts in 1976–7, compared with 75 per cent in 1967–8.

It is not surprising that government subsidies to local authorities have increased enormously and that the demand for such housing has exceeded the supply. Not only does policy in no way guarantee that the 'needy' can obtain accommodation, as reflected in record priority waiting lists, but it also has meant that the mobility of the workforce is severely curtailed. This is because possessing council housing in one area does not give an entitlement to similar housing in another area (in fact, local authorities with severe 'resident' qualifications positively discourage it). One result is desperate advertisements in newspapers for 'council house exchanges' – the inefficiency of bartering at its worst. The typical narrow spread of rents relative to household incomes over different sizes of accommodation also means that there is little incentive for families to move to smaller accommodation in the face of family size decreases, especially when the children of the family set up their own households. Finally, the lowness of rents has meant that not only have the financial costs borne by taxpayers and ratepayers increased considerably in recent years but that all new building is now almost entirely financed by taxpayers and ratepayers.

Positive policy in the public sector is becoming increasingly more expensive and counterproductive. If government wishes to improve the access to local authority housing for poor families and deprived groups, and also provide greater independence for tenants to exercise tenure choice, then rents must be allowed to rise to reflect the real costs of accommodation. Thus a move towards the establishment of 'economic' rents within the local authority sector is a prerequisite for the establishment of an equitable and efficient allocation and distribution of local authority houses. Schemes based on economic rents have been examined by Gray[15] and Meade[16] and a detailed study of alternatives has recently been expounded by Grey, Hepworth and Odling-Smee.[17] Such a rationalization does not necessarily imply that the overall subsidies to local authority houses and households be reduced, as many claim, but it would mean that subsidies would be more equitably and efficiently distributed on the criterion of inability to pay. Appreciation of the real housing costs to society would not only improve consumer sovereignty but would also overcome the extraordinary administrative and financial complexities that currently abound in housing authorities. Better-off tenants facing a rise in rents under 'economic' determination would be able to choose among paying the higher rent and bearing an appropriate share of the economic costs, purchasing their present home, given the greater financial incentive, and purchasing another house in the private sector. Poorer tenants would be cushioned from the introduction of economic rents through rent rebates based on ability to pay, which in no way would prejudice their security and could more effectively raise their standard of living.

The introduction of economic rents for council housing could stimulate increased voids and sales to sitting tenants at market prices and provide a larger supply stock and additional finance to meet the needs of poor tenants and those currently denied access. Producer sovereignty, so evident in paternalistic local authority letting rules and in administrative procedures that 'choke-off' applicants, would soon disappear as consumer sovereignty became better established.

Privately rented housing

Although private rented housing now constitutes only about 15 per cent of total housing stock, it has remained one of the most politicized targets of housing policy since rent controls were first introduced in 1915, when 88 per cent of the total housing stock was privately rented. The Rent Act 1965 provides the basic framework of the present legislation, and with the Rent Act of 1974, the vast majority of tenancies are now potentially subject to rent regulation. The Green Paper referred any proposals for the reform of this sector to a *Review of the Rent Acts*.[18] This document declared that the then Labour Government wished to see an increase in the supply of rented accommodation. The results of the review have not been published, but it is difficult to see how the supply of rented accommodation could be increased given the uncompromising statement that in no way would the principles of full security of tenure and current rent regulation be undermined in any new policy initiatives. Although rent control has militated against new private letting, rising real incomes and tenant aspirations, more profitable forms of investment opportunity and competition from heavily subsidized local authority housing have also been important factors in the demise of the private landlord. While rent controls are popular with existing tenants, they restrict resource allocation and have effects on the distribution of income, not only between tenants but between landlords and tenants. Regulated rents below market level simply increase demand and reduce supply in the short run, leading to a sustained economic shortage, unless an increased supply of housing in the long run is forthcoming.

Present policies in the private rented sector, particularly, discriminate against the poor. By definition, the poor cannot easily purchase their own homes and thus face the private or public rented sectors. They have virtually no chance of access to the former, but may find accommodation in the uncontrolled resident landlord sub-sector or pay black market rents. In the controlled private rented sector, landlords faced with a fixed rent have every incentive to discriminate against tenants who they may think are unreliable, uncreditworthy or immobile, and favour the young, professional and childless couple. Thus families who are poor or large, or who comprise immigrants, have even less access to privately let accommodation than might first appear.

The excess demand for housing leads to increases in waiting lists of local authorities, with ramifications for homelessness and squatting. Landlords denied an economic return under rent regulation and the prospects of uncertain repossession fail to maintain their properties. It is hardly believable that increasing homelessness is compatible with the present increasing empty accommodation. Properties have decayed before their time due to lack of repair and maintenance, necessitating slum clearance, probably at the final expense of the local authority. Some landlords resort to harassment, and properties have been sold for owner-occupation or left vacant in the hope of a change of legislation. The plight of prospective tenants is no less gloomy, and the increase in squatting has prompted new legislation in an attempt to plug a further hole in housing policy. The economic effects of rent control and the policy options facing government are examined in the next chapter in this book.[19]

Although successive governments have stated that they wish to curtail the decline of private letting and even rejuvenate it, there is little prospect unless present legislation is changed. Structural reform requires a phased abolition of rent control, as now administered, and the introduction of contracts of fixed and certain security periods. In addition, rent allowances, as currently administered, should be phased out and income support provided on ability to pay principles. This would be compatible with the principles discussed for a reform of the public rented sector, with equity and efficiency prevailing within and between tenure groups. The prevailing injustices facing both landlords and tenants arise, in particular, from the Rent Act 1974 and pilot studies have shown that there have been adverse effects on the attitudes of landlords[20] and supply of rented accommodation.[21] A political commitment towards gradual repeal of the Rent Acts, together with income support for the poor, would be unlikely to bring an immediate response from landlords who have learned by experience. However, greater flexibility in policy, such as the gradual removal of the cumbersome mechanism now involved in the implementation of control and the repossession of property, would at least slow the decline of a tenure for which there is an evident demand.

Conclusion

Movement towards an efficient and effective housing market requires a uniform approach within all the sub-markets. While reform may now be long overdue, especially in the public sector, any acceptable structural change requires that social justice is seen to be applied to all tenures. The housing problem of today does not centre on shortages or general poor quality but on issues, enunciated in the Green Paper, of access, opportunity, independence, mobility and sustained house investment. They are not marginal issues, as suggested in the Green Paper, but problems arising from the present system. In its defence of the status quo, the Labour Government appeared to take the view that any structural change would involve substantial income distribution and financial implications for many families and thus even discussion, yet alone gradual implementation was out of the question.

If the objectives, as laid down in the Green Paper, are to be met, then the present incompatible tenure strategies require fundamental reform. If it is public policy to improve the size and quality of the housing stock beyond what would prevail in the free market, then it must resort to a relative subsidy to all sectors and apply this to the supply of new houses and the maintenance of the existing stock. The demand subsidies, as currently administered, simply distort the distribution of households over the housing stock and result in under-occupation, rigidity of markets and the denial of consumer choice. It is illogical for those who wish to destroy the market mechanism in housing completely by the municipalization[22] of all rented accommodation and nationalization of building societies to argue that people cannot afford to pay market prices for accommodation in the private and public housing sectors. Under the market mechanism, the price of any good is set by the interaction of supply and demand so that market prices are just as much determined by consumers as by producers. If prices are too high, then vendors and landlords have to reduce them if they are going to sell or let property. It follows that landlords cannot 'exploit' tenants in free market conditions. The conditions prompting exploitation, black markets, harassment, discrimination and homelessness arise from the inflexibility of government control.

A long-term stable solution which is internally consistent must involve the gradual removal of indiscriminate and tenure-based demand subsidies and a redirection of funds towards the poorer households. This paper has argued in favour of a number of broad reforms relevant to each tenure. First, owner-occupied houses must be accepted as goods and as such liable to Schedule A tax and capital gains tax. Tax neutrality principles would be met vis-à-vis the treatment of other investment assets, including the treatment of houses which are let and currently liable to income tax on net rental income, and capital gains tax. Second, there must be a pricing system for all rented accommodation, both in the private and public sector, which reflects the level of rents that would be paid in the absence of government intervention. Third, there should be reform of the present subsidy system towards a system that does not provide subsidies in an indiscriminate, unjust and inefficient manner and which really is based on principles of ability to pay applied comprehensively, irrespective of tenure. While it must be accepted that there would be transitional costs involved, it is by no means true that they need be substantial or that they do not justify an approach towards a housing system which would be consistent, equitable and efficient within and between all housing tenures. The Green Paper suggested that the benefits of structural change would not justify the costs involved. This argument would be more convincing if the Labour Government had at least explored the causes of the present housing problems. The omission of an analysis of the costs and benefits of structural reform in housing was a disappointment in a Green Paper that was conceived as a major review of housing finance.

Notes and References

1. *Housing Policy: A Consultative Document* (1977), Cmnd. 6851, H.M.S.O., together with a supporting Technical Volume in three parts.
2. E. Craven (1975), 'Housing' in R. Klein (ed.), *Inflation and Priorities*, Centre for Studies in Social Policy.
3. D. C. Stafford (1973), 'A Survey of Recent Developments in Housing Legislation, Policy and Administration', *Social and Economic Administration*, Vol. 7, No. 2 and in M. H. Cooper (ed.), *Social Policy* (1974), Basil Blackwell.
4. D. C. Stafford (1976), 'Government and the Housing Situation', *National Westminster Bank Review*, November.
5. *Widening the Choice: The Next Steps in Housing* (1973), Cmnd. 5280.
6. A. Murie (1976), *The Sale of Council Houses: A Study in Social Policy*, Occ. Paper No. 35, Centre for Urban and Regional Studies, University of Birmingham.
   C. Edwards (1978), 'Public Finance, Local Housing Policy and the Sale of Council Houses', *Public Finance and Accountancy*, March.

7. R. L. Harrington (1972), 'Housing – Supply and Demand', *National Westminster Bank Review*, May.

8. D. G. Mayes and D. C. Stafford (1977), 'The Effects of Inconsistent Government Policy in the British Housing Market', *The Banker's Magazine*, February.

9. M. Clarke (1977), 'Too Much Housing', *Lloyds Bank Review*, No. 126, October.

10. J. Black (1974), 'A New Policy for Mortgages', *Lloyds Bank Review*, January.

11. D. C. Stafford (1977), 'Britain's Housing Problem', *Building Societies' Gazette*, June.

12. A. J. Merrett and A. Sykes (1965), *Housing Finance and Development*, Longmans. Building Societies' Association (1976), *Evidence Submitted by the Building Societies' Association to the Housing Finance Review*.

13. J. Revell (1973), *U.K. Building Societies*, Economics Research Papers, University College of North Wales, Bangor, reprinted in *Housing Finance – Present Problems* (1974), O.E.C.D.

14. D. C. Stafford (1978), *The Economics of Housing Policy*, Croom-Helm.

15. H. Gray (1968), *The Cost of Council Housing*, Research Monograph No. 18, Institute of Economic Affairs.

16. J. E. Meade (1972), 'Poverty in the Welfare State', *Oxford Economic Papers*, 24, No. 3.

17. A. Grey, N. P. Hepworth, J. Odling-Smee (1978), *Housing Rents, Costs and Subsidies*, The Chartered Institute of Public Finance and Accountancy.

18. Department of the Environment (1977), *The Review of the Rent Acts – A Consultation Paper*.

19. M. H. Cooper and D. C. Stafford (1980), 'The Economic Implications of Fair Rents' in R. A. B. Leaper (ed.), *Health, Wealth and Housing*, Basil Blackwell.

20. B. Paley (1978), *Attitudes to Letting in 1976*, Office of Population Censuses and Surveys, Social Survey Division, H.M.S.O.

21. D. Maclennan (1978), 'The 1974 Rent Act – Some Short Run Supply Effects', *The Economic Journal*, Vol. 88, June.

22. M. Wicks (1973), *Rented Housing and Social Ownership*, Fabian Tract No. 421, Fabian Society.
B. Douglas-Mann *et al.* (1973), *The End of the Private Landlord*, Fabian Tract No. 321, Fabian Society.

CHAPTER FIVE

The Economic Implications of 'Fair Rents'[1]

MICHAEL H. COOPER and DAVID C. STAFFORD

The legislative framework

Rent control has been an important and controversial component of United Kingdom housing policy since it was first introduced as an emergency measure during the First World War.[2] For the following forty years, successive Rent Restriction Acts have attested to the prevailing political view that rent control was a necessary, if essentially temporary, imposition. In the period following the Second World War, rents were kept frozen at 1939 levels and as late as 1954, landlords were able to raise rents only by predetermined amounts and then, only if compensating repairs to property were undertaken. The Rent Act of 1957, however, provided for rent increases for some five million controlled tenancies and permitted decontrol of properties falling vacant and re-let. This was intended as the first stage towards the piecemeal dismantling of rent control, but many of the provisions of the Act were never actually implemented and no further decontrol measures were ever enacted.[3] The Rent Act 1965 marked the introduction of a formal rent regulation procedure, embodying the notion of a 'fair rent', new security of tenure provisions, and a statutory control system for the future regulation of rents. Since 1965, rent control measures have been progressively extended, particularly with the introduction of the Rent Act 1974, and today control is applied to almost all permanently rented private dwellings. Ironically, the increase in the size and complexity of the recent Rent Acts has been inversely related to the absolute and relative significance of the private rental sector.[4]

The Rent Act 1965, which was consolidated with other existing legislation in the Rent Act 1968, was a major influence on the supply of rented accommodation between 1965 and 1974, for it made vital the distinction between unfurnished and furnished housing. All lettings by private landlords of unfurnished dwellings with a rateable value at the time not exceeding £400 in Greater London and £200 elsewhere were to become regulated tenancies and subject to 'fair rent' registration and security of tenure. This security provided for a regulated tenancy to be transmitted twice to members of a tenant's family at his death. 'Fair rents' were to be determined by rent officers and ratified by a rent assessment committee. The 1965 Act distinguished three separate markets for rented accommodation – the regulated unfurnished market, the unregulated furnished market, and the old controlled housing – which were to be gradually phased into a new regulated sector.

Of critical consequence for rental housing, of course, were the determining criteria laid down for the assessment of a 'fair rent':

(a) In determining for the purposes of this Act what rent is or would be a fair rent under a regulated tenancy of a dwelling house regard shall be had, subject to the following provisions of this section, to all circumstances (other than personal circumstances) and in particular to the age, character and locality of the dwelling house and to its state of repair.

(b) For the purposes of the determination it shall be assumed that the number of persons seeking to become tenants of similar dwelling houses in the locality on the terms (other than those relating to rent) of the regulated tenancy is not substantially greater than the number of such dwelling houses in the locality which are available for letting on such terms.

Under (a) a 'fair' rent is determined by reference to the attributes of the property and not to the financial or personal circumstances of the tenant. Under (b) the scarcity of the accommodation is seemingly to be ignored. The intention, however, would appear to be that only 'abnormal' scarcity should be ignored and the rent set at a level where all 'need' is met.

In a perfectly competitive market context, the absence of such 'scarcity' would be achieved in the long run at the equilibrium level. The implication of this interpretation is that, unless long-run equilibrium (assuming a perfectly competitive market) is already achieved, the 'fair' rent is permanently less than the market clearing one and conditions are created such that there is no incentive for landlords to increase the supply of accommodation. Moreover, the application of 'fair' rents and the introduction of rent allowances in 1972 may be interpreted to mean that a 'fair' rent is a rent that families can 'afford' to pay.[5]

The Rent Act 1974 was directed at extending the legislation already governing unfurnished accommodation to the furnished sector. On the request of either landlord or tenant 'fair rents' would be assessed by rent officers and security of tenure automatically extended. At the time of the Act, there was a great deal of uncertainty as to its provisions, owing to the publication delay that resulted from industrial action by Her Majesty's Stationery Office, and although the Act was originally conceived as a way of controlling a hitherto relatively buoyant free market, the effect of the legislation was to create new 'loopholes'[6] (as the Rent Act of 1965 had before it). No longer was the legislative distinction between furnished and unfurnished accommodation a determinant for regulatory purposes; it now rested upon the residential status of the landlord. Since 1974, a resident landlord, subject to certain conditions, has been able to claim exemption for this property, but almost all other accommodation is subject to both rent regulation and security of tenure provisions. The only exemptions are in the cases of lettings by educational institutions and accommodation for bed and breakfast and holiday letting purposes.

The private rented sector is practically unique in having so much complex legislation formulated and implemented by successive governments on the basis of either pure political dogma and/or unsubstantiated conventional wisdom. Apart from the most general data derived from the quinquennial census, very little accurate information exists on, for example, the composition of the rental market which could be employed to either condemn or condone policy to date. The very few studies that have been undertaken in the United Kingdom have examined the ownership characteristics of the rented sector within given city boundaries (for example Lancaster[7] and Edinburgh[8]). More recently, Maclennan has re-searched the Glasgow furnished rented sector and in particular the short-run supply effects of the Rent Act 1974.[9] No monitoring or evaluation of the effects of the new legislation appears to have been undertaken and there is no consistent and comprehensive published government data on rent levels (apart from aggregate data on registered rents), vacancy rates, or on the composition and income of either tenants or landlords.

The characteristics of the rented sector

Notwithstanding the dearth of data and the proliferation of complex legislation, the privately rented housing market embraces a number of characteristics relevant to policy analysis:

(a) It is a sector that has undergone a sustained decline in the number of dwellings, both absolutely and relatively, as gradual replacement and augmentation by local authority, housing association and owner-occupation has taken place. In 1914 about 90 per cent of the total housing stock was privately rented, but by 1939 this proportion had fallen to 58 per cent. This relative decline was attributable mainly to the rapid increase in owner-occupation and local authority housing, for the absolute net decrease in privately rented houses was only of the order of 0.5 million. While 1.5 million houses were sold for owner-occupation, nearly one million new or converted houses were added to the private rented sector during the inter-war period. Since the war, both the absolute and relative decline has been faster. Again, sales for owner-occupation have been important, but in contrast to the inter-war period there have been only 0.4 million new or converted houses added to the private rented sector. By

1976 the private rented stock, which had stood at 7.1 million in 1914, had fallen to 2.8 million, representing only 15 per cent of total stock and providing housing to some 20 per cent of all households.

(b) According to the 1971 census, there is a wide diversity of households in rented housing and a marked contrast between furnished (resident and non-resident landlords) and unfurnished tenancies (regulated and controlled), as defined under the 1965 Rent Act. The unfurnished sector comprises mainly the elderly, the low-income households, and tenants who have occupied their homes over many years. By contrast, the furnished sector comprises mainly the young, the single, the above average income, and the fairly mobile households. Similarly, landlords of unfurnished property tend to be in the older age groups and have generally either inherited or purchased their let property many years ago. Their low incomes (often pensions) and the low-income yield on their investment (notwithstanding availability of improvement grants), have precluded substantial improvement and maintenance of their properties. In the case of furnished tenancies, a large number of landlords are either resident or are company landlords. The balance comprises landlords who let on a largely ad hoc basis.

(c) The geographical distribution of the private rented sector is uneven and tends to be concentrated within inner city areas. London alone accounts for over 25 per cent of private rented dwellings and about 37 per cent of all households in furnished dwellings.[10] A number of the larger university cities also contain a relatively high proportion of private lettings.

(d) According to the 1971 England and Wales House Condition Survey, 70 per cent of private rented dwellings were built before 1919 and the majority of the balance were built in the interwar period. Some 40 per cent of private sector dwellings lack one or more basic amenities, 30 per cent are in disrepair and about 20 per cent are statutorily unfit for habitation.

The purpose here is to examine, in the light of the present legislative framework and the concern over the decline in the number and quality of rented properties,[11] the alternative strategies now available to government, which are compatible with recently declared objectives. To this end, an examination of the general theoretical consequences of rent control will be followed by an appraisal of these objectives and an examination of the current constraints. The alternative strategies will then be assessed with the aid of some fairly restrictive assumptions and simple models.

The general economic effects of control

In this analysis of the general consequences of rent control two models with restrictive assumptions are elaborated. The first model employs a neo-classical but ad hoc conventional supply and demand analysis of the effects of control under the assumption of homogeneous units and sites with a control system that imposes a ceiling on the rent of the dwelling units. The second model of the rented housing market assumes that homogeneous housing *services*, rather than homogeneous housing units, are traded in the market and also specifically distinguishes between the short and the long run.

(1)   SIMPLE EQUILIBRIUM MODEL

Implied within a simple neo-classical equilibrium housing model (Figure 1) of the effects of rent control would be the following assumptions:

   (a)   all dwelling units are homogeneous and have the same site values, that is the level of housing services yielded by each dwelling unit is not variable;
   (b)   the rental market for dwelling units is perfectly competitive;
   (c)   the market demand curve *DD* for dwelling units slopes downwards;
   (d)   the market supply curve *SS* for dwelling units slopes upwards on the presumption of increasing costs. Since the market model is not derived from an explicit model of the firm, no specific reference is made to whether *SS* represents the short or long run. More realistically, *SS* may be presumed to be

perfectly inelastic in the short run, on the grounds that the number of dwellings units cannot be altered due to (i) the smallness of annual production in relation to total market stock, (ii) the spatial immobility of houses, and (iii) the high capital/output ratio of housing.

In Figure 1, it is assumed that the market is in equilibrium with Q_0 dwelling units and a rent of P_0 each. A ceiling rent of P_1 which is below the equilibrium rent of P_0 for all dwelling units is then applied. It might be considered more realistic to postulate the freezing of rents at P_0, and then to examine the effects of an increase in demand (for example increased household formation) on the housing market. This approach is adopted by Lindbeck,[12] but does involve explicit assumptions on the price elasticity of supply in the short and long run.

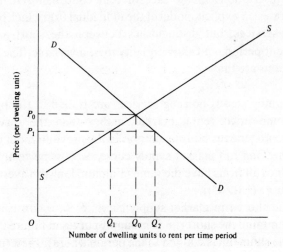

FIGURE 1

As a result of the imposition of a maximum rent of P_1, the model yields a number of important predictions:

(a) the number of occupied dwelling units will decline to Q_1;
(b) there will be excess demand of $Q_2 - Q_1$ dwelling units. Such excess demand can lead to any one, or all, of the following consequences; (i) non-price rationing (tenant discrimina-

tion), (ii) increased owner-occupation, (iii) the development of black markets, (iv) increased demand for housing in other rental sectors (local authority housing), (v) multiple accommodation, and (vi) increasing homelessness;

(c) any subsequent increase in demand will lead to increased excess demand, but would not affect the number or rent of dwelling units;

(d) any increase in landlord costs will shift the supply curve upwards and lead to a further reduction in dwelling units offered for rent.

(2) EXPLICIT MODEL OF THE FIRM WITH A QUALITY VARIABLE

This model, developed by Frankena,[13] achieves a greater reality for policy prescriptions in the face of rent control, for it not only incorporates an explicit model of the individual firm which provides housing services, but distinguishes between the short and long adjustment period, and allows quality to be a variable. The specific assumptions are that:

(a) homogeneous housing services are traded in the perfectly competitive rental market, rather than the services of homogeneous housing units as in the previous model;

(b) the long run market supply curve, $S_1 S_1$, is perfectly elastic since all firms have the same minimum long run average cost curve (LRAC);

(c) the short run market supply curve, $S_2 S_2$, is constructed by summing the short run firm supply curves in Figure 2;

(d) the short run is defined as the period where no new firms can enter the market and existing firms can adjust quality, but some costs are fixed. Figure 2 incorporates the short run average cost curve (SRAC), the average variable cost (AVC), and the short run marginal cost (SRMC).

In Figure 2 it is assumed that initially the firm is in equilibrium producing q_0 housing and operating at zero profits and that the market for housing services is in long-run equilibrium, so that Q_0

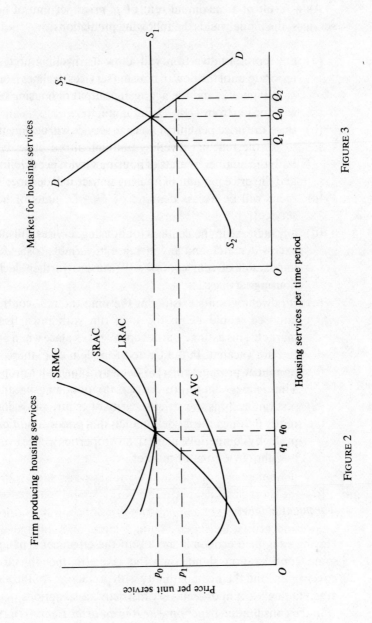

FIGURE 3

Market for housing services

Housing services per time period

FIGURE 2

Firm producing housing services

Price per unit service

Housing services per time period

units of housing services are traded at a rent of p_0 per unit.

As a result of a maximum rent of p_1 price per unit of housing services, the model yields the following predictions:

(a)   the representative firm will allow its dwelling units to deteriorate until the flow of housing services declines from q_0 to q_1 in Figure 2, and the aggregate output of housing services will decline from Q_0 to Q_1 in Figure 3;

(b)   since the price per unit of housing service will decline from p_0 to p_1, the rent per dwelling unit will also decline, because both the number of units of housing service per dwelling unit and the price per unit of housing service will decline;

(c)   there will be excess demand of $Q_2 - Q_1$ units of housing service;

(d)   any increase in the demand for housing services will increase excess demand, and any increase in variable costs after the imposition of rent control will cause a further decline in housing services;

(e)   *all* dwelling units existing at the time the rent control was imposed would be in the long run withdrawn from the market. This assumes no decontrol takes place when properties are vacated. In the United Kingdom case, there are no imminent prospects of rent decontrol for re-let properties. Thus, unless there are barriers to obtaining vacant possession, such as the strict security of tenure provision currently existing, the model predicts that under conditions of a perfectly competitive market, all properties will be eventually withdrawn from the market.

The policy problem

Having examined economic models of the effects of rent control, some consideration should now be given to the objectives of government and their compatibility with predictions of the models, albeit taking account of their very restrictive assumptions.

In the consultation paper on *The Review of the Rent Acts*, 1977, a number of objectives that should be met in new proposals to halt the decline in the number and quality of rented houses were specified:

(a) to safeguard the interests of existing private tenants;
(b) to ensure that fit private rented houses are properly maintained and kept in repair;
(c) to promote the efficient use of housing and to encourage, for example, the letting of property which might be available for only short lets;
(d) to ensure that the methods and criteria for the determination of rents are tailored to meet the difficulties faced by landlord and tenant;
(e) to simplify the law on private renting and to make for a speedier and more effective resolution of landlord/tenant disputes;
(f) to provide for a legislative framework which maintains a fair balance between the interests of tenants and landlord so that private rented accommodation can contribute effectively to meeting housing needs and choices whilst evolving into social forms involving, and acceptable to, existing landlords and their tenants.

The justification for attempts to increase the supply of rented accommodation stems mainly from the existing financial commitment to housing and the inability of government to increase its current levels of provision. The growth and cost of housing programmes of both local authority and housing associations has been considerable in recent years[14] and now represents nearly 10 per cent of total public expenditure. Notwithstanding this growth in expenditure, the increase in homelessness and the apparent stability of waiting lists for local authority housing suggests that a large group of individuals and households will continue to face acute problems. This is particularly true of the young, single and mobile, and households without children, who are currently often ineligible for such types of housing. Further, although the newly introduced House Investment Programmes for local housing authorities have a strong bias towards the revitalization of inner city areas, their success can only be limited given the present deteriorating and blighting private rented properties which are concentrated in such areas.

In fact, recent legislation[15] and the Government's commitment to mitigate the problems of the inner city has so far led to an extremely modest redirection of public expenditure of about £100 million per year[16] in favour of newly designated areas, representing one per cent of total local authority expenditure.

In so far as the present legislative framework for the control of rents is concerned, there are a number of additional aspects which appear to militate seriously against either the stability or expansion of the sector. First, adherents to maintenance of rent control frequently argue that it contributes to a higher general housing standard. This seems paradoxical. Housing consumption depends on the stock of existing dwellings. If rent control is removed, the quantity of housing demanded may well be reduced, but the overall consumption of housing in the short run, since the supply is relatively inelastic, would not be affected. It is the imposition of rent control which results in an expansion of tenants' consumption of other commodities, due to the income and substitution effects and the spill-over of unsatisfied demand in the rented housing sector to other markets. In addition, rent control diminishes the incentive to 'ration' accommodation, because it encourages the continued occupation of large houses by small families, who would, in a free market, either sub-let or move to smaller dwellings.

Second, a rent that denies a return competitive with alternative investments is going to encourage neither new construction for rental nor new lettings from the existing housing stock. The situation is aggravated if rents are not permitted to rise during periods of rapid price increases for both new building and the repair and maintenance of existing stock. At present, rent reviews generally take place every three years, and given the rate of price inflation, there is a considerable lag before rents can rise to compensate for these increases. If there is no compensation, and landlords are making losses, then they will have every incentive to reduce the housing services provided, particularly so far as the physical aspects of the property are concerned. The resultant lack of maintenance and repair will be aggravated by the uncertainty of repossession of the property, given the security of tenure provisions that currently exist.

Third, rent restrictions have obvious implications for income distribution. Insofar as the tenant pays a rent below market equilibrium, the tenant is receiving a subsidy which implies a redistribution of income from landlords to tenants. Without accurate data on the relative income position of landlords and tenants, however, no quantitative statement can be made on the welfare implications of such an outcome. Nevertheless, it is clearly a random redistribution, and it raises the policy issue of whether, if rent control is to continue, landlords or the state should be responsible for any resulting subsidy.

Fourth, rent restriction evidently militates against the mobility of labour. Tenants will clearly not only be reluctant to vacate existing controlled dwellings, but find it difficult to find comparable housing elsewhere during conditions of excess demand.

Fifth, rent control poses as big a problem for new entrants to the market as for existing tenants who wish to move. Recent evidence suggests that search costs for accommodation can be considerable with complex effects on potential tenant welfare.[17]

Finally, given the government objectives and constraints and the features of rental housing, it can be contended that a return to an uncontrolled rented sector (unless phased over many years) is unlikely to prove politically acceptable to any government. At the other extreme, municipalization[18] is unlikely to be either politically acceptable or financially possible. What is feasible, however, is the design of policies which accept the current reality of comprehensive rent control and attempt, through fiscal measures, to retain, at worst, the current stock of rented housing and, at best, to revitalize and increase the supply of rented housing.

Policy strategies

Although the concept of a 'fair rent' is now a central element in United Kingdom housing policy, its theoretical underpinning remains obscure. What precisely is implied by a 'fair rent' and what, if any, is its relationship to economic forces?

Figure 4 represents a model embracing the following assumptions:

(a) all housing units are assumed homogeneous with the same site value, and each family can possess only one dwelling unit;

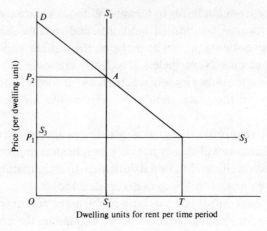

FIGURE 4

(b) OS_1 is the actual stock of housing to rent and S_1S_1 is a perfectly inelastic short run supply curve;

(c) S_3S_3 is the long run supply curve assuming a perfectly competitive market with all firms having the same long run average cost curves and no technological or pecuniary externalities.

P_1 is the 'fair rent' because it would be the rent ruling in a competitive market without scarcity, given constant cost conditions, that is the long run perfectly competitive equilibrium rent level. Hence, 'fair rent', P_1, is defined at a level where, in the absence of abnormal circumstances, need would be equated to supply with neither landlord nor tenant penalized. By the determination of the 'fair rent' and the provision of rent allowances, the Government assumes that OT families are ready and able to pay a rent of P_1. In this context, it is fair to both landlords and tenants.

The model assumes an initial situation of disequilibrium with P_1 rent prevailing as the 'fair rent'. OT families are ready and willing to pay P_1, but supply in the short run is only OS_1. In the short run, therefore, equilibrium can be achieved only at a rent of P_2. In the long run, new entrants would ensure that, assuming a perfectly competitive market, a rent of P_1 would ultimately be attained and everyone (OT families) would or could be housed.

Figure 5 makes the rather more realistic assumption that long run supply is subject to increasing costs and that the supply curve therefore slopes upwards from left to right. In this situation no obvious long run solution suggests itself.

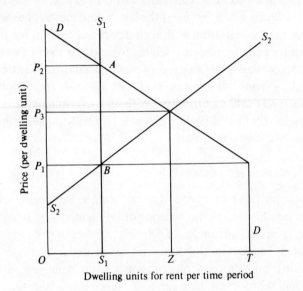

FIGURE 5

Faced with this situation, what can the State do? A number of possibilities present themselves, but they all pose difficulties.

(1) CONTROL RENTS AT P_1

Controlling rents at P_1 represents a perpetuation of the present policy of 'fair rent' levels. Theoretically, it implies the transference of P_1BAP_2 supplier surplus to the consumer and prevents the suppliers of dwellings from 'exploiting' the short run shortage situation. This rent is 'fair' in that it fully meets the long run supply price of OS_1 units. The problem with this 'solution' is that it gives the supplier no incentive to overcome the obstacles to increasing supply even in the long run. In addition, it is a very unstable solution, as landlords know that there are OS_1 people willing to pay a rent of P_2 or more and they will be accordingly reluctant to grant tenure to their sitting tenants. Once the rent is at the controlled level of P_1, it will be politically difficult to remove the control. At the controlled rent of P_1, there will be excess demand of S_1T (OT families are willing and able to pay the 'fair' rent) and a queue will form.

Some of the enhanced consumer surplus will find its way back to those landlords willing to bend the law or find means of evading it. A black market will form with such devices as charges for fixtures and fittings (OS_1 families are willing to pay in excess of even a rent of P_2). Moreover, with this excess demand, landlords will attempt to gain utility from rationing by prejudice (colour, creed, a ban on children, and the like). Of course, without Government provision of housing, S_1T will still go homeless or be forced to share housing units in extended family units.

(2) CONTROL RENTS AT P_3

The logic for this conception of a 'fair rent' is that it represents the market equilibrium in the absence of the 'temporary' supply constraint. It has the advantage of offering suppliers some inducement to expand supply in the long run, even under increasing cost conditions, and protects the consumer from being asked to pay more than the 'normal' long run cost. Nevertheless, shortage of S_1Z units would remain with S_1T homeless in the short run and ZT in the long run.

(3) ALLOW RENTS TO RISE TO P_2

This would effectively mean the abandonment of 'fair rents' in the short run in anticipation that in the long run equilibrium would be achieved at P_3. It is evident, however, that in the short run, landlords would gain a considerable surplus but, given freedom of entry, in the long run there would be an apparent strong incentive to expand supply to OZ units. In this case, no rationing by means other than ability and willingness to pay is either necessary or probable. There would, of course, remain an unmet need of ZT even in the long run.

(4) SUBSIDIZE DEMAND

Under this strategy, the State would remove rent controls, but acknowledge that 'needs' outstrip ability to pay and so subsidize demand either at a flat rate per unit of housing or ad valorem.

In Figure 6, the short run effect of removing controls at P_1 and subsidizing demand by $P_2 P_4$ per unit would be to simply increase rents to P_4, but in the long run the shift in the demand curve to the right would give a new long run equilibrium output which coincided with need (OT units) at a rent of P_5. The demand curves $D_1 D_1$ and $D_2 D_2$ will both 'kink' at OT units of housing and rents of P_1 and P_5 respectively. This follows because it is assumed that every family is willing and able to pay a rent of P_1 (and, with assistance, a rent of P_5) for some standard accommodation unit of given quality and location, and that no family can demand more than one unit. Demand is therefore perfectly inelastic up to an including the 'fair rent' level.

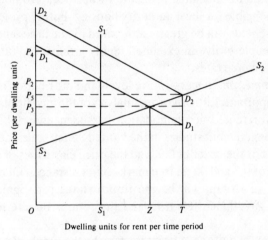

FIGURE 6

The tenant himself is paying a rent of P_1 and the landlord is receiving a rent of P_5, with the State paying the difference. The tenant is now paying $P_1 P_3$ less than he would have in the former equilibrium position and the landlord is receiving $P_3 P_5$ more. The relative gains to the tenant and the landlord of the State subsidy will, of course, depend upon the elasticities of supply and demand. The greater the elasticity of supply and the lower the elasticity of demand, the greater will be the relative gain of the tenant from any given subsidy and vice versa. In the case of an ad valorem subsidy, the gap between the two demand curves would widen or narrow, depending upon whether it was progressive or regressive.

Conclusions

The foregoing analysis has been based upon simplistic assumptions regarding the position and shape of the demand and supply curves for housing to let. Reliable data as to their actual shapes and position are critical. The main factors affecting the demand function would appear to be:

(1) *The 'growth in household' function* – the impact of household formation will be influenced by availability conditions and the price of housing in alternative sectors, especially the local authority and housing association sectors. There is little doubt that many families will continue to be unable to secure owner-occupied housing and remain ineligible for local authority housing. Future projections of such households will be greatly influenced by the tastes and willingness of people to live in extended family groups, and future marriage and divorce rates.

(2) *Incomes and prices* – future levels and distribution of income will be important. Little rigorous analysis of the income elasticity of demand for rented accommodation has been undertaken in the United Kingdom but studies in the United States[19] calculate income elasticities of the order of 0.9, and the price elasticities of supply in the range of 0.3 and 0.7 in free market circumstances. Of particular relevance in Britain will be the future status (or stigma) of the landlord, government controls and the returns on alternative investments.

However, of more specific interest is why the supply of accommodation continues to contract. While this chapter has concerned itself with an analysis of the effects of rent control, it can in no way be assumed that it has been a principal or even major factor in explaining the contraction of the market. Public aspirations, rising real incomes and the growth of building societies have undoubtedly attracted many tenants out of the private rented sector into owner occupation. In addition, there has been 'unfair' local authority competition with only the excess demand in this sector spilling over into the private rented sector. Further contributory factors might include taxation policy in respect of both landlord and tenant, redevelopment programmes, and the tremendous political uncertainty surrounding the rented sector since the First World War.

More recently, the Rent Act 1974 has not only extended rent control, but has also given full security of tenure to the majority of rented properties. These measures may be predicted to increase the uncertainty relating to landlords' ability to repossess or dispose of property when desired, and therefore, have an important impact on investment, maintenance and letting decisions. Such increased risks can induce some landlords to cease letting at the earliest opportunity, while continuing landlords may attempt to contain risks by letting to transient groups and adjust the level of housing services provided. Either one of these effects is sufficient to militate strongly against the Government's major objectives – the provision of a stable supply of furnished accommodation at a decent standard with full security of tenure for 'poor families' within the sector.

These demand and supply influences serve to emphasize that the models examined in this text make simplistic assumptions regarding the shape of both the demand and supply curves, and the homogeneity of the units traded. In addition, it assumes that the State is in a position to identify the demand and supply relationships at different rent levels.

Any attempt to determine an economic interpretation of a 'fair rent' is fraught with difficulties. The legal definition provides scope for highly subjective interpretations by rent officers and social commentators. Here we have explored the implications of just one such interpretation.

Notes and References

1. Based on two articles originally published in *Social and Economic Administration*, Vol. 9, No. 1, Spring 1975; and Vol. 10, No. 1, Spring 1976.
2. F. W. Paish (1952), 'The Economics of Rent Restriction *Lloyds Bank Review*, April.
   E. H. P. Brown and J. Wiseman (1964), 'Rent Control' in *A Course in Applied Economics*, Pitman.
   F. G. Pennance and H. Gray (1968), *Choice in Housing*, Institute of Economic Affairs.

F. G. Pennance (1975), 'Recent British Experience: A postscript from 1975', in *Rent Control: A Popular Paradox*, The Fraser Institute.

3. J. Greve (1965), *Private Landlords in England*, Occasional Paper on Social Administration, No. 16, Bell.

4. D. C. Stafford (1976), 'The Final Economic Demise of the Private Landlord', *Social and Economic Administration*, Vol. 10, No. 1, Spring.

5. M. H. Cooper and D. C. Stafford (1975), 'A Note on the Economic Implications of Fair Rents', *Social and Economic Administration*, Vol. 9, No. 1, Spring.

6. A. Henry (1975), 'The Implications of the Rent Act, 1974', *Housing Review*, March–April.

7. J. B. Cullingworth (1963), *Housing in Transition*, Heinemann.

8. B. Elliot and D. McCrone (1975), 'Landlords in Edinburgh', *Sociological Review*, Vol. 45.

9. D. Maclennan (1978), 'The 1974 Rent Act – Some Short Run Supply Effects', *The Economic Journal*, Vol. 88.

10. Department of the Environment (1977), *The Review of the Rent Acts – A Consultation Paper*.

11. *Housing Policy: A Consultative Document* (1977), Cmnd. 6851, Ch. 8.10, H.M.S.O.

12. A. Lindbeck (1967), 'Rent Control as an Instrument of Housing Policy' in A. A. Nevitt (ed.), *The Economic Problems of Housing*, Macmillan.

13. M. Frankena (1975), 'Alternative Models of Rent Control', *Urban Studies*, No. 12.

14. D. C. Stafford (1978), *The Economics of Housing Policy*, Croom-Helm.

15. *Policy for the Inner Cities* (1977), H.M.S.O.

16. A. J. Harrison & C. M. E. Whitehead (1978), 'Is there an Inner City Problem?', *Three Banks Review*, No. 119, September.

17. D. Maclennan (1977), 'Search in a Model of Housing Choice', *Centre for Environmental Studies*.

18. M. Wicks (1973), *Rented Housing and Social Ownership*, Fabian Tract, No. 421, Fabian Society.
B. Douglas-Mann *et al.* (1973), *The End of the Private Landlord*, Fabian Tract No. 312, Fabian Society.

19. F. de Leeuw and N. F. Ekanem (1971), 'The Supply of Rental Housing', *American Economic Review*, 61.

PART III

Health

CHAPTER SIX

The Royal Commission on the National Health Service [1]

MICHAEL RYAN

Whatever its achievements and shortcomings, the state-provided system of medical care in the United Kingdom has never suffered from a lack of published comment, appraisal and recommendations for reform of various kinds. In this plethora of documentation much is mere pamphleteering with very limited value for the process of policy-creation. Nevertheless, a large amount of well-informed and largely dispassionate advice is available to assist Ministers in the task of deciding on adjustments in the sub-systems, programmes and practices of the Health Service. In addition to reports from departmental committees and the Central Health Services Council (a statutory advisory body)* Ministers can turn to the findings of research undertaken in universities and other non-governmental organizations. These sources can be supplemented, obviously enough, with unpublished information and evaluation supplied through the civil service and party political machinery.

In view of this, it is highly pertinent to ask why the Labour Government chose to create yet another source of advice in the form of the Royal Commission on the National Health Service. That no broad-ranging inquiry yielding conclusions of general interest had been undertaken since the mid-1950s is a relevant but

* The Council was abolished in 1980.

by no means a sufficient explanation. The same can be said of the more contingent justification (discussed below) that was advanced by the then Prime Minister in 1975. Given that the very Government which established the Royal Commission had refused to take such action in the previous year, there exists a *prima facie* case for seeking an explanation in terms of pressure-group activity; and key events that occurred on the medico-political scene during the intervening period tend to endorse this view.

In the following account, the reconstruction of events has obviously been undertaken without the benefit of official records of relevant discussions which took place at the Department of Health and Social Security and elsewhere. That sufficient published information is available to attempt a detailed reconstruction is testimony to the coverage which the quality press and some of the medical journals habitually devote to relations between doctors and the state. (In social policy studies generally, it may be said, the strong emphasis on pressure-group activity and conflict has been fostered by the richness of non-official source material.)

The public justification

Perhaps appropriately in this connection, it was the news media and not Parliament who were first informed, on 16 October 1975, that the Government had decided to appoint a Royal Commission on the Health Service. Its terms of reference were given as being: 'To consider in the interests both of the patients and of those who work in the National Health Service the best use and management of the financial and manpower resources of the National Health Service.'

When Parliament reassembled a few days later, the Prime Minister made a statement to the House of Commons which contained an ostensible 'explanation' of the decision to initiate an independent examination of these large issues. In this context it is relevant to quote an observation made by Gerald Rhodes[2] in his scrupulous study of committees of inquiry (under which term Royal Commissions are embraced). 'Most commonly', he writes, 'either no reason at all is given for the appointment of a committee, or else reference is made to the particular event or circumstance immediately preceding the appointment.' On this occasion, however, what the Prime Minister had to say amounted to something of a reasoned case.

Mr Wilson began by noting that a great deal of concern had been expressed in the House and outside it about the state of the Service. He said that the N.H.S., along with other public service industries, was 'under severe pressure from the economic difficulties which the country faces'. This pressure, he continued, had been accentuated by the effects of reorganization of the administrative structure (the Labour Government were strongly critical of this reform enacted by their predecessors). He also referred to 'the unrest which followed from the Service's employees falling behind in pay before the substantial pay increases which they received over the last twelve months'. But perhaps the most significant features of the situation were the rising expectations resulting from advances in medical science and the possibilities of new and higher standards of care. In the years ahead, he continued, 'pressure on the nation's resources would make it impossible to do all that was desirable'; it was essential that 'profound and careful thought' should be given to the question of how the available money and manpower could best be deployed.[3]

As a preliminary comment on what the Prime Minister said, it is necessary to emphasize that none of the factual statements can be faulted. Nevertheless, the reference to obtaining an optimum use from scarce resources was no more than a truism which has long formed part of the stock-in-trade of Ministers and planners in this field as in others. Indeed, the tension between rising expectations and the greater potential of medical technology on the one hand, and the constraints arising from limited finance and manpower on the other, can be said to constitute a basic feature in the architectonics of the Service.

However, the main difficulty about Mr Wilson's 'explanation' is that it bears a strong resemblance to what he said when, in August 1974, he refused the request of representatives of the health-care professions for an independent inquiry into the financing of the N.H.S.[4] Of course fifteen months is a long time, not only in Wilsonian politics and, as the saying goes, circumstances alter cases.

The background of conflict[5]

The key to the Prime Minister's change of mind must be sought primarily in the crisis of relationships that arose between the Government and the medical profession, more specifically the consultants, without whom the state-provided hospital service could hardly continue to function. The attitude of the consultants, it can be argued, was fundamentally an adverse reaction to the unacceptable prospect of status impairment. Central to an understanding of their actions is the long-standing antagonism of many doctors towards the prospect of full-time salaried service. Broadly speaking, this is held to entail the transformation of a free and learned profession into a group of employees docile to the demands of the State, whose power over them would reside largely in its monopoly of health-care facilities. The Wilson Government triggered off fears of this prospect with proposals concerning two inter-related issues: the introduction of a new type of contract for consultants and the phasing out of pay beds from Health Service hospitals, as promised in Labour's Election Manifesto.

Though full of potential for conflict, these two issues were initially the subject of traditional 'behind-the-scenes discussions', following the return to power of Labour in the spring of 1974. Pressed to enquire into the terms of employment of senior medical and dental staff in hospitals, the Government established a joint working party under the chairmanship of the Parliamentary Under Secretary for Health, Dr David Owen. Its terms of reference included consideration of 'arrangements for private practice'. Conceivably, the two sides could have agreed on some sort of trade-off with concessions by both, had they remained free to negotiate in private.

However, all chances of a deal were to vanish in the wake of overt political action taken by members of the National Union of Public Employees (N.U.P.E.) and the Confederation of Health Service Employees (C.O.H.S.E.). These two unions had long pressed for the abolition of pay beds and, in the early summer of 1974, their members sought to bring it about immediately by taking industrial action on a localized basis. Thus, at Charing Cross Hospital in London some staff threatened to withdraw services, including domestic, catering and linen services from the private wing unless it was closed by the end of the month in question, June 1974.

How did the doctors react? As a riposte they asked the Secretary of State to restore normal working at Charing Cross and other hospitals affected by the ban on private patients, backing up this request by saying that if no action had been taken by Monday 8 July all consultants would be advised to work strictly according to their contracts, and to refrain from a variety of non-clinical work such as attending committees. On Friday 5 July negotiations were held under the chairmanship of the Secretary of State for Social Services, Barbara Castle. The outcome of these crisis talks was that N.U.P.E. and C.O.H.S.E. instructed their members to discontinue their action and await the report of the Owen working party. Furthermore, the Secretary of State gave a pledge that no arbitrary reduction in pay bed numbers would occur while the report was awaited.

Almost immediately after the threatened work to rule was called off, the Hospital Consultants and Specialists' Association held a mass meeting which left the general public in no doubt about the likely effect of the Government's pursuit of their election pledge. As could easily have been predicted, in the face of an external threat whole-time consultants closed ranks with part-timers (whose contract enables them to undertake private practice) and they voted overwhelmingly for the retention of pay beds within the Health Service. The strength of their determination was borne out by the heavy defeat of a motion to the effect that, while every effort should be made to retain pay beds, no pressure should be put on the Government by the threat of industrial action that would be detrimental to the care of patients. Moreover, the President of their Association, which represents about 5,000 doctors, was able to point out that despite a recent dispute with the British Medical Association (B.M.A.), both bodies had stood solidly together during the crisis. Indeed, it was an interesting and important feature of the situation that, so far as can be seen, the B.M.A.'s Secretary played a key co-ordinating and initiatory role in dealings with Barbara Castle – action which served both to strengthen the consultants and to validate the B.M.A.'s claim to speak on behalf of both main branches of a frequently disunited profession.

It was also the Secretary of the B.M.A. who at this time protested strongly against the constitutional impropriety of the proposal to phase out pay beds by administrative fiat, insisting that the policy would be legal only if Parliament sanctioned it by means of an amending act. In the event, this contention was tacitly accepted by the Government and, after prolonged and bitter conflict, the relevant legislation reached the Statute Book some two years later. The Health Services Act 1976, it should be added, provided for the withdrawal of 1,000 pay beds within a period of six months, but assigned to an independent Health Service Board the task of phasing out the majority of beds and the facilities for private out-patients. By the time of writing (August 1978) only a further 433 pay beds had been withdrawn, leaving a total of 3,011 in Great Britain as a whole.

It is appropriate now to look in detail at events which occurred late in 1974 and in 1975. Broadly speaking, this account serves to point up the mutual interdependence of Government and hospital doctors: this resides in the possession by one of the costly fixed capital, and by the other of inalienable specialist skills which are together indispensable for a modern hospital service. In the context of the basically ideological dispute over pay beds, this interdependence can be seen as the underlying reason for the Government's decision to accept the demands of the medical profession for the establishment of a Royal Commission.

Following the second election of 1974, Barbara Castle informed M.P.s that action to phase out pay beds would be taken during the coming session. This announcement, made on 1 November, was followed by a very angry reaction from the specialists who resented (among other things) the pre-emption of discussions by the Owen working party. Some consultants in the north of England started an unofficial work-to-contract but their action was soon overtaken by events. On 6 November the doctors' side of the Owen working party examined not only the timetable for phasing out the majority of pay beds but also the proposed new contract, which contained a 'full commitment allowance'. Taking the two documents together, the consultants expressed their fears about being lured into becoming full-time salaried employees of the State. The following day the Secretary of State was asked to produce, within a period of three weeks, a contract to which the consultants could give their agreement in principle. B.M.A. members received copies of the Association's *Sanctions Plan for Emergency*, the first stage of which was non-cooperation, and the second, withdrawal from the Service.

On 20 November Mrs Castle presented to the consultants what came to be known as her 'take it or leave it' contract. They decided to leave it, and to start working to their original contracts. Although this is not the place to analyse the course of their action, which lasted from early January until mid-April 1975, it is necessary to emphasise that it became closely interlinked with industrial action over pay beds.

Despite the fact that the Secretary of State accepted that the work-to-contract was not directly connected with the pay beds issue, in the author's view she was open to the charge of tacitly condoning what can only be described as bully-boy action by members of N.U.P.E. It is far from clear precisely how many private beds were effectively closed down by union action, or for how long, but the Merseyside region was particularly affected, and in South Wales union militancy took an ugly form. For example, in March at Morriston Hospital, Swansea, N.U.P.E. members resolved to ban all services for a twenty-eight-bed surgical ward to which one private patient had been admitted. For a period of over twenty-four hours the services to the ward in question had to be provided by volunteers, whom the branch secretary abused as 'blacklegs and scabs'.[6] At national level C.O.H.S.E. issued a threat to the effect that if the Government gave no promise of action before 8 May it would consider taking country-wide industrial action.

This was a deadline which Mrs Castle managed to meet. On 5 May she announced that the programme for phasing out would be carried out under legislation to be introduced as soon as Parliamentary time was available. A few months later, in August 1975, she published a consultative document which was intended to prefigure the proposed Bill.[7] Thereafter, it became apparent that a majority of doctors were being impelled towards an extreme position by the Government's determination to ignore warnings about the harm they would cause – a determination which a leader in *The Times* described as their 'readiness to set ideology above the real interests of Britain's health services'.[8]

The Government's move

The Government also had to reckon with the action of junior hospital doctors who were conducting a militant campaign over their terms of contract and level of remuneration. That discontent had become dangerously virulent by early October 1975 was signalled by the intervention of the President of the Royal College of Surgeons. Only very rarely do the Royal Colleges become visible on the medico-political scene, being debarred by their charters from trade union activity intended to further the interests of doctors. But it was on the question of standards in medical practice – and hence the safety of patients – that Sir Rodney Smith sounded a note of alarm in public: morale in the service was as low as it could be. He referred to emigration and a shortage of young British graduates wishing to enter the speciality of surgery – a situation which threatened a slide in standards, with the consequent danger of people dying from unsuccessful operations.[9] The Government's continued refusal to concede the demand for an independent inquiry was liable to be interpreted by doctors and the Parliamentary Opposition – and not by them alone – as irresponsible obduracy.

The issue of an inquiry came up at the press conference which had been hastily convened by the Secretary of State later on the same day as Sir Rodney Smith's statement, apparently in order to counter the effects of what he had said. On this occasion, Mrs Castle was described as giving 'a conciliatory impression – which contrasted with the intemperate and abrasive utterances she had made earlier in the year. She repeated earlier assurances that the Government did not intend to abolish private practice and that nothing she was proposing would debar patients from seeking private treatment. Although she had not excluded the possibility of an independent inquiry, she still had to be convinced that it would be useful.[10] However, she was also reported as saying, in a most revealing aside: 'There might be a case for holding one just for the therapy of the profession'.[11] On the following day, 10 October, the Secretary of State reiterated her scepticism: 'I must say I am a little doubtful whether an inquiry would help us find new sources of money for the Service'. But her mind was not closed, she said, to an inquiry into 'areas of general concern about the N.H.S. and its resources and priorities'.[12] During this final stage of the 'lead-in' period, the question presumably received attention from the Cabinet, and it is an intriguing possibility that the statement quoted above echoes a Cabinet decision. Whatever the truth about this conjecture, only six days later Mrs Castle announced the appointment of the Royal Commission.

The Government thus conceded a demand which the medical profession had made first in 1965 and reiterated with increasing frequency following the issue of Mrs Castle's consultative document. Initially, the demand seems to have arisen from the expectation or, less confidently, the hope that an independent inquiry would recommend additional sources of finance for the Service and increases in existing charges. (At the 1964 Annual Representative Meeting of the B.M.A., a majority of more than two-thirds advocated retention of the prescription charge, thus reversing a policy that had stood for twelve years.)[13]

The doctors' preoccupation with finance for the Service and methods of revenue-raising persisted after the prospect of legislation on pay beds became imminent,[14] and indeed may have been a tactically disastrous diversion of energies. Immediately after the appearance of Mrs Castle's consultative document in August 1975, the B.M.A. might have been politically adroit to punch home the message that the proposed withdrawal of pay beds now overshadowed other issues and had implications so potentially serious for the Health Service as to justify, in itself, the appointment of an independent inquiry.

As it was, immediately after announcing the appointment of the Royal Commission, the Prime Minister was able to affirm that legislation would be introduced to phase out pay beds. So in a meaningful sense the doctors had been hoist with their own petard. By establishing an independent inquiry, the Government could be portrayed as having acted responsibly in offering a concession that justified a reduction of hostilities. But no procrastination over pay beds was entailed. Hence, no storm of protest would arise from Labour backbenchers and there could be no justification for C.O.H.S.E. and N.U.P.E. members attempting to take the law into their own hands. Whatever judgement is made of the overall strategy of the Wilson Government, their tactics must surely be regarded as revealing great sophistication.

A taxonomy of committees

Having examined the circumstances surrounding the appointment of the Royal Commission, it is appropriate now to take up the problematic question of the outcome of the Commission's work. This discussion can be pursued against the background of a taxonomy of committees which Gerald Rhodes[15] elaborated. His four-fold classification runs as follows:

(1) *Committees set up reluctantly by a government under pressure with the object of staving off that pressure*: committee may well fail to agree, but in any case reports likely to be accepted to the extent that they recommend no action or only minor action.

(2) *Committees set up to postpone an awkward issue*: reports likely to be accepted to the extent that they indicate a solution not likely to be too troublesome.

(3) *Committees set up because the government is in doubt how an issue should be resolved*: reports likely to be accepted to the extent that they indicate that an acceptable solution is possible.

(4) *Committees set up where government is fairly clear what course to adopt but needs independent backing before doing so*: reports likely to be accepted to the extent that committee provides this backing.

Did the Commission conform to type?

The Royal Commission on the National Health Service can be allocated to the first category without much difficulty. In so far as the Government had ensured that the Commission could not be employed as a stalling device in respect of pay beds, it had not bought the doctors off. But the doctors could hardly denounce the machinery that had been created at their insistence, and hence, in the short term, the wind was taken from their sails.

It is next necessary to ask whether there is evidence that members of the Commission are likely to find themselves in disagreement. When attempting to answer this question one moves only too rapidly into the quicksands of pure conjecture. However, it is revealing to categorize the sixteen members according to the various interests or general approaches which they can be held to represent. (One categorization is recorded in the notes.[16]) Even the vestigial biographical data published with the announcement of their names does make clear that a number of members have a direct or indirect link with the Health Service, and further investigation makes it possible to extend the list. (Only five are health-care professionals as such: three doctors, one dentist and a nurse.) So it hardly seems fanciful to suggest that, given their previous experience and present office or occupation, the majority of Commissioners will carry into their deliberations a reasonably strong commitment to the broad principles of the Service.

But that does not rule out the possibility of minority reports, and it is important to note that the Chairman, Sir Alec Merrison, clearly indicated that unanimity will not be contrived through the avoidance of controversial issues. After the names of the Commission's members had been announced – somewhat belatedly – in May 1976, Sir Alec was reported as saying that, 'they would not duck issues because they were politically sensitive'.[17] Later, in October of the same year, he announced that the Commission would monitor important policy decisions such as the principles of re-allocation of resources (the R.A.W.P. policy) or the rate of withdrawal of pay beds. If it considered them wrong, it would say so before making its final report and, if the Commissioners were divided, something would be said 'giving both points of view'.[18] Up to the time of writing, rather disappointingly, no interim statements have appeared and hence it is impossible to identify dissenting groups or individuals.

Another factor which may perhaps militate against unanimity is the Commissioners' evident concern to sound out opinions as widely as possible. Although talk of a dialogue with the man in the street would be an exaggeration, the Commission has surely made itself unusually and commendably accessible to the influence of groups and individuals. Thus, in May 1976, the Chairman issued a request for views on which problems were the most important for in-depth examination, and in October of the same year a booklet was published to explain in outline the Commission's programme of work.[19] This booklet stated that more than a thousand replies to the Chairman's request had been received and that the list of topics singled out for examination had been influenced by the views expressed. But public opinion was assigned a further role in that the Commissioners said they expected to modify their programme in the light of evidence which would be submitted, and of their own investigations.

While a researcher cannot obtain access to the full collection of evidence, he can look over the Commission's shoulders – up to a point – by obtaining copies of submissions from their authors and by reading summaries of them in the press. As might be supposed, some of the opinions expressed are essentially non-controversial, except perhaps among a few groups of technocratic specialists. (An example is the view of the Committee of Professors of Clinical Pharmacology and Therapeutics that there should be more effective administration and control of drug therapy through the wider application of clinical pharmacology.) However, it is not difficult to find a variety of highly disputatious recommendations for change.

One striking set of examples is provided in the evidence submitted by N.U.P.E. Among their more contentious proposals are:

(a) legislation to absorb all private practice into the N.H.S.;
(b) transfer to the N.H.S. of local authority services which relate directly to the provision of health care;
(c) N.H.S. management bodies to consist half of persons elected by the electorate as for local government and half of persons selected from and elected by all grades of N.H.S. staff by means of the trade union machinery;
(d) the abolition of the independent contractor status of family doctors and dentists in favour of a salaried employee status;
(e) the abolition of charges and the N.H.S. portion of the National Insurance contribution paid by employees and employers.

As would be expected, N.U.P.E. is not alone in advancing radical proposals. Thus the Chairman of the B.M.A.'s Negotiating Sub-committee expressed the view that 'The Royal Commission is our last chance this century to do something fundamental about the Service'.[20]

It is a predictable but crucial point that the recommendations of certain organizations such as N.U.P.E. and the B.M.A. are mutually exclusive, to a greater or less extent. So if the Commissioners reproduce the divisions of opinion in the evidence, they are likely to issue minority reports and notes of dissent or reservation. But this presupposes that the Commission is no more than – to quote a line from Samuel Taylor Coleridge – 'A vain, speech-mouthing, speech-reporting Guild'.

Moreover, the Commissioners are in a position to examine controversial issues with greater objectivity, rigour and breadth of vision than can be expected of any interest group or political party. After all, their conclusions will be influenced not only by the evidence submitted by individuals and organizations, but also by impartial research which they themselves caused to be undertaken. The high quality of this commissioned work is evident already, interestingly enough, since the findings of three research studies were published in the summer of 1978 in order to inform and stimulate discussion of the issues they deal with.[21]

A possible outcome

Consideration must finally be given to the question of Governmental reaction to the conclusions presented by the Commission. If this Commission conforms to Rhodes's first category in respect of outcome as well as origin, its recommendations (whether unanimous or a majority verdict) are likely to be accepted to the extent that they entail no action or only minor action. And indeed there are strong reasons for supposing that radical changes in the organization and financing of the Service will not emerge.

As for possible recommendations about organization, it would be somewhat surprising if the Commissioners did not advocate the abolition of one tier in the management structure in order to simplify decision-taking and reduce the overlap of functions. The need for such a reform is recognized by large numbers of people working within the Service, and not only by them. In April 1978 the Conservative Party committed themselves to making the N.H.S. 'more local' by abolishing Area Health Authorities and strengthening management at district level. If the Opposition were to win the impending election, they might well proceed to implement this policy on the basis of their mandate without waiting for the Commission to confirm its validity. The point here, however, is that the proposal could hardly be described as having far-reaching implications likely to evoke a major political row.

With regard to methods of financing the Service, the Commission cannot fail to be aware of pressures operating to preserve the *status quo ante*. Even if a majority of the Commissioners were prepared to recommend raising a substantially larger proportion of revenue from charges of various kinds (which seems unlikely), they would do so in the almost certain knowledge that a Labour Government would reject the proposal for ideological reasons. Similarly they could assume that the Conservative Party in office would probably go little further than increasing the prescription charge (as they are committed to doing) on the pragmatic ground that the introduction of sizeable payments at the time of receipt would be highly unpopular with most of the electorate.

It is relevant to refer at this point to the only other full-scale examination of the Service carried out by a Government-appointed committee of inquiry. (The fact that it was not a Royal Commission has no significance here.) As I have argued elsewhere, the appointment in 1953 of a five-man committee to examine the cost of the N.H.S. apparently resulted from the Conservative Government's hope of independent support for increased payments by users of the Service.[22] In the event, though, the Guillebaud Report[23] arrived at the conclusion that no convincing case had been made out for imposing new charges to be borne by the patient. More generally, it was notable for providing a 'shot in the arm' for an institution that was subjected to considerable criticism from a variety of quarters – then as now.

The importance of the Merrison Report, appearing in 1979, may similarly reside in its broad endorsement of the organization and operation of the Service at a time when its survival into the 1980s is by no means assured. That a serious malaise now exists in the Service can hardly be doubted, not least because of the industrial militancy displayed by many groups of health-care workers in the recent past. But it is essential to distinguish between the attitudes of the Health Service pressure groups who favour changes of various and often irreconcilable kinds and the attitudes of the majority of the electorate who, at a high level of generality, expect Governments at least to ensure that access to medical and allied services remains on the same basis as at present.

In conclusion, most voters, broadly satisfied with the Service they know, would be opposed to radical change in the fundamental and interrelated principles of the N.H.S.: State responsibility, comprehensive care, universal coverage of the population and little or no payment at time of consumption. Given that the Commissioners evidently attach considerable weight to the views of the general public, they are likely to bear that consideration very much in mind when framing their report. Any of their recommendations liable to infringe those principles will almost certainly be ignored by political parties seeking support from the electorate.

Notes and References

1. First appeared as an article in *Social and Economic Administration,* Vol. 11, No. 3, Autumn 1977.
2. Gerald Rhodes, *Committees of Inquiry,* Allen and Unwin, 1975, p. 51.
3. H. C. Debs, Vol. 898, Cols. 35–36, 20 October 1975.
4. *British Medical Journal,* 10 August 1974, p. 424.
5. Passages in this section draw on the author's article: 'Hospital Pay Beds: A Study in Ideology and Constraint', in *Social and Economic Administration,* Vol. 9, No. 3, Autumn 1975, pp. 164–183.
6. *The Times,* 26 March 1975.
7. Department of Health and Social Security, Scottish Home and Health Department, Welsh Office, *The Separation of Private Practice from National Health Service Hospitals: A Consultative Document,* August 1975.
8. *The Times,* 17 May 1975.

9. *The Times,* 9 October 1975. See also his letter published in *The Times* on 30 September 1975.
10. *The Times,* 9 October 1975.
11. *British Medical Association News Review,* November 1975, p. 106.
12. *The Times,* 10 October 1975.
13. *British Medical Journal,* Supplement, 25 July 1964, p. 75.
14. Thus the Secretary of the B.M.A., in a statement on the action of junior hospital doctors over their contract, made the point that: 'So far there is no evidence of a desire on the part of the Government to fundamentally rethink the financing of the N.H.S. or to consider whether there is any better way of finding the necessary resources. Such an inquiry is long overdue and should be put into effect quickly if confidence is to be restored'.
Source: *British Medical Journal,* 18 October 1975, p. 181.
15. Gerald Rhodes, *Committees of Inquiry,* p. 192.
16. The categorization most relevant to the argument in the text is as follows:

Representatives of Health Service professions and employees
Dr Cyril Taylor, G.P. in Liverpool.
Dr Christopher Wells, G.P. in Sheffield.
Professor Ivor Batchelor, Professor of Psychiatry at Dundee University.
Professor Paul Bramley, Professor of Dental Surgery at Sheffield University.
Professor Jean McFarlane, Professor of Nursing at Manchester University.
Miss Audrey Prime, Staff Side Secretary, General Whitley Council for the Health Services of Great Britain.

Representatives of relevant statutory agencies
Sir Thomas Brown, Chairman, Eastern Health and Social Services Board, Northern Ireland.
Sir Simpson Stevenson, Chairman, Greater Glasgow Health Board.
Ann Clwyd, Member, Cardiff Community Health Council.
Lady Sherman, Social Services Committee of the London Borough of Hackney.

Persons with relevant research interests
Professor Alan Williams, Professor of Economics at York University.
Miss Kay Richards, Senior Lecturer, National Institute for Social Work Training.

Mr Peter Jacques, Secretary of the Social Insurance and Industrial Welfare Department of the T.U.C.

The Chairman, Sir Alec Merrison, is Vice-Chancellor of Bristol University, but cannot be classified as an outsider since he chaired the Committee of Inquiry into the Regulation of the Medical Profession which reported in 1975. The Commission's one lawyer, Mr C. M. Clothier, QC., was also a member of that Committee. Only Mr Frank Welsh, a director of Grindlay's Bank Ltd and a number of companies, appears to have no direct or indirect connection with the National Health Service.

17. *The Times*, 7 May 1976.
18. *The Times*, 20 October 1976.
19. Royal Commission on the National Health Service, *The Task of the Commission*, H.M.S.O., October 1976.
20. *British Medical Association News Review*, January 1976, p. 137.
21. Royal Commission on the National Health Service, *The Working of the National Health Service*; *Management of Financial Resources in the National Health Service*; *Allocating Health Resources: a commentary on the report of R.A.W.P.* All H.M.S.O., 1978.
22. See the author's article: 'Free at Time of Use: a Study of Charges and Costs in the National Health Service', *Social and Economic Administration*, Vol. 7, No. 3, September 1973, pp. 219–234.
23. *Report of the Committee of Inquiry into the Cost of the National Health Service*, Cmd. 9663, H.M.S.O., 1956.

Postscript

In July 1979, over three and a half years after the announcement of its appointment, the Royal Commission presented its report to Parliament. At an estimated cost of almost £1 million, the Commissioners' investigations gave rise to a lengthy document containing a total of twenty-two chapters. It is clearly impossible to precis its contents in the space available here and what follows is no more than a summary assessment linked with the preceding part of this chapter, prepared before the Report was published.

As for the broad approach underlying the report, the Commissioners make a point of recording that it would have been wrong to have interpreted their terms of reference 'in a narrow financial and administrative context' (1.6). They attempted to take 'the widest possible view of the N.H.S.' and consider that, as a result, important topics had been dealt with cursorily, perhaps even superficially (22.3).

Whatever judgement is formed about the quality of their analysis of major issues, there can be no denying that the Commissioners cover an impressive range of topics. The final chapter (which is also published separately) reflects this range and diversity in putting forward no less than 117 specific recommendations for action. These are grouped under the following headings:

services to patients
the N.H.S. and its workers
the N.H.S. and other institutions
management and finance.

Other categorizations are possible and it seems helpful to identify a number of recommendations as having the common objective of endorsing existing good practices and encouraging their wider dissemination or more vigorous implementation. For example, the Commissioners state that health departments and health authorities should continue to give financial support and encouragement to voluntary effort in the N.H.S. Similarly they consider that all hospitals should provide explanatory booklets for patients before they enter hospital.

It is possible to relate recommendations labelled in this way with the likelihood of their acceptance. The chances of rejection must be slim for the two examples just cited but others that can be placed in the same category are less likely to succeed on grounds of cost. At the time of writing there can be no certainty that the Government will agree that plans for the expansion of community nursing should be continued and the existing technical college/dental hospital training schemes for dental technicians should be expanded.

A second category of proposals (which overlaps the first) can be identified as those which evidently entail substantial increases in the allocation of personnel and finance to the N.H.S. and related agencies. Within this category can be included an interesting collection of proposals concerned with the promotion of research; the most ambitious of these advocates the establishment of an Institute of Health Services Research. Taken as a whole, this category can be placed a little further along the scale of acceptability that runs from completely unobjectionable to highly controversial. A few of the proposals that can be assigned to it are certainly unacceptable to the present Government on grounds of policy.

That is most obviously true for 'the gradual but complete extinction of charges' which is estimated to cost the taxpayer some £200 million. It is not certain that the Commissioners had an opportunity to revise their text after the General Election of April 1979 but they would have known that the proposal would be rejected since the Conservative Party Manifesto had contained a promise to increase charges. As it happened, the increases came into effect a few days before the Commission reported: from 16 July prescription charges rose to 45p per item and the maximum charge for dental treatment became £7 (but no change occurred in respect of N.H.S. glasses).

Here it is relevant to add that whereas the Commissioners gave no indication of the relative importance they attached to abolishing charges, they do assign a 'top priority' tag to another item entailing substantial expenditure. This is the need for 'extra funds to permit much more rapid replacement of hospital buildings than has so far been possible' (10.74). Also by contrast, this is an issue on which a measure of agreement exists between the Commission and the Government. Thus in the week after publication of the report the North West Regional Health Authority was able to announce the largest programme of hospital building ever sanctioned for that region: over a period of ten years a total of some £172 million will be spent on upgrading and replacement.

Although the general tendency of the report is to increase the cost of the Service substantially, it would be misleading not to indicate that a few proposals conduce to the saving of resources due to enhanced managerial efficiency. Under this heading can be placed the recommendation that below the regions in England and below the health departments elsewhere in the United Kingdom, generally one management level only should carry operational responsibility for services and for collaboration with local government. A second example – the more striking on account of its boldness – is provided by the proposal that the formal responsibility of the Department of Health and Social Security (including its accountability to Parliament) should be transferred to the English regional health authorities. It can be added that the first example largely coincides with – and consequently helps to legitimate – the Government's previously announced commitment to simplify the administrative structure of the N.H.S. and devolve management authority to the lowest effective level.

A further set of recommendations (which again are not totally separable from the previous group) can be described as statist strategies. Despite the fact that their primary or ostensible object may be to increase efficiency and effectiveness, they would serve to greatly enhance the powers reposed in Health Service and related bureaucracies. This threat may appear remote in some instances – such as the introduction of a salary option for G.P.s. On the other hand, the B.M.A. could be pardoned for interpreting it as the first step on a slippery path which leads to all N.H.S. doctors becoming full-time salaried employees of the State. Suspicions of this kind are all the more likely to be aroused due to the Commissioners' lack of sympathy for the concept of an independent professional contractor, an attitude that is implicit in the recommendation that Family Practitioner Committees in England and Wales should be abolished and their functions assumed by health authorities. This step, in the Commissioners' words, 'must allow [the authorities] to influence more positively than they can at the present the distribution and quality of surgeries and other practice premises, the balance and relationship between hospital and community care, the movement of staff across institutional boundaries and deputising services' (20.57). Moreover, the Commissioners unquestionably move into the sphere of high politics by proposing that the Health Services Board (created by the Labour Government to phase out pay beds) should be given responsibility to consider, and power to control, the aggregates of beds in private hospitals and nursing homes when any new private development is considered in a locality. Even before the General Election it was well known that the Conservative Party intended to abolish this Board as one means of ending Labour's 'vendetta' against private medical care.

The foregoing paragraph was not intended to imply that the

report, taken as a whole, should be regarded as a crypto-political document. Out of the fourteen Commissioners who signed it (there were two resignations) only a minority were members of the Labour Party who could be expected to bring specifically Socialist doctrines to bear on their inquiries. What is surely the more significant factor – and one that helps to explain the unanimity of the report – is the close connections with the Service of almost all members prior to their appointment. This background in fact receives mention and is presented as a virtue: '. . . we have felt it right to play to our strength, which we see as the wide experience we possess collectively in N.H.S. matters and matters which affect the N.H.S.' (1.10). So the statist coloration can be ascribed at least as much to circumstance as to the influence of doctrine.

Turning back now to the origins of the Commission, it may appear ironic that in 1975 Barbara Castle expressed scepticism about the potential usefulness of an inquiry then being demanded by the doctors. For in the event, the Royal Commission gave weighty support to the existing method of financing the Health Service very largely from general taxation when they dismissed the case for a change to an insurance-based system. One main disadvantage to such a scheme, say the Commissioners, is that there are groups in the community who are both bad health risks and too poor to pay high premiums; a second is the high cost of administration. Perhaps more influential in practice, however, will be their comments on partial insurance financing – a concept which has been advocated in both B.M.A. and Conservative Party circles. In one form this would entail restricting free use of the N.H.S. to people below a certain income level, leaving the wealthier to take out private insurance cover. The Commissioners consider (with good reason) that the arrangement would produce a dual standard of care and they go on to state: 'We would have serious reservations about actively encouraging a system in which the richer members of our society received better care than the less well off' (21.23).

Finally, reference can be made to the general endorsement of the Service which may be thought implicit throughout the report and is explicit in more than one passage. The character of this overall assessment is well suggested by the words '. . . we must say as clearly as we can that the N.H.S. is not suffering from a mortal disease susceptible only to heroic surgery' (22.4). Another leit-motif is conveyed in the sentence: 'In our review of the N.H.S. as it exists we found much about which we can all be proud' (22.86). That verdict occurs in a section headed 'The Future' and its location there is especially appropriate since the Commissioners have done much to ensure that the Health Service should continue into the 1980s without being subject to fundamental changes.

Editor's Post-postscript.   In December 1979 the Government published its consultative document, *Patients First*, advocating a reduction in N.H.S. administrative tiers by abolishing multi-district area authorities, but keeping the family practitioner committees, and in general accepting many of the recommendations of Royal Commission Report.

CHAPTER SEVEN

How Not to Regulate the Medical Profession[1]

ALAN MAYNARD

First doctor:	What did you charge her?
Second doctor:	£200.
First doctor:	What had she got?
Second doctor:	£200.
	(G. B. Shaw *The Doctor's Dilemma*)

Introduction

The objectives of this chapter are to appraise critically the regulation of doctors, and to indicate how the failure to recognize that the role of this group is critical in the provision of health care services has led to outcomes throughout the world which may be viewed as both inefficient and inequitable. Throughout, the analysis is concerned with health-care services, and it must be emphasized at the outset that such services may have little to do with improving the health status of individuals in the community. Health care is merely one input into activities which generate the outcome of good health. I will indicate that the productivity of health care may be very low, and it is possible that if a policy objective is to improve health status in an efficient manner, policy makers may need to shift resources out of health-care systems into other sectors, or at least to allocate incremental resources to other activities that improve health status more efficiently.

The main body of the text is divided into three sections. The first is concerned with the institutional arrangements by which physicians regulate themselves. In the second section it will be argued that because of the inappropriateness of these regulatory devices, health-care systems tend to be inefficient in their outcomes. The third section will extend this argument and examine the effects on the equity or 'fairness' with which health-care is delivered. A brief concluding section will summarize the discussion and argue that the present system of regulating physicians is inefficient, inequitable and unethical.

The regulation of physicians

Some professions, of which medicine is one, license practitioners and, by so doing, affect the quality and the quantity of practitioners. Often the regulatory power of the profession is sanctioned by the state. Trades or professions tend to arise when the practitioners are self-employed, highly paid and operate in fields which require substantial training. There are two conflicting 'explanations' of the existence of professions: the public interest argument, and the self-interest argument.

The arguments contained in the public interest rationale of licensing are based on the belief that the individual is not the best judge of his own welfare. There are three strands to the arguments. The first strand is that the supply of information about the efficiency of medical care therapies is inadequate. The patient is uncertain about the nature of the health care product and, as Arrow[2] has argued, licensing could be seen as an insurance against uncertainty because it could, in theory at least, remove or mitigate this problem. It is also argued that licensing increases information by establishing minimum standards for entrants. Licensing, at worst, ensures that all practitioners have some minimum standard of competence.

This argument is not without its problems. First, licensing tends to affect only new entrants. Those physicians registered before licensing is started, or registered prior to changes in licensing qualification rules, are not affected by the rules or changes in them. Thus, new entrants may be qualified, but established practitioners may be incompetent when their skills are compared to present-day registration criteria. A good example of this is the application of tests of competence in language, particularly to immigrant doctors in the United Kingdom: only potential new entrants are being tested; those immigrant doctors already at work in this country are not.

The second problem with the uncertainty argument is that licensing gives no information about the degree of heterogeneity in the standards of those registered. In fact, the profession has made advertising illegal so that patients encounter great difficulties if they attempt to acquire information about the relative skills of local doctors. Third, licensing raises the costs of entering the medical profession because educational standards are raised. This tends to inflate the 'price of the trade', or the physician's salary. Thus, if uncertainty is reduced, the cost may be substantially increased.

Moore[3] has argued that an effective and simple alternative to this type of 'public interest' argument would be the replacement of licensing by certification. Such an arrangement would certify as a practitioner anyone who achieved some minimum standard in a testing procedure. This mechanism would pay no regard to the amount of training, but would assess only the quality of the training outcome. Such a proposal begs an explicit set of criteria that have to be met before certification. These could be high (as now), or low, as in the Swiss Canton of Appenzell. There anyone who is certified as being of good character by the police (that is anyone with no criminal record) can practise as a doctor. This has led to a health service industry in which 'quacks' exceed registered medical practitioners, the number of medical practitioners has been constant since 1860, and the income of 'quacks' is about the same as registered practitioners. This fascinating case indicates that patients are prepared to use 'quacks' and so have reduced the demand for registered practitioners, who are expensive to train.

Where practitioners themselves regulate training and limit competition, availability of information may be a major problem. One may well ask whether the lack of public knowledge about the profession makes licensing necessary, or whether indeed the licensing process and the profession inhibit the flow of information.

If the information argument is discounted, two other arguments remain for those who maintain that licensure is in the public interest. The first of these is the 'society knows best' argument. Its proponents assert that even if the information flow is 'adequate', individuals would make the 'wrong' decisions. Moore[3] quotes the American economist J. M. Clark: 'The growth of scientific knowledge of mental and physical health and disease is working a revolution in this matter, undermining the idea that each individual is the best judge of his own welfare.' To argue that the licensed professional is a better judge of the welfare of society is a value judgement with which not everyone would agree.

The final item in the 'public interest' set of contentions is the externality argument, which asserts that licensing may be necessary because the social costs of medical activity may exceed the private ones. For instance, if incompetent physicians diagnose illness incorrectly, their mistakes may contribute to the spread of contagion and the propagation of an epidemic. The costs of such errors to society exceed the costs to the individual physician. This argument has some appeal, but licensing in such circumstances would be sensible only if it can be shown that by making available more competent physicians epidemics would be avoided and that patients would not forgo this more expensive medical advice. First then, licensing may not necessarily generate more efficient physicians to reduce the chances of epidemics and the externality problem arising. Second, it is debatable that self-regulation of physicians results in better evaluation. Third, even if more efficient physicians are produced, the increased costs of the service, expressed in terms of prices or taxes, may affect utilization and generate new externality problems.

The 'public interest' arguments in favour of licensing are fraught with difficulty. Some of the arguments reflect differences in value judgements and cannot be refuted by evidence. Those arguments which can be tested empirically have often not been adequately tested, and the circumstantial evidence which is available would tend to make most observers wary of the argument's validity.

If licensing is not in the public interest, is it in the interests of the profession?

Whether the self-interest argument is discussed broadly, as by Stigler,[4] or narrowly by Moore,[3] the validity of the arguments seem superior, logically and empirically, to those that have been discussed in the preceding paragraphs on the public interest rationale. However, like all theories and evidence, they are not unambiguous and the reader is warned to be wary of assuming that correlation implies causation either in whole, or in part.

Stigler argues that licensing is merely one part of regulation by the state. His central idea is that regulation is sought, acquired, designed, and operated primarily for the benefit of those who are regulated. He further argues that occupational licensing is a possible use of the political process to improve the economic circumstances of the regulated group. The licence is an effective barrier to entry because occupational practice without the licence at best runs foul of opposition engendered by facts and myths about quacks, and is at worst illegal.

Moore and Stigler both conclude that the powers resulting from professional organization have increased both the monetary and intangible life-time rewards for the professionals. The evidence about the monetary returns to medical training in the United Kingdom is quite clear. Because of the system of subsidies (student grants and the funding of teaching hospitals) the private cost of indulging in medical training is quite small, and consists largely of income forgone during the period of training. The private benefits in terms of life-time earnings are substantial and so it is not surprising to find very high estimates, in excess of 20 per cent (Walker)[5] of the rate of return to medical education. The returns to society are much lower because it has to finance most of the high cost of training (about £40,000 in 1975). Whether we look at cross-section earnings distributions (for example the New Earnings Survey) or life cycle characteristics, the financial rewards for medical practitioners are very high.

Friedman and Kusnets[6] have argued that beneficial outcomes in terms of the rewards to members of the profession have been achieved by crude but simple economic behaviour. They argue that the American Medical Association in the period after the Flexner Report (1911) used its control over entry to reduce the supply of physicians and to inflate their salaries. They conclude that the manipulation of the supply of practitioners would not have raised professional incomes in the period 1911–39 by 20 per cent over and above expected values if supply had not been manipulated in this manner. Similar outcomes from the activities of professionals in the United Kingdom were discussed with great clarity by Dennis Lees[7] over a decade ago.

Not only may professionals use their power to inflate their incomes, but they may also use their power to affect other aspects of their jobs. It has been shown, for example, that the profession has used its power to discriminate against Jews in the United States (Kessel),[8,9] against blacks and against women (Frech).[10] Furthermore, professional power gives control over medical education curricula, and can prevent competition within the profession.

The extent to which such powers are used varies from one health-care system to another. It is difficult to generalize about the outcomes of the regulation process, but the contention here is that professionalization has led to activity which has no incentives in it for the pursuit of either efficient or equitable outcomes with regard to the delivery of health-care. By prohibiting advertising and severely circumscribing competition, both within the profession and from outside it, for example osteopaths (Lees),[7] profession regulation may have inhibited the development of efficient therapies. By being unwilling to accept significant regional differentials in pay, the profession may have contributed towards the geographical inequality in the distribution of health-care inputs which is to be found in most Western health-care systems. By controlling the content of medical education, the professionals have inhibited technical change and contributed towards the preservation of dubious, or worthless, practices.

The efficiency of health-care delivery

It was emphasized earlier that there is a difference between the demand for health and the demand for health-care. While most consumers may seek 'good health', health care may not always contribute to the attainment of this state. In this section my objective is to show that there is considerable evidence which leads us to doubt that health care induces beneficial changes in health status. Yet despite this evidence, the profession has failed to develop effective measures to combat inefficient practice and, indeed, has prevented their development.

One of the principal exponents of this view that many health-care procedures are of little value is A. L. Cochrane,[11] who is himself a medical practitioner. In his book he advocates the increased use of evaluation techniques. Cochrane was one of the main forces behind Mather's study[12] of coronary care. This study used randomized control techniques, so that for the sample alternate patients were placed in intensive-care units or their own homes after the attack. The study was, however, opposed by the profession, which took the position that intensive-care units were more effective, and that it was unethical to risk life by using such methods. However, the work of Mather and his co-authors showed that there was no difference in survival rates for the two groups of patients, and questioned the need for expensive intensive-care in many cases. It seems that most patients with a coronary arrest die within six hours of the onset of the illness. If they survive this period, care in the home or in the hospital appear to be equally effective. However, hospital care clearly consumes many more N.H.S. resources than care in the home does. We need to use therapies which are effective medically and consume the fewest resources; that is, we have to use cost-effective techniques.

What Cochrane demonstrates – and this can also be seen in some of the literature cited in the Priorities Document (Department of Health and Social Security)[13] – is that there has been relatively little systematic analysis of the effectiveness of alternative medical therapies. This conclusion is also borne out by the work of Bunker, Barnes and Mosteller.[14] Medical therapies have been applied in every country in the world and their effectiveness in maintaining life and/or improving health status, however measured, has been taken on faith rather than in relation to hard facts. At its crudest this line of argument asks, for example, for any disease category, why there are variations in length of stay, or, across disease categories, why there are large variations in, for example, catering costs. The more sophisticated type of this argument seeks to analyse the relative effectiveness of competing therapies. (For a recent survey of the methodology of this work see Alderson.)[15] More recently, this type of analysis goes on to inquire into the costs of the alternative therapies and to insist that policy makers are not interested only in identifying effective therapies but cost-effective therapies. (For a survey of this work see Drummond.)[16]

One conclusion to be derived from the work of Cochrane and other writers is that medicine is not an exact science. It is an art, which could, however, be improved by a severe dose of scientific method. Only if hypotheses are formulated and tested in a clear scientific fashion can the present deplorable level of ignorance about the effectiveness of alternative therapies be dissipated.

The work of T. McKeown (1976) consists of an attempt to identify by systematic anlysis the causes of the decline in mortality in the United Kingdom since the nineteenth century. The decline in mortality since 1838 has been due mainly to the decline in infectious diseases and during the period 1838 to 1935, mortality was not influenced substantially by immunization or medical therapy. McKeown argues that, while exceptions to these smallpox, diphtheria, syphilis, tetanus, diarrhoeol diseases and some surgical conditions were exceptions to these generalizations, these conditions made only a small contribution to the overall decline in mortality. In the period since 1935, the trends of the preceding century for many infectious disease categories have continued. The significance of the contribution of medicine to this trend is disputed by McKeown, although his work has been criticized by some historians (Razzell).[17]

The implication of the McKeown analysis is that the causes of the decline in mortality are environmental. If health-care programmes are to contribute effectively, then, the most productive method from the point of view of improved health status would be of an ecological, rather than of an engineering approach. Improved living standards and water supplies, for example, may contribute more to community health than the use of medical therapies of dubious value.

The arguments of physicians such as Cochrane and McKeown have been replicated and elaborated by other writers. Illich[18, 19] has reasoned that medical practice is ineffective and the side-effects of therapy can be life-threatening. He argues that at its extreme, health-care can generate a hell for its victims. Navarro[20] analyses health-care from a Marxist perspective, and claims that the outcomes are related to the class structure and the distribution of power in society. His criticisms are similar to those of Cochrane, McKeown and Illich. However, although he also seeks cost-effective health-care, he differs in advocating a radical change in the structure of society.

As a result of this and similar work by others, there is now a considerable amount of evidence to indicate that many medical therapies are ineffective at best and damaging at worst. However, despite this growing body of evidence, the profession has been unwilling to develop incentive systems that could lead to the adoption of more effective procedures. This unwillingness could be interpreted as another example of the pursuit of policies not conducive to the attainment of outcomes in the public interest. The licensing arrangements appear to have offered little incentive for the pursuit of 'good practice' and have even inhibited the attainment of such a goal in some cases.

The adoption of such mechanisms as differential remuneration systems, budgetary systems, peer review and medical audit could, by changing monetary and non-monetary incentives, encourage practitioners to pursue more effective procedures. Differential remuneration systems could, by generating appropriate financial rewards, give practitioners incentives to adopt particular techniques or work in particular geographical areas. The efficiency of these techniques is not clear (see Maynard),[21,22] but their potential is attractive and needs to be tested rigorously in carefully controlled experiments.

New budgeting systems would seem also to be potentially very productive as a means of inducing more effective use of health-care resources. The variety of such schemes is considerable. For instance, in the Westminster Hospital experiment (Coles, Davison and Wicking;[23] Brent Health District[24]) the management team of physicians and nurses were made accountable for their budget. The decision-maker (the clinician) was the budget holder and responsible with others for spending. The Westminster Hospital work consisted of monitoring the effects of this innovation on decision-making. It was found, for instance, that fewer X-rays and diagnostic tests were carried out under the new regime. These tests reduced ward budgets and clinicians were more careful in using these costly facilities. The Westminster Hospital experiment was one of five which the Department of Health tried to initiate. The others failed to get past the planning stage because of opposition, largely from medical practitioners.

Peer review, a mechanism by which peers or equals can monitor and influence the behaviour of individual physicians, and medical audit, a mechanism by which a third party can monitor and influence their behaviour, are both mechanisms which may be adopted more extensively in the years to come as a means of increasing the efficiency with which health-care resources are used. Peer review appears to be more effective in reducing deviance from group norms when the groupings are small. But, as the group grows in size, deviant behaviour (in relation to the group norm of 'good practice') reasserts itself. The initial definition of 'good practice' is important to the effectiveness of the review.

The medical audit system, if effective, should reduce deviance from the externally determined group norms. But first, it is difficult to identify qualified third parties who are competent to determine norms. Lack of technical expertise may lead the third party to establish conservative norms that have only minor effects on medical practice. In addition, the auditor can control only relative costs, that is the costs of one practitioner *vis-à-vis* another. If absolute cost norms are not effectively established, the medical auditor may control relative costs but leave absolute costs uninhibited.

The incentives to develop such mechanisms as peer review and medical audit are limited. In the United Kingdom groups of physicians use the relatively crude data produced by the hospital activity analysis to discuss individual behaviour and establish norms. One innovation is the idea that the Ombudsman should have the authority to investigate clinical practice (House of Commons).[25] Also, the Health and Safety Executive have become interested in health care, as their remit is to protect the health and safety of the consumer. They have now defined patients as consumers and are examining how they may best protect their clients. The Department of Health and Social Security has reacted to the demands of the Ombudsman and the activities of the Health and Safety Executive by formulating its own proposals for review and audit. At the time of writing (September 1978) these proposals are still secret but they have provoked a reaction in the medical profession which consists of a desire to set up review and auditing procedures controlled by doctors before such procedures are imposed on doctors by outside bodies. These latter developments may, if permitted to flourish, lead to medical audit in the N.H.S. Such developments are essential if scarce resources are to be used efficiently.

In this section an attempt has been made to indicate that the effectiveness, in terms of clinical outcomes and costs, of many established and widely used medical therapies is dubious, if not absent. Much more detailed research into the efficiency and cost-effectiveness of alternative therapies must be carried out quickly and throroughly. Only when such research activity has compensated for past sins of omission, and has become established policy for testing all new therapies, will it be possible to acquire a comprehensive picture of the efficacy of medical practices.

However, acquisition of such information by itself will not change behaviour. Decision-makers, usually clinicians, should be given their own budgets and made responsible for their efficient allocation. Greater variation in remuneration systems and budgeting schemes could create incentives to practise efficient and cost-effective medicine. Only if experiments with alternative incentive schemes are carried out and monitored will it be possible to identify those procedures which are efficient. Only if the profession is prepared to be more flexible in the regulation of its members and prepared to innovate will the present inefficiency of health-care be reduced and the interests of the patient and society be served.

The equity of health care systems

Equity or fairness is, like beauty, in the mind of the beholder. The concept of equity is value laden, and because values differ, concepts of equity also differ. Rawls[26] maintains that no inequality is just unless:

(a) that inequality is to the advantage of the most unfortunate individual;

(b) that inequality is derived from positions or offices held in society that are equally available for all to compete for on a basis of their ability.

Although these simple rules are not without their difficulties, they can be taken as one set of criteria by which the outcomes of health-care systems can be adjudged fair or just. However, the definition of outcome in the health-care industry has, of necessity, been restricted because there is no accepted measure of the 'output' of the industry. We are limited in our judgements to analysis of the distribution of inputs, and to appraisal of available care by different socio-economic groups. Regardless of the nature of the health-care system significant inequalities may still exist.

One indicator of inequality in the distribution of health care is geographical variation in the distribution of manpower. Table 1 shows details of the geographical distribution of physicians in France in 1975. The average physician endowment per 100,000 population in 1975 was 146.5, but the distribution was highly skewed. Only six areas had endowments above the national average and of these only three (Paris, Languedoc-Roussillon, and Provence – Côte d'Azur) had endowments at least 30 per cent above the average. The worst endowed areas (Picardie and Basse-Normandie) had an endowment equal to only 67 per cent of the national average, and a further ten areas had endowments below 80 per cent of the average.

A similar inequality in the distribution of physicians can be seen in West Germany too. The Berlin and Hamburg areas have endowments over 50 per cent above the national average (see Table 2). Niedersachsen is the worst endowed area, 19 per cent below the national average, and as can be seen by comparing Tables 1 and 2, the number of areas below the average and the extent to which they are below the average, is smaller in West Germany than in France. By the beginning of the 1970s West Germany had a very large stock of physicians (174 per 100,000) which had grown by 18 per cent in the preceding decade and was set to grow more rapidly in this decade. Despite this large stock and its high actual and planned rate of growth, the inequalities between the Lander (States) has remained much the same since 1960.

The remuneration systems of French and West German physi-

TABLE 1   *Regional distribution of physicians in France, 1975.*

Region	Number per 100,000 population	Endowment as a percentage of the national average
Paris	218.0	148
Champagne-Ardenne	104.6	71
Picardie	98.8	67
Haute Normandie	105.5	72
Centre	111.8	76
Basse-Normandie	97.9	67
Bourgogne	111.7	76
Nord-Pas-de-Calais	113.1	77
Lorraine	114.6	78
Alsace	136.8	93
Franche-Compté	102.9	70
Pays de la Loire	108.8	74
Bretagne	114.0	78
Poitou-Charentes	111.6	76
Aquitaine	149.9	102
Midi-Pyrénées	160.5	109
Limousin	122.5	84
Rhône-Alps	129.4	88
Auvergne	127.6	87
Languedoc-Roussillon	190.6	130
Provence-Côte d'Azur	199.9	136
Corse	148.7	101
All France (national average)	146.5	100
All France (except Paris)	129.5	88

Source: 'Santé et Sécurité Sociale' (1977), Ministère de la Santé, Paris.

cians are similar in some respects. The French physician who works in the community is paid a fee per item of service (for further details see Maynard).[27] In the early 1970s the fees in the Paris region were higher than those elsewhere and this tended to reinforce distribution inequalities. More recently, the differential has been reversed, but its magnitude is relatively small and its effect on the geographical distribution is also likely to be quite small. In West Germany the fee setters have attempted to create payment differentials to rectify the geographical imbalances. However, as in France, the profession has resisted the introduction of significant differentials and so this policy instrument has failed to make a significant impact on distributional outcomes.

TABLE 2   *Regional distribution of physicians in West Germany.*

Region	Number per 100,000 population	Edowment as a percentage of the national average
Berlin	297	170
Hamburg	263	151
Bremen	193	110
Hessen	192	110
Baden-Württemberg	177	101
Bayern	175	100
Saarland	170	98
Schleswig-Holstein	162	93
Nordrhein-Westfalen	160	92
Rheinland-Pfalz	150	86
Niedersachsen	141	81
West Germany (national average)	174	100

Source: Hochschulabsolventer im Beruf: Document 1. *Ausbildungsbedarf für Mediziner bis zum Jahre 2000*, McKinseys and Co. Inc., Bonn 1974, page 62.

TABLE 3   *Regional distribution of physicians in England.*

Region	Number per 100,000 population	Endowment as a percentage of the national average
Northern	98	95
Yorkshire	96	93
Trent	85	82
East Anglia	94	91
North-West Thames	124	120
North-East Thames	122	118
South-East Thames	120	116
South-West Thames	121	117
Wessex	97	94
Oxford	101	98
South-Western	96	93
West Midlands	96	93
Mersey	100	97
North-Western	98	95
England	103	100

Source: Department of Health and Social Security (1976), 'Health and Personal Social Service Statistics', H.M.S.O., London.

In the United Kingdom payment differentials and labour direction have been used to reduce geographical imbalances. Table 3 shows details of the geographical distribution of physicians in England, where the dispersion around the average is not as large as that in France and West Germany. The worst off region is Trent, and the best endowed are the Thames regions around London. It is not clear how much salary differentials and labour direction have contributed to this outcome Both policies have been aimed largely at the distribution of general practitioners. Salary differentials have included designated area allowances whereby G.P.s practising in under-provided areas have received additional payments. Labour direction has been of a negative type, that is, physicians have not been told where to work, but merely where they cannot work (in particular in 'over-doctored' areas such as the South-West). The efficacy of these policies has not, however, been tested in a systematic manner. (Cooper and Culyer;[27,28,29] Maynard,[30] Maynard and Tingle).[31]

Inequalities in geographical distribution of one type of manpower input is merely one facet of this problem. As others have noted, these inequalities are paralleled by differences in other input and expenditure characteristics (Cooper and Culyer,[28,29,30] Maynard,[31] Maynard and Tingle).[32] Furthermore, there is evidence that relative deprivation in one input area is not compensated for by over-endowment in other input areas: areas that are badly off for one type of manpower or capital are badly off for most types of manpower and capital. Nor are those areas with low endowments compensated with better quality inputs. As Lavers and Rees[33] have shown, the better endowed areas tend to attract the better quality staff.

Another indicator of equality is the utilization of health services by differing socio-economic groups. The evidence about the effects of pricing in health-care systems has been summarized by (Maynard).[22] In those health-care systems where the extent of pricing is limited, as in West Germany and the United Kingdom, the amount of evidence about utilization of health-care by differing socio-economic groups is also limited. Rein[34] concluded that the lowest socio-economic groups made the greatest use of health services in the United Kingdom, and that the care they received appeared to be of an equivalent quality to that received by other socio-economic groups. This conclusion was countered by Townsend.[35] Le Grand (p. 132)[36] presents evidence derived from the Government's General Household Survey which is also different to Rein's finding: '... the upper two socio-economic groups appear to receive 40 per cent more expenditure per person ill than the lower two'. Various North American authors, such as Beck[37] and Salkever[38] present data which indicate that those with higher incomes tend to make greater use of health services even when they are free – that is, when no prices are charged at the point of consumption. Available evidence does, however, seem to indicate that the removal of financial barriers leads to increases in the utilization rates of those who had previously 'under-used' the services.[39]

The absence of a measure of 'output' makes it necessary for all the analysis to be in terms of physical inputs (for example physician) or expenditure costs. These indicators are crude, but they do show that whatever the nature of the health-care system, the inequalities that exist are substantial and extensive. In terms of the Rawlsian principles set out at the beginning of this section, it is reasonable to conclude that Western European and North American health-care systems do not seem to be just or fair. Clearly the information that is available about the distributional effects of varying health-care systems is incomplete, but the available pieces of this jigsaw, seem to indicate that the Rawlsian principles are not met.

Conclusion

The first section of this chapter indicated that the way in which the medical profession regulates itself by licensing is of dubious value. The 'public interest' arguments in favour of licensing appear to be weak and the forces of self-interest permit the profession to pursue pecuniary and non-pecuniary ends that may not be in the interests of society. The licensing regulations give no incentives for the inefficiency and inequity of Western health-care systems to be mitigated. Indeed, by permitting the profession to regulate itself in the way it does, society may be ensuring the maintenance of inefficiency and inequality by permitting unethical practices to continue.

One version of the Hippocratic Oath to which all physicians are supposed to adhere states the following:

> I swear by Apollo the healer, by Aesculapius, by Hygeia, by Panacea and by all gods and goddesses, making them my witness, that I will fulfil this oath and indenture to the best of my ability and judgement.
>
> I will hold my teacher in this art equal to my own parents; I will share my livelihood with him; I will provide his necessities if he is in want; I will look upon his offspring as my own brothers and will teach them this art, if they wish to learn, without any fee. I will teach by example, oral instruction, and by all other means to my sons, the sons of my teacher and to pupils who have sworn the Oath of a Physician but to no one else. I will treat the sick to the utmost of my ability and judgement but never to their hurt or for any wrong purpose. I will never administer a poison if asked to do so nor will I suggest any such thing and I will not assist a woman to procure an abortion, but will keep both my life and my art pure and holy. I will not use the knife, not even upon sufferers from the stone, but will give place to those who practise this craft. Into whatever houses I enter, I will enter to help the sick and ill and will abstain from all intentional wrongdoing and harm and especially I will not seduce any man or woman, bond or free. And whatever I see or hear when attending the sick, or even apart therefrom, which ought not to be told, I will never divulge but hold as secret.
>
> If I hold to this oath and do not break it, let it be mine to enjoy life and art alike with good repute among all men at all times. But if I break this oath and fall into wrongdoing, may the opposite be my fate (Cartwright, p. 41).[40]

Careful reading of this oath and a comparison of the obligations it places on the practitioner with what the practitioner does might lead us to conclude that many doctors violate this code, particularly in the light of arguments presented by Cochrane, McKeown, and others. The resource misallocation and the inequity imposed on society by such actions can be reduced only if practitioners adopt a scientific approach to the analysis of cost-effectiveness of medical therapies. Such an approach will be adopted only if the institutional arrangements of health-care systems provide adequate pecuniary and non-pecuniary incentives to medical decision-makers.

Such changes in the regulation and organization of health care will not come quickly. At present medical education teaches the aspiring doctor to do everything possible for the individual in his care. This 'individualistic' ethic ignores the fact that there may be patients outside the doctor's hospital or surgery who could use the facilities to greater advantage than those at present in receipt of care. Health-care resources are scarce and it is not possible to treat everyone. Criteria have to be established to decide who shall live, and at what level of health we shall enjoy. Establishing explicit, efficient and equitable allocation procedures in health care requires the doctor to give up his 'individualistic' perspective and adopt a social, or opportunity-cost view of the world: resources used to improve my health status are resources denied to you for the improvement of your health status. Clearly, the challenges of the analysis for the medical profession and society in general are very significant.

Notes and References

1. First appeared as an article in *Social and Economic Administration*, Vol. 12, No. 1, Spring 1978.
2. K. J. Arrow (1963), 'The Welfare Economics of Medical Care', American Economic Review, 53, 941–73. Reprinted in M. H. Cooper and A. J. Culyer (eds) (1973), *Health Economics*, Penguin.
3. J. G. Moore (1961), 'The Purpose of Licensing', *Journal of Law and Economics*, 4, 93–117, p. 103.
4. G. J. Stigler (1971), 'The Theory of Regulation', *Bell Journal of Economics and Management Science*, 2, 1, 3–21.
5. A. Walker (1974), 'The Rate of Return to Medical Education', unpublished mimeograph, University of York.
6. M. Friedman and S. Kusnets (1945), *Income from Independent Professional Practice, National Bureau of Economic Research*, New York.

7. D. Lees (1966), *The Economic Consequences of the Professions*, Institute of Economic Affairs, Research Monograph, number 2, London.
8. R. A. Kessell (1958), 'Price Discrimination in Medicine', *Journal of Law and Economics*, 1, 20–54.
9. R. A. Kessell (1970), 'The A.M.A. and the Supply of Physicians', *Law and Contemporary Problems*, Health Care, 35, 2, 267–83.
10. H. E. Frech (1974), 'Occupational Licensure and Health Care Productivity: the issues and the literature' in J. Rafferty (ed.), *Health Manpower and Productivity*, D. C. Heath and Co. Lexington Books.
11. A. L. Cochrane (1972), *Effectiveness and Efficiency: Random Reflections on Health Services*, Nuffield Provincial Hospitals Trust.
12. M. G. Mather *et alia* (1976), 'Acute Myocardial Infarction: home and hospital treatment', *British Medical Journal*, 1, 925–929.
13. Department of Health and Social Security (1976), *Priorities for Health and Personal Social Services in England*, H.M.S.O., London.
14. J. P. Bunker, B. A. Barnes and F. Mosteller (1977), *Costs, Risks and Benefits of Surgery*, Oxford University Press, New York.
15. M. Alderson (1976), *An Introduction to Epidemiology*, Macmillan, London.
16. M. Drummond (1978), 'Evaluation and the National Health Service', in A. J. Culyer and K. G. Wright (eds), *Economic Aspects of Health Services*, Martin Robertson, London.
17. P. E. Razzell (1977), 'Review of McKeown's Modern Rise of Population', *Economic History Review*, 30, 1, 192–193.
18. I. Illich (1975), *Medical Nemesis*, Calder and Boyar, London.
19. I. Illich *et alia* (1977), *Disabling Professions*, Marion Boyars, London.
20. V. Navarro (1977), *Medicine under Capitalism*, Prodist and Croom Helm, New York and London.
21. A. Maynard (1978), 'The Containment of Health Care Costs in the United Kingdom' in S. Schwitzer (ed.), *Cost Containment in Health Care Systems: papers presented to the Fogarty Conference in Washington D.C., 1976*, U.S. Government Printing Office, Washington, D.C.
22. A. Maynard (1979), 'Medical Care and the Price Mechanism' in K. Judge (ed.), *Pricing and the Social Services*, Macmillan, London.
23. J. Coles, A. Davison and I. Wickings (1974), 'Control of Resources', *Health and Social Services Journal*, 84, 4413, 2654–5 (18 November).
24. Brent Health District (1975), *Evaluating Management Information Presented to Clinically Accountable Teams*, Westminster Hospital Management Research Project, 1973–74.
25. House of Commons (1977), *Report of the Select Committee on the Ombudsman*, H.C. 45, H.M.S.O., London.

26. J. Rawls (1971), *Theory of Justice*, Oxford University Press, London.
27. A. Maynard (1975), *Health Care in the European Community*, Croom Helm and University of Pittsburgh Press, London and Pittsburgh.
28. M. H. Cooper and A. J. Culyer (1970), 'An Economic Assessment of Some Aspects of the Operation of the National Health Service', Appendix A of *Health Services Financing*, British Medical Association, London.
29. M. H. Cooper and A. J. Culyer (1971), 'An Economic Survey of the Nature and Intent of the British National Health Service', *Social Science and Medicine*, 5, 1–13.
30. M. H. Cooper and A. J. Culyer (1972), 'Equality in the National Health Service: intentions, performance and problems in evaluation'. In M. H. Hauser (ed.), *The Economics of Medical Care*, Allen and Unwin, London.
31. A. Maynard (1972), 'Inequalities in Psychiatric Care in England and Wales', *Social Science and Medicine*, 6, 221–227.
32. A. Maynard and R. Tingle (1976), 'The Objectives and Performance of the Mental Health Services in England and Wales in the 1960s', *Journal of Social Policy*, 4, 2, 151–168.
33. R. J. Lavers and M. Rees (1972), 'The Distinction Award System in England and Wales', in *Problems and Progress in Medical Care*, seventh series, Nuffield Provincial Hospitals Trust and Oxford University Press, London.
34. M. Rein (1969), 'Social Class and the Utilisation of Medical Care Services', *Hospitals* (Journal of the American Hospitals Association), 1 July.
35. P. Townsend (1974), 'Inequality and the Health Service', *Lancet*, 1, 1179–82.
36. J. Le Grand (1978), 'The Distribution of Public Expenditure: the Case of Health Care', *Economica*, 45, 178, 125–142.
37. R. G. Beck (1974), 'Economic Class and Access to Physician Services under Public Medical Care Insurance', *International Journal of Health Services*, 3, 3, 341–355.
38. D. S. Salkever (1975), 'Economic Class and Differential Access to Care', *International Journal of Health Services*, 5, 3, 373–95.
39. P. E. Enterline, V. Salter, A. O. McDonald and J. C. McDonald (1973), 'The Distribution of Medical Services Before and After "Free" Medical Care: The Quebec Experience', *New England Journal of Medicine*, 289, 22, 1174–78.
40. F. F. Cartwright (1977), *A Social History of Medicine*, Longmans, London.

CHAPTER EIGHT

The Demand and Need for Dental Care[1]

MICHAEL H. COOPER

The problem

The particular dilemma with which this chapter is concerned arises from the fact that there is a clear gap between the need for dental care as perceived by the providers of such care and the actual utilization of dental services by the populace at large. There is ample evidence to show that the need for care as assessed by practitioners greatly exceeds the public's demand for it.[6,8,11] Further, any given individual's unconstrained 'want' for dental intervention (his own perception of his needs) tends to exceed his actual demands (expressed wants) in all countries regardless of their particular method of allocating and financing dental care. Formidable barriers exist between an individual's want for dental care and its finding expression as a demand. One such barrier is, of course, the individual's 'ability to pay', but this is only one of many. In theoretical terms, an individual's 'need' for dental care is likely to exceed his 'want', which in turn exceeds his actual 'demand' (Figure 1, overleaf).

Should all dental needs be met?

With a given state of dental technology and population at risk, it

160　　*Michael H. Cooper*

Want	*Demand*	*Need*
An individual's own assessment of his dental state. His 'want' for better oral health. The demand for dental intervention is derived from this basic want.	Those of his 'wants' that the individual converts into demands by seeking the assistance of a dental practitioner.	A state of oral health deemed as in 'need' of intervention by a dental practitioner.

Dilemma All needs do not find expression as demands nor are all demands necessarily needs.

FIGURE 1　*The basic dilemma*

may be reasonably hypothesized that past a certain level of provision each additional unit of dental intervention will have a diminishing marginal impact upon the nation's oral health. The actual shape of a curve traced out in this manner (the 'marginal benefit' curve) is of critical importance to policy considerations. In Figure 2 (below) the total need for dental intervention, given the current state of knowledge, is equal to *OB*. The marginal benefit, as

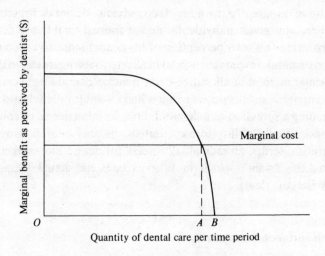

FIGURE 2　*Marginal benefit curve (1)*

perceived by the providers of dental care, however, past a certain critical point, falls away rapidly to zero. Over the range *AB* the marginal cost in terms of the goods and services foregone (the opportunity costs) exceeds the marginal benefits. Dentists, however, may feel that it is their professional duty to make any intervention which they see as yielding positive benefit to the patient. They would aim to supply *OB* interventions per time period as, beyond that point, marginal benefit would be zero (each successive unit adding nothing to total benefit). If patients, however, had the necessary knowledge of costs, were forced to bear them, and had the same perception of benefits as their dentists, they would stop at *OA*, as this is the point where marginal cost and benefit are equated. To go beyond this point is to sacrifice more in alternative goods and services than the additional benefits derived are 'worth'. More dental services can be gained only at the expense of something else. In this particular case, however, the implied 'waste' from ignoring costs and providing dental care free at the point of consumption may be economic in the sense that the costs of estimating the waste and removing it may exceed potential saving. In a positive price market, to the extent that prices indicate the actual resource costs of dental provision, the waste will be avoided by consumers equating their perception of the 'value' of the marginal benefit gained to the value of the marginal goods and services foregone.

In practice a more realistic shape for the marginal benefit curve might be that depicted in Figure 3. Here marginal benefit smoothly descends from an initially high level to zero, but with a very long tail offering the promise of positive but relatively trivial benefits well short of their opportunity costs. The total benefit from intervention may be immense, but the marginal benefit slight. In support of Marginal Benefit Curve (Figure 1) it might be said that a 'rotten tooth' is a 'rotten tooth', but it could be treated with a ten-minute extraction or by a one-hour gold inlay; by hammer and chisel or by oral artistry. The need for intervention ranges from emergency salvaging to cleaning and polishing at shorter and shorter time intervals. For example, as dental plaque forms continuously on tooth surfaces, we could all be thought of as perpetual patients in constant need of treatment. It would be possible to conceive of an open-ended treatment with no foreseeable end in sight! There appears to be, for example, no doubt that the professional cleaning and polishing of teeth at fortnightly intervals (plus instruction on oral health care) over a two-year period reduces the plaque detectable without staining to zero.[4] There is ample evidence that dentists vary considerably in what they consider appropriate treatment for any given patient.[9] In practice over the operationally relevant area of choice, need is likely to be a continuum with no self-evident point at which the marginal benefit quickly descends to zero.

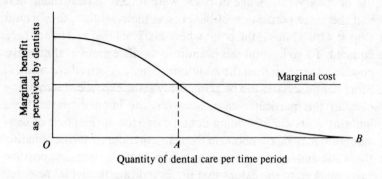

FIGURE 3　*Marginal benefit curve (2)*

In the case of Marginal Benefit Curve (2) in Figure 3 it is clear that costs could never be ignored: the implied waste would be substantial. Over the entire range $A-B$, marginal costs exceed benefits. Even if dental care were made available free of charge at the time of consumption, supply would have to ration demand by availability to something approximating to OA. Faced with zero prices and with the same perception of benefits as the profession, rational consumers, if unrestrained by availability, would expand their demand to OB (that is until marginal benefits were zero). Clearly all need probably could not, and certainly should not, be met.

In practice it is improbable that the public would be prepared to forego the necessary resources to make even OA dental care available. The marginal benefit curves we are considering reflect only the suppliers' (dentists') view of the potential benefits to be reaped. This is most unlikely to coincide with the view of the public at risk. The public's estimation of the probable marginal value to them of going to the dentist is likely to fall well short of the professionally perceived marginal benefit. The summation of patient views is represented by the marginal value line in Figure 4.

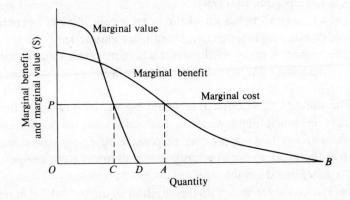

FIGURE 4   *Marginal value and marginal benefit*

In Figure 4 the consumer will clearly be willing to purchase only *OC* dental care at a price of $*OP* (equal to the marginal costs of providing that care). Even if the price were zero at the point of consumption, he would still only demand *OD* (beyond that his perception indicates benefits to be zero). In fact, as Figure 4 has been drawn, no degree of subsidization, including 100 per cent, would lead the consumer to demand the level of care deemed rational by the benefit/need model (*OA* care), still less the elimination of all need (*OB*). It is not, of course, claimed that this is the case, merely that it is at least a theoretical possibility.

In Figure 4, marginal value is shown to exceed marginal benefit for low volumes of intervention. That this is at least possible can be seen from considering the patient who presents with decay and sets a high value on the extraction of the affected teeth. The dentist, however, may set a very low benefit score to such an outcome, greatly preferring restorative treatment. In medicine, of course, it is commonly asserted that the marginal value line for health interventions is likely to lie above and to the right of the marginal benefit line. That is to say, that both want and demand exceed need and have to be restrained by availability or positive prices.[7]

There appear to be at least three possible objectives for a dental system:

(i) to meet all needs (*OB*);
(ii) to meet all needs up to the point where marginal benefit equals marginal cost (the benefit/need model);
(iii) to meet want up to the point where marginal value equals marginal cost (the value or utility model).

The third of these objectives would be met by ensuring a free market in which there were no restrictions on entry into the profession (so that supply was responsive to price), there was reasonably good access to information, and prices were competitively determined among large numbers of providers and demanders. The major problem with this solution would be that it ignores the unequal distribution of incomes and hence ability to pay (many may be willing but unable to pay $*OP*), and would only meet those wants which were able to find expression, given budgetary constraints and a willingness to sacrifice other goods and services. From a paternalistic view *OA* would remain the preferable objective, and given the view that no man is indifferent to his brother's fate, may even be consistent with the normal utility model. I may get positive utility (benefit) from your consumption of dental care; indeed, being rational, I would willingly make transfers of tied purchasing power, until the marginal utility to me of your consumption equalled the marginal utility of my own. Society might, therefore, attempt to bribe those seen as in need to consume more dental care than they themselves see any point in consuming. The only definite conclusion which can be reached, is that in no circumstance (except possibly that illustrated in Figure 2) is it rational to aim to provide *OB* dental care (that is, meet all need).

The demand process

As need and demand are not the same things, the question as to which the dental system is primarily concerned with becomes critical. In a market system with prices that reflect costs, need as such is relevant only in so far as effective demand happens to reflect relative needs. Needs which are not matched by a willingness and ability to pay the going price simply find no outlet.

(1) THE DEMAND FOR ORAL HEALTH

Before discussing the process by which a demand for dental inter- vention s created, it is important to state that the demand for oral health is not synonymous with the demand for dental care. Clearly, dental sickness is not simply a matter of random misfortune. To a large extent an individual's state of oral health is the outcome of past collective and individual decision making. Fluoridation of public water supplies and personal diet and hygiene are examples. Although the demand for dental care is derived from the demand for oral health, the relationship may be complex. A decline, for example, in the demand for oral health will eventually increase the demand for salvage intervention. Eating sweets and cleaning one's teeth once a month in unfluoridated water will lead to a demand for extractions if nothing else.

An increase in the demand for oral health would almost certainly in the long run have a favourable impact on the volume of need for dental intervention. Periodontal disease, which leads to a heavy toll of teeth, is a social disease related heavily to class and educational status.[15] Further, doubts are expressed in the dental literature as to the effectiveness of much standard dental procedure directed to- wards the control of the disease,[10, 12] whilst the attempt to use the dental consultation, as a means of educating the patient into a better oral health life style, might be likened to a surgeon giving his patient advice as he lay on the operating table.

(2) THE WANT FOR DENTAL CARE

Apart from the actual physical state of an individual's mouth (itself a legacy of past action and inaction), a large number of variables will affect an individual's state of self-perceived want. Amongst the more obvious of these are:

(i) his degree of oral awareness,
(ii) his understanding of what is normal,
(iii) his threshold of tolerance,
(iv) his appreciation of what benefits are possible.

His view of these things will be, in turn, greatly influenced by the prevailing view of his society and reference group, his upbringing, his formal educational attainments, his class, and his general state of contentment with life.

(3)   THE DEMAND FOR DENTAL CARE

With any 'given state of want' an individual's demand for dental intervention will be determined by the actual costs involved in consultation and his ability to meet them. His want expresses his degree of willingness to seek care, while the costs are the barriers he has to surmount. Although it is perfectly possible, in theory, to construct a demand curve with respect to any variable influencing demand, it is traditional to relate demand to price, holding all other variables constant. The logic of this is simply that, in the short run, it is price that is most likely to change significantly. Thus, holding the price of all other goods and services, taste, income and other factors constant, it is possible to draw a demand curve for dental care with respect to price (in essence a marginal valuation curve) as in Figure 5. Given a supply curve of SS (drawn on the assumption that technology, prices of other goods and services, factor prices and supplier motivation all remain constant) the market clearing, or equilibrium, price would be OP. Those willing and able to pay OP would get dental treatment (OA) and the others would have to go without. Demand at zero price would have been OB and so there would be an AB unmet 'need', as perceived by consumers. Want might well exceed even OB as barriers to demand would exist even at zero price at the point of consumption. Further, it should be noted that all consumers, other than the marginal ones, value dental care higher than OP and that as a consequence, consumers as a whole would enjoy a surplus equal in area to PDF.

Empirical evidence from the United States suggests that the demand for dental care is, in practice, very strongly related to price.[8]

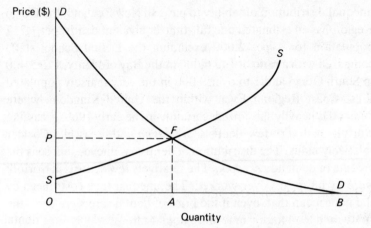

FIGURE 5   *Demand and supply of dental care*

A 10 per cent increase in price is associated with a 15 per cent decrease in demand and vice versa. More technically the elasticity of demand with respect to price ($\delta q/\delta p \cdot p/q$) is about 1.5.

Among the other influences, on demand income appears the next most critical. Indeed, the elasticity of demand with respect to income ($\delta q/\delta y \cdot y/q$) appears to be also around 1.5. In terms of cross-sectional data, in 1969 those with incomes in excess of $15,000 a year consulted dentists more than twice as frequently as those with less than $5,000 a year.[14] In 1975 white Americans consulted dentists 1.7 times as frequently as their black countrymen (their DMF scores, however, were higher). Over 60 per cent of the black poor had not visited a dentist for over two years.[13, 14]

The third most important influence appears to be time costs, which are related to geographical access (travel time) as well as to waiting and treatment times. Surveys have shown that manual workers in particular are very sensitive to time costs, often in the form of income foregone during wating or travelling.[6] Lu Ann Aday has shown the very high time costs faced by the poor, minority groups, and those living in unfashionable urban and rural areas.[2, 14] These groups have to travel further and wait longer than the rest of American society. The very unequal distribution of dentists in the United States is, of course, to some extent a reflection of the very unequal distribution of 'ability to pay'. In New Zealand, the Otago Region has an estimated one full-time equivalent dentist per 1,217 population (or 1 per 2,000 excluding the Dental School staff) compared with a ratio of 1 to 6,000 in the Bay of Plenty, 1 to 5,400 in South Otago and 1 to over 8,000 in the very sparsely populated West Coast Region.[9] Even within the United Kingdom, where demand is heavily subsidized, certainly in the early 1960s areas like Norfolk had very few dentists *per capita* and areas like Chester relatively many. The distribution of dentists is uneven, but so is the volume of demand *per capita*. The relatively few dentists in Norfolk were by no means over-worked. The unequal time costs faced by the poor mean that, even if the price of dental care were zero, the rich would tend to consume more dental care.

Other variables affecting demand include anticipated pain, fear, the psychological costs of entering, albeit temporarily, an alien middle-class environment, and so on. In terms of Figure 4 (page 000), it is clear that even in the absence of positive prices other costs would stop demand well short of OD and, with positive prices, short of OC.

(4)   DEMAND FOR WHAT KIND OF DENTAL CARE?

The actual demands made upon dentists may, of course, not correspond with what they wish to provide. Patients may demand extraction and dentures, while dentists wish to provide restorative treatment and continuing maintenance in accordance with their judgement of the patient's need. It is interesting to speculate on why the dental patient has never as fully abdicated his discretion to his agent, the dentist, as he has in medicine to the doctor.[7]

(5)   THE NEED–DEMAND GAP

Figure 6 presents an overview of the demand process. Many wants, of course, never find any expression as demands. Newman and Anderson[11] found that some 45 per cent of those with bleeding gums, 25 per cent of those with toothache, and 61 per cent of those with loose teeth sought no treatment. The presence of such symp-

WANT
(physical state: societal norms: education: thresholds)

▼

BARRIERS
(fees: time costs: psychic costs: pain: income)

▼

DEMAND

▲

NEED
(available resources: technological know-how)

FIGURE 6   *The demand process*

toms, however, doubled both the consultation rates and expenditures, compared with those without symptoms, irrespective of sex, age or racial group.

Need consistently appears to outstrip both demand and want. In the United Kingdom Bulman[6] and his team found 90 per cent of non-denture wearers and 75 per cent of the sample population in need of dental treatment. Over 75 per cent of those with their own teeth had some decay present, and 70 per cent 'needed' periodontal care. Significantly, lay perception of need showed little relationship to actual need as assessed by dentists. Many denture wearers, for example, appeared content with teeth in need of repair or replacement. Some 60 per cent of the sample considered themselves to be fit.

Although it is difficult to make comparisons between the Bulman study and that carried out in Canterbury (New Zealand) for the World Health Organization (W.H.O.), the findings do not appear inconsistent.[5] The W.H.O. study suggests that 55 per cent of the thirty-five to forty-four-year-old group had either full or partial dentures. Bulman's team found figures of 56 per cent for the thirty-six to forty-year-olds, and 58 per cent for the forty-one to forty-five-year-old groups in their study of Salisbury (England). Similarly, both studies revealed steep class gradients. In Darlington 52 per cent of classes I and II and 70 per cent of classes IV and V wore dentures compared with 20 per cent for class I and 84 per cent for class VII in Canterbury. The really striking finding of the W.H.O. study, however, was that whereas 36 per cent of the thirty-five to forty-four-year age group in Canterbury had full dentures, the corresponding figures for Trondelag (Norway), Hannover (Germany), Sydney (Australia) and Yamanashi (Japan) were 6 per cent, 2 per cent, 13 per cent and 0 per cent respectively. In the Bulman study the figures for the thirty-six to forty-year age group were 24 per cent for Salisbury and 25 per cent for Darlington, but for the forty-one to forty-five group the figures increased to 32 per cent and 49 per cent respectively. Careful research into the reasons for these dramatic variations is clearly imperative.[16]

SUPPLY

In Figure 5 (page 000) it was assumed that supply was responsive to price and that, if demand increased as in Figure 7, supply would expand to meet it. Suppose, for example, that incomes increase, causing an outward shift in the demand curve to $D_2 D_2$. Prices would then rise to OP_2 and supply would expand to OB. In practice, however, entry into the profession is subject to a long gestation period and not a little professional birth control. A much more likely supply curve, at least in the short and medium runs, is depicted in Figure 8. Here, any shift in the demand curve simply results in an increase in professional fees (from OP to OP_2). Clearly, an increase in demand is unlikely to lead to any increase in the volume of need being met, unless (i) there is excess capacity already in the market, or (ii) there is some elasticity of supply.

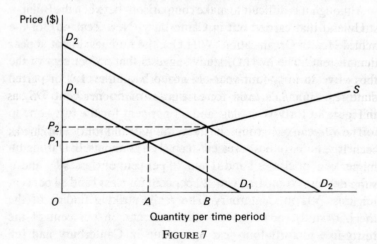

FIGURE 7

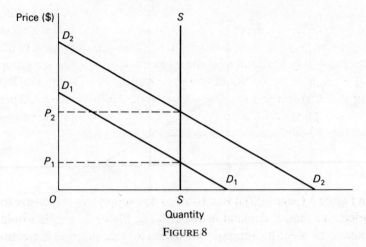

FIGURE 8

How to narrow the need/demand gap?

From the analysis so far three basic approaches to reducing unmet need suggest themselves:

(i) with a given state of want lower the barriers to care (fees, time costs);
(ii) increase the want for oral health (education);
(iii) increase the supply of dental care and/or improve its productivity and geographical distribution.

Unless there is excess capacity in the system, any attempt to achieve (i) or (ii) without (iii) will simply lead to the same volume of dental care, but at higher prices. An increase in supply, however, if fees were allowed to find their new level would, even with a given state of want and demand, increase utilization from OS_1 to OS_2, as in Figure 9.

The effect of policy option (ii) on the demand for dental care as such is, of course, not clear. Increasing the want for oral health might lead to better hygiene and diet and fluoridation of water supplies, and thus to less need for dental intervention. Equally it might lead to an increased demand for dental intervention to meet the backlog of unmet need and neglect and to maintain newly restored oral health once established.

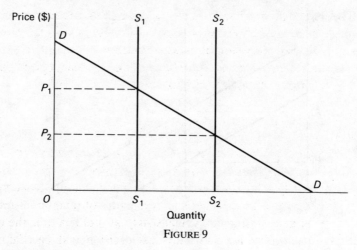

FIGURE 9

What should be the state's role?

Given the option map, the question arises as to what extent the profession can provide its own remedies and to what extent the state should increase its intervention. Further, what form should any such intervention take?

Those who favour state intervention in the dental market might do so for any or all of the following reasons:

(i) market imperfections (such as consumer ignorance, consumer uncertainty, monopolistic supply conditions, absence of price competition);

(ii) a belief that dental care should be distributed according to relative need and not according to ability to pay;

(iii) concern for the unequal distribution of purchasing power – income should be redistributed from rich to poor, fit to sick, young to old;

(iv) the existence of external benefits to society as a whole, over and above those accruing to the actual consumer of care;

(v) to rationalize by negative direction the distribution of dental manpower and to plan and co-ordinate future supplies;

(vi) to evaluate alternative methods of achieving a given objective;

(vii) pure paternalism ('experts know best').

The actual nature of any state intervention could take many forms, including:

(i) Subsidizing supply (for example free education, incentive payments to work in certain areas);
(ii) subsidizing demand (zero or token payments by the patient, the remainder from tax);
(iii) state insurance to pool risks with, or without, state subsidies and with, or without, co-insurance or deductibles;
(iv) intensive oral health education programmes;
(v) state provision of selected services (for example dental nurses and fluoridation).

State intervention might be universal or restricted to selected groups of dependent or high-risk sections of the community (the young, the poor, the sick, expectant mothers, and others). It might be restricted to geographical areas of high deprivation. In any event, the objective would need clear definition and progress towards it, monitoring and evaluation.

Whatever approach is adopted, the need to increase the level of dental awareness in society seems clear, as does the need to ensure that all have reasonable physical access to dental care.

Lessons from overseas

The American experience clearly demonstrates that income and prices are strong determinants of demand.[2,8,14] The British, on the other hand, have shown that merely making a health-care service available, free of charge at the point of consumption, does not in itself guarantee equal access to that care for equal needs, or that more needs will be met as a consequence.[7] Time costs and other barriers can be formidable. One cannot, moreover, make use of even a zero-priced good if it does not exist. Being told that my local garage is giving away cars is of little consequence if, when I arrive to collect one, I am told, 'We do not actually have any, but if we did, they would be free.'

State provision suffers from the problem of a tax illusion. The

174   *Michael H. Cooper*

public tends to regard taxation not as the public price for public goods, but rather as confiscation. They are consequently reluctant to pay it. The further apart the act of payment and the receipt of benefit, the greater the reluctance to pay seems to become. Once paid, however, there is sometimes a determination to use the service to the hilt (fortunately, or unfortunately, in dentistry the non-price costs militate against this). The main rationale for the State provision of a health service is the claim that rationing by availability is more equitable than rationing by ability to pay.[7]

Other dilemmas

This chapter set out to analyse one dilemma but not to provide any answers. There are, of course, other dilemmas which have not been touched upon:

  (i) the relationship between inputs and outputs (that is, do more dentists lead to better or worse dental health?);
 (ii) the optimal mix of inputs (for example, dentists, dental nurses, hygiene teachers);
(iii) the optimal level of skills (for example are dentists over-trained for the work they do?);
(iv) how is supply determined (is it, for example, responsive to price, need, political pressures, whim?).

Conclusion

We clearly need to know a lot more about why people choose to consult a dentist. Even more important, why do so many choose *not* to do so? *Is it their fault or ours?* Is it lack of physical access, high time costs, fear, poverty, ignorance, or something else? It must be admitted that whatever efforts are made, some people will continue to make use of a dentist only in a crisis. Time spent cleaning teeth or visiting dentists for maintenance care represents real costs (to which fees must be added), and this has to be matched against only the *possibility* of some benefit at some future date. People gain real utility from eating sugary snacks between meals, and many regard fluoridation as an infringement of basic individual liberty. Knowledge may be a necessary condition for changing oral habits and consultation rates, but it is unlikely to be a sufficient one. People have a multiplicity of objectives, many of which conflict. Behaviour depends not only upon the value attached to a given outcome (its opportunity costs), but also on the probability that any given action will lead to the desired outcome, and doubts clearly still exist. Little progress is likely until we have good information on a regular basis as to the state of oral health in our community and ongoing research into the variables which affect it.

Notes and References

1. First appeared as an article in *Social Policy and Administration*, Vol. 13, No. 2, Summer 1979.
2. Lu Ann Aday and R. Eichorn, *The Utilization of Health Services: Indices and Correlates*, D.H.E.W., H.S.M. 73–3003, Washington, 1972.
3. H. Allred (ed.), *Assessment of the Quality of Dental Care*, London Hospital Medical School, 1977.
4. P. Axelsson and J. Lindhe, 'The effects of a preventive programme on dental plaque, gingivitis and caries in Schoolchildren', *Journal of Clinical Periodontology*, 1,125, 1974.
5. H. Brown (ed.), *Oral Health Needs of the Adult Population*, University of Otago, 1977.
6. J. S. Bulman *et al.*, *Demand and Need for Dental Care*, Oxford, 1968.
7. M. H. Cooper, *Rationing Health Care*, Halsted Press, J. Wiley, New York and Croom Helm, London, 1975.
8. P. Feldstein, *Financing Dental Care: An Economic Analysis*, Lexington Books, 1973.
9. *Health Manpower Resources*, Management Services and Research Unit, Department of Health, N.Z., 1978.
10. L. M. Lightner, P. P. Crump *et al.*, 'Preventive periodontal treatment procedures: results after one year', *J.A.D.A.*, 78:1043, 1968.
11. J. F. Newman and Odin W. Anderson, *Patterns of Dental Service Utilization in the U.S.A.*, University of Chicago, Research Series No. 30, Chicago, 1977.

12. *Periodontal Disease*, W.H.O., Technical Rep. Ser. 207, 1961.
13. U.S.P.H.S., *National Center for Statistics, Series III*, No. 12 and No. 23, Washington, Undated.
14. U.S.H.R.A., *Health of the Disadvantaged*, D.H.E.W., H.R.A., 77–628, Washington, 1977.
15. J. Waerhaug, 'Epidemiology of periodontal disease: A Review of the Literature' in S. P. Ramfjord *et al.* (eds), *World Workshop in Periodontics*, Ann Arbor, 1966.
16. W.H.O., *International Collaborative Study of Dental Manpower Systems in Relation to Oral Health Status*, 1979.

CHAPTER NINE

The Growth of the British Medical Association[1]

PHILIP R. JONES

There are two very good reasons for pursuing an enquiry into the growth of the B.M.A. In the first instance the B.M.A. is not a closed shop and membership rests on a voluntary basis.[2] Discussion of why the B.M.A. has grown may then cast light on the question of why individuals choose to act collectively in the pursuit of common goals. Secondly, there can be little doubt that the B.M.A. has exerted considerable influence upon medical practice in the United Kingdom. It is appropriate, therefore, to question the basis upon which it can claim to be the 'voice of the profession'.[3]

The British Medical Association began life in 1832 as the Provincial Medical and Surgical Association. The early years were clearly ones of considerable difficulty.[4] Membership remained low until the early 1850s, though in 1856 the association assumed a national character by adopting the name of the British Medical Association. The success of the B.M.A. in the twentieth century stands as a marked constrast with those humble origins, and such a transformation invites enquiry. For by the 1950s the B.M.A. was to embrace some 80 per cent of the profession[5] and its absolute membership would rise to 64,000.[6] In the 1970s it was the second largest medical association in the world,[7] and in the United Kingdom its name has become synonymous with the medical profession as such.[8]

The following graph (Figure 1) shows the growth of membership

177

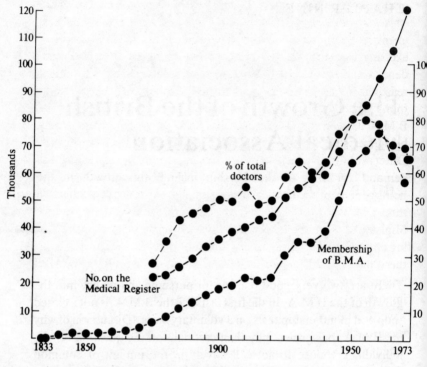

(Source: B.M.J.s and General Medical Registers)

FIGURE 1   *Membership of the B.M.A., 1832–1973*

of the B.M.A. This has been set against the growth of numbers on the Medical Register, which is the proxy normally used for the medical profession.[9] It should be noted, however, that figures for B.M.A. membership and numbers on the Medical Registers include overseas doctors. The fall in proportionate membership in the 1960s is in part explained by the fall in overseas membership of the B.M.A., as branches in New Zealand and Australia assumed independence.[10] Supplementary data will be employed when discussing the development of the B.M.A. in the United Kingdom during the post-war period.

The question of whether membership of an association is voluntary is a moot point. Associations may not openly assume the status of closed shops but nevertheless may still possess informal mechanisms for putting pressure on individuals to join.[11] It is possible to unearth occasions when the B.M.A. may be thought guilty of exerting pressure on doctors to pursue its policy. Yet such incidents hardly dominate the Association's history and one might reasonably accept that doctors actually choose whether or not to join.[12] The doctor may be viewed as a potential consumer of the B.M.A. One might then expect that demand for membership may be influenced by the level of income and the price of the good. Other variables which may also be important in explaining the demand for B.M.A. membership include the growth in the homogeneity of the medical profession, the existence of a collective threat to the profession, recognition of the association by the Ministry of Health, changes in the work environment and advertising and recruiting campaigns by the Association. Such variables as these have found prominence in research on the growth of trade unions and associations. The intention here is to examine the importance of each to the B.M.A.'s growth. Obviously, proxies will have to be employed for certain of the variables. For example, for the growth of homogeneity in the work force one can look to the extent to which recruitment to the profession has been concentrated from the middle class. For the existence of a collective threat one can look to changes in the income of doctors and to extensions of government activity in the medical market. Though for some of the variables data may be too weak to substantiate a precise measure of their importance, it may still be possible to offer some discussion on their part in the growth of the B.M.A.

Doctors' incomes

An examination of doctors' incomes and B.M.A. membership might easily lead to two lines of reasoning. First, that membership of the B.M.A. may increase as income rises. The real cost of membership may be falling in such periods and also individuals may credit the association with promoting prosperity of the profession.[13] Second, that membership growth is stimulated by falls, or threatened falls, in the level of real income. Essentially, the reasoning is that it is a feeling of grievance on the part of individuals which leads them to join associations.[14]

Looking at the time-series data on the growth of the B.M.A., there appears some reason for believing that threatened or actual falls in income have been a stimulus to growth. The period 1875 to 1890 was clearly a high growth period, with percentage membership increasing from 27.53 per cent to 46.8 per cent. This growth rate was considerably faster than in the following fifteen years, when membership density rose from 46.8 per cent to 50.7 per cent. During the nineteenth century doctors felt aggrieved over a number of issues. Their treatment under the Poor Law, in the Armed Forces and in public health, and competition from quacks and from the Friendly Societies and medical clubs caused considerable resentment. Yet, within this period, the late 1880s mark a watershed. In almost all areas relief had been won.[15] The Medical Amendment Act of 1886, which further restricted entry into the medical profession, may perhaps be taken as representative of this. Little progress had been made against the Friendly Societies and the Medical Aid Institutions, but in all other areas the doctor's life was notably improved.

In the early 1900s membership grew slowly and indeed in 1908 it fell. From 1910 it was rejuvenated, such that in 1912 it exceeded 64.11 per cent of the profession. This must obviously be interpreted as a reaction to the announcement of Lloyd George's National Health Insurance Bill. Wider intervention of the state into the medical market posed a potential threat to doctors' incomes and to their clinical freedom. The B.M.A. proved successful in its defence of the profession. It radically altered the provisions of the Bill, but failed to appreciate that in so doing the profession had become inclined towards the scheme. It refused to compromise on one remaining issue and was humiliated when doctors deserted to join the scheme which the Association had helped to make so attractive.[16]

Membership once again fell, and by 1918 only 45.5 per cent of the profession were members. It was at this time that the Association had difficulty in pursuing a claim for higher fees and the potential threat of the state was again brought to the fore. The B.M.A. argued the need for a capitation fee of thirteen shillings and sixpence but arbitrators to the dispute in 1920 awarded only eleven shillings, though by the end of 1921, the Government was proposing a reduction in remuneration to a fee of nine shillings and sixpence. The profession accepted the cut in the capitation fee in the interests of the need for national economy, but by 1924 the Government proposed a further reduction of either eight shillings and sixpence for a period of three years or eight shillings for a period of five years. However, agreement could not be reached, and after a threat of mass withdrawal of doctors' services, the matter was referred to a court of inquiry, which finally fixed a fee of nine shillings. This controversy clearly reflects the profession's fears of the monopsonistic powers of the Government. It explains why, by 1930, the B.M.A.'s membership had risen once more to 64.5 per cent of the whole profession.

In the early 1930s the density of membership of the B.M.A. once again fell. This appears strange in view of the fact that in 1931 the Government had cut renumeration again by 10 per cent. However, it must be noted that in 1934 this cut was reduced to 5 per cent, and by 1935 the full rate was restored. Furthermore, doctors were beginning to enjoy the increasing value of the pound (fixed income groups were 50 per cent better off in real terms throughout the 1930s than, for example, in 1920).[17] While most general practitioners were not well-to-do they were comfortably situated, with a net average income in 1936–8 of about £1,000.[18] Indeed, in 1939 the British Medical Journal (B.M.J.) suggested that conditions in the National Health Insurance Scheme were such as to induce a 'better class of man' to enter general practice.[19] In the light of this evidence it would appear that the 1930s gave doctors somewhat less cause for concern, and appropriately membership fell off.

The remarkable rise of percentage membership in the 1940s must be related to the prospect of the introduction of the National Health Service (N.H.S.) after the Second World War. The Government was proposing to take responsibility for 95 per cent of the medical market, and this was to affect hospital doctors as well as general practitioners. If anxiety characterized the profession in 1911, then in 1944 one could safely describe a state of panic as proposals from the Brown Plan were leaked.[20] Membership reached an unprecedented 80 per cent of the profession, and interestingly it did not fall off, but continued increasing even after the negotiations. Two explanations might be offered for this. First, the B.M.A. did not appear humiliated at the end of the struggle, but rather bowed gracefully to the inevitable. On 20 May 1948, and before the inception of the N.H.S. in July, the B.M.A. Council led by Dr Guy Dain took note of the 1913 collapse and resolved to accept the N.H.S. Second, and perhaps of more importance, conditions of remuneration were not fully settled on entry into the N.H.S. The reports of the Spens Committees settled the net income of doctors in 1939 values. It was to await the Dankwerts Adjudication of 1952 for the 'betterment factor' to be settled, and for incomes to be settled in post-war values.

The B.M.A. has published figures showing membership in the 1950s as a percentage of the total working profession in the United Kingdom. These have been set out in Table 1. Membership density did not fall very quickly in the 1950s, and this period was one when

TABLE 1

Year	Membership as a % of the total profession in the United Kingdom	Membership as a % of the working profession in the United Kingdom
1946	N.A.	75 (approx.)
1947	75	77.5
1948	76	78.7
1949	76	78.0
1950	77	85.0
1951	76.6	85.0
1952	74.0	84.0
1953	72.0	81.0
1954	71.0	80.0
1955	71.0	80.0
1956	71.0	80.0
1957	70.3	79.2
1958	70.2	79.0
1959	70.5	79.3
1960	70.9	N.A.
1961	71.2	N.A.
1962	71.0	N.A.
1963	70.8	N.A.

Source: British Medical Journals

all professions were finding it difficult to maintain their relative income position *vis-à-vis* salary earners.[21] The medical profession as a whole found the Dankwerts award eroded by inflation. By 1959, for example, G.P.s' average earnings had increased by 9 per cent but prices had risen by one-third, so reducing the real value of income by about 20 per cent. During this period the community's standard of living, in terms of Gross National Product (G.N.P.) per head at constant factors cost, rose by 22 per cent.[22] In 1958 the B.M.J. reported that 'Doctors are united in considering that the Government, by its apparent repudiation of the Spens Report, has broken faith with the profession'.[23] Even so, in 1956 G.P.s with the average number of patients (but with no other source of income) were in the highest 2.4 per cent of British income receivers. Sixty-seven per cent of doctors questioned in a Gallup Poll in June 1956 stated that if they had the chance to vote again in favour of starting the N.H.S. they would vote in the affirmative.[24] Clearly, then, there was discontent at the failure of remuneration to match inflation, but doctors were not bitter about the N.H.S. Hence the conclusion that B.M.A. membership would fall very slowly.

The Royal Commission's Report in 1960 did much to redress the grievances of the profession.[25] Between 1960–1 and April 1971 it was claimed that there were increases of 83 and 131 per cent in the average remuneration of hospital doctors and G.P.s respectively. The average increase for all, weighted according to the numbers in each category, was 106 per cent, as compared with an increase in salaries during the same period of 102 per cent.[26]

The crises of the 1960s and 1970s have taken the form of disputes over the appropriate remuneration differentials between various sections of the profession. Fears have arisen within sections of the profession that they have been poorly dealt with by comparison with others. It would follow from the hypothesis we are pursuing that these fears lead to the formation of sectional associations, and this, of course, is precisely what has happened. The general practitioners, perhaps still a little envious of the treatment consultants had experienced under Bevan in 1948, finally protested at their conditions by forming the General Practitioners Association (G.P.A.) in 1963. The junior hospital doctors, concerned with poor promotional prospects to consultant posts, followed suit in 1966 with the Junior Hospital Doctors Association (J.H.D.A.). Both 'Ginger Groups' to the Association have proved their worth. In three to four years each sectional group has registered notable gains; the Review Body on Doctors' Remuneration improved the lot of G.P.s in 1966[27] and junior hospital doctors in 1970.[28] General practitioners' conditions were so markedly improved in the 1960s that the G.P.A. has fallen from prominence.

The lesson of the G.P.s and junior hospital doctors were not wasted on the consultants. In 1969 the Regional Hospital Consultants and Specialists Association was revitalized on a national basis. In 1974 the teaching hospital consultants asked to join their association, and the name was changed to The Hospital Consultants and Specialists Association (H.C.S.A.). The 'Ginger Group' strategy had clearly caught on. Many doctors became members of both the B.M.A. and one of these sectional associations. Out of 2,114 replies to a questionnaire issued by the Regional Hospital Consultants and Specialists Association, 1,427 answered that they were also members of the B.M.A.[29] In 1975 the B.M.A. declared its membership to be 62.85 per cent of the profession in the United Kingdom.[30] It is fair to suggest that had the nature of the grievances faced in these years been different there would not have been a fall. That is to say that, if doctors had felt the grievance to the profession as a whole and not solely to a section of the profession, those members of the G.P.A., J.H.D.A. and H.C.S.A. who are not members of the B.M.A. would instead have become members of the B.M.A.

During the 1970s the sectional fears of the medical profession have been obvious. In 1974, when negotiating a new contract with the Department of Health, consultants were made very aware of the Labour Party's continued intention to phase out pay beds in National Health Service hospitals. Agitation by the ancillary hospital workers' trade union, the National Union of Public Employees (N.U.P.E.), brought this question acutely to the fore. In 1975 junior hospital doctors became aggrieved at the manner in which their new contract was to be priced. Though general medical practitioners may have expressed solidarity with their hospital colleagues on these issues, it was the hospital doctors who played the active role of invoking industrial action, by working to contract to underline their claims.[31] Indeed, in the nature of the disputes the differences between the hospital doctors were sometimes emphasised. Noel and José Parry draw attention to the fact that the claims of part-time consultants to be working well beyond their requirements was questioned in the light of a Junior Hospital Doctors Survey on the work and commitment of junior hospital doctors.[32] Clearly, these years have emphasised the threat to individual hospital groups within the profession, and the J.H.D.A. and H.C.S.A. have become established. By 1977 the membership of the J.H.D.A. was estimated at about 5,500 out of approximately 17,500 junior doctors. The H.C.S.A. experienced a membership rise of 250 per cent between 1972 and 1974, and in 1977 claimed some 5,000 members or 40 per cent of consultants.[33]

Evidence therefore suggests that the existence of collective threats induce individuals to join associations. Initially, the B.M.A. was a direct beneficiary of the advent and growth of state intervention in the medical market. Ironically, the American Medical Association (A.M.A.), which might be viewed as more successful in resisting this trend, has relied more intensely on exerting pressure on individual doctors to ensure high and well-behaved membership.[34] In recent years, however, the B.M.A. has found difficulties as the problems within the N.H.S. have served to exacerbate traditional rivalries in the profession.

In general, over the period as a whole, however, it is also fair to argue that the economic position of doctors has improved together with the membership increase. Routh points to the favourable increase in G.P.s' remuneration between 1913/14 and 1960,[35] and the increase in average remuneration in the 1960s has already been referred to.[36]

Group cohesion – the social background of doctors

The feeling of collective solidarity among doctors may well run much deeper than just a willingness to protect common goals. The professionalization of medicine, and the rising status it has enjoyed, have attracted to the profession individuals from a quite narrow spectrum of society. It has been argued that collective identity, prompted by homogeneity in the work force, will explain the growth of associations.[37] It is clear the B.M.A. has grown during a period of increasing homogeneity in the social background of recruits to the medical profession.

In the era prior to the medical acts of 1858 and 1886 doctors emerged from all levels of society. Those in the higher classes adopted the position of physician, while the 'less well-bred' might entertain prospects of becoming a surgeon. Even the members of the lower social classes might, through apprenticeship to an apothecary, have learned something of the art of medicine and later set up practice. Merskey[38] has commented:

> The period in question was a seminal one in English, if not in British Medicine. The basic professional structure, established for more than a century, was changed as a result of many different influences. These included economic and social upheavals, the aftermath of the French Revolution and Napoleonic wars, the rapid growth of the population increases in the size of cities, the spread of commerce and, equally with all the rest the development of scientific knowledge. Medicine was a profession in which an able youth could cross social barriers. It attracted extracts from a large range of social classes – from the respectable poor youth who went as an apothecary's apprentice, to the graduate of Oxford or Cambridge from a relatively affluent family – and in the midst of a world in social and intellectual ferment, it underwent vigorous although often bitter developments.

With the success of the medical reform movement led by the B.M.A. this tendency of social integration within medicine was to end. The requirement of qualifications dependent on success in examination, and the increasing length of the curriculum preceding the examination, was to permit only the more affluent classes to consider medicine. The fact that the status of the medical practitioner was rising, with the increasing middle class as patrons, meant that the sons of the middle classes felt the long training worthwhile. There remained in the 1880s only one practical means of entry into the profession for the poorer classes. This relied upon the system of 'covering'. Qualified practitioners would build up large practices by supervising unqualified practitioners. The unqualified might then learn something of medicine at very little cost while still receiving a small income. Eventually, they would attend for examination at the medical colleges of London. Yet this avenue was closed in 1891, when the General Medical Council (G.M.C.) declared all medical practitioners guilty of unprofessional conduct if they engaged in 'covering'.

The restriction of entry to the profession from the lower classes meant that in 1944 it was estimated that 80 per cent of the population (the manual, lower clerical, and distributive workers) were contributing only about 5 per cent of the nation's doctors.[39] The fact that the state began to subsidize the costs of a much more expensive medical training does not appear to have made a great deal of difference. In 1954 a London medical student paid at most about 19 per cent of the cost of medical training.[40] Yet, a report showed that in 1955–6 the proportion of students admitted whose fathers were manual workers was lower in medicine than any other faculty. For Oxford, this percentage in medicine was 5 per cent, at Cambridge 6 per cent, London 13 per cent, and for all universities 15 per cent.[41]

If there was to be a trend towards taking slightly more recruits from the lower classes, this has recently been sharply reversed. In 1961, 68.9 per cent of final year medical students were drawn from the Registrar General's social classes I and II, while only 31.1 per cent were drawn from combined classes III, IV and V. Social classes I and II make up only 18.3 per cent of the total, while classes III, IV and V make up 81.7 per cent. In the succeeding five years 1962–6, the balance of intake altered. Of first year medical students entering in 1966, the proportion drawn from classes I and II had risen to 74.7 per cent, while social classes III, IV and V had fallen to 24.2 per cent of the intake.[42]

In 1976, S. P. B. Donnan undertook a survey of medical students to determine the changes which had occurred since the 1966 investigation.[43] He quite confidently claimed that a greater proportion of final year students had fathers from social classes I or II in 1975 than in 1966. In the surveys 34.1 per cent of final year students were from social class I and 35.7 per cent from social class II in 1966. In 1976 these figures were 40.1 per cent and 39 per cent respectively.

The degree of selectivity in the medical profession is perhaps more fully appreciated when it is realized that the Robbins Committee found 59 per cent of all undergraduates in universities drawn from classes I and II in that year, and this compared with 73 per cent in medical schools.[44] The desire to draw students from the homes of higher social classes seems to be a tradition that has survived the introduction of the grants system. The Royal College of Surgeons suggested for example,

There has always been a nucleus in medical schools of students from cultured homes. . . . This nucleus has been responsible for the continued high social prestige of the profession as a learned profession. Medicine would lose immeasurably if the proportion of such students in the future were to be reduced in favour of precocious children who qualify for subsidies from the local authorities and the State purely on examination results.[45]

A trend during the history of the B.M.A. to recruit doctors from a social background very similar to theirs was supplemented by a significant rise in the percentage of the profession that have been 'self-recruited', that is, themselves the sons of doctors. Kelsall has traced the growth of this phenomenon and compared it with that of other professions. He found, for example, that at Cambridge, between 1850 and 1899, 29 per cent of medical students were sons of doctors, while between 1937 and 1938 this was 56 per cent.[46] Clearly, one factor which could explain the rise in self-recruitment in medicine between 1850 and the late 1930s was the ability to hand on a practice to a son, or to take him into partnership. In a survey conducted for the academic year 1955–6, it was recorded that 17 per cent of all medical students were the sons of doctors.[47] Research conducted for the Royal Commission on Medical Education showed that in 1966 just over one-fifth[48] of medical students had medical fathers. Donnan's study gave reason to believe that the proportion of students whose fathers were doctors was lower in 1975 than in 1966, but that the proportion with either parent medically qualified was not significantly different. In 1966, 21.2 per cent of first year students had medical fathers and 23.3 per cent had either parent medically qualified. In 1975 these figures were 15.6 per cent and 22.4 per cent respectively.[49]

The nineteenth century marked the culmination of a process, which had been apparent in the eighteenth century, of excluding women from the emerging medical profession.[50] The twentieth century still bears evidence to indicate such exclusion. Quotas of women students have been employed by medical schools and they were condemned by the Todd Commission on medical education.[51] As such, in surveys comparing 1975 with 1966, there was a markedly greater proportion of female students.[52]

Yet if entry is so restricted, an even greater degree of common identity is imposed on the entrants during their education. It is the view of Hill that, 'The aim and object of medical education is to educate a student to become a member of the profession of medicine rather than a mere scientist or technologist'.[53] The comparative isolation which a medical student experiences for some six years fosters a social dependence on, and identity with, the dominant professional ideology, and throughout training a knowledge of the ethics and values of the profession are imbibed. The profession has recommended maintaining the isolation of the student. The recommendations of the Royal Commission on Medical Education for closer integration of the medical schools with the mainstream of academic life in the universities were opposed by many teaching hospitals.[54]

The profession, then, has developed a strong common identity.[55] The B.M.A. grew up in a tradition of passing on practices from father to son. Indeed, the B.M.A., and membership of it, has become a traditional part of the profession.

Recognition by the Ministry of Health

In analysing membership increases in white collar unions, G. S. Bain has ascribed great importance to the attitudes of employers.[56] Three lines of reasoning were used to relate union growth to union recognition by employers. The first of these was the belief that white collar workers identify with management and will reject what management rejects. The second was the suggestion that membership of an unrecognized union may become a barrier to promotion. Third was the argument that management recognition will make unions more able to achieve their aims *vis-à-vis* remuneration and job regulations.

In looking to the medical profession it seems hardly likely that the first two lines of argument are applicable. In the first instance, doctors have shown a distrust of lay interference in their work. Most certainly they do not identify with lay administrators or managers and, if anything, resent their potential interference. Secondly, while B.M.A. members and officials do hold positions on committees within the N.H.S., there is no evidence that advancement of a doctor's career was dependent on membership of the B.M.A. Nevertheless, the third line of reasoning suggested by Bain may have relevance to the medical profession. There is within the literature on medical politics a seminal work whose thesis is that the B.M.A. shares a unique and 'intimate' partnership with the D.H.S.S. in the administration of the N.H.S., and that, when allowed to flourish without outside interference, this relationship assists the B.M.A. in achieving its aims.[57] Success in negotiations is, it is argued, directly related to the degree to which this relationship between the B.M.A. and the D.H.S.S. holds.

H. Eckstein is not unique in pointing to this partnership. Evidence exists to substantiate the argument that it has existed since the introduction of the National Health Insurance Service (N.H.I.S.). Indeed, Dr Alfred Cox, a former medical secretary of the B.M.A., noted that the controllers of the National Health Insurance Commission realized it was in their interests 'to deal with an established organization which they believed had learned by experience'.[58] Stevens also draws attention to the way in which the Ministry of Health rallied to the aid of the B.M.A.[59] In the 1963–5 confusion on remuneration the B.M.A. and its leaders were under heavy criticism from the profession. The Minister of Health (Anthony Barber) intervened to establish a new working party to deal with the problems of general practice, and in an open letter to the B.M.A. expressed his concern over the discontent of G.P.s. Such a gesture might be interpreted as an attempt to pacify G.P.s, who at the time, were feeling somewhat betrayed by the B.M.A. Stevens commented that in the situation 'the Ministry would be forced to take a stronger planning initiative both to safeguard general practice and to reinforce the professional associations whose strength was essential to running the health service'.[60] More recently, the difficulty which the J.H.D.A. and H.C.S.A. experienced in applying for negotiating rights with the D.H.S.S. suggest that the partnership with the B.M.A. continues to be valued in the 1970s.[61]

The precise importance of B.M.A. and Ministry relations is, however, questionable. Eckstein illustrated his argument by comparing a situation in which this relationship flourished with one in which outside interference destroyed it. In the early 1950s the Ministry decided to make over 1,000 Registrars redundant and to advise them to accept less suitable posts. Discussions between the B.M.A. and the Ministry led to a step-by-step reversal of this policy, so that in 1954 the number of redundancies was only 100 or so. This success was contrasted with negotiations over the 'betterment factor' to be applied to doctors' remuneration set by the Spens Committee. Here the Ministry was under the shadow of the Treasury. Negotiations were to become deadlocked and Mr Justice Dankwerts and his working party ended the conflict. Yet, while Eckstein refers to such negotiations as unsuccessful, Marriot and Thomas are not convinced.[62] Their argument is that at the end of the conflict the doctors did get what they wanted. As a contrast to Eckstein, they see no reason to stress the precise constitutional setting in explaining the success of negotiations. An examination of medical politics in the United Kingdom, the United States and Sweden lead them to present a hypothesis of negotiations which is independent of different institutional settings.

A. J. Willcock's analysis of negotiations is another that calls into question the value of the B.M.A.–Ministry relations. In his opinion the relative success of the B.M.A. with the Ministry, as compared with other pressures, is explained simply by the bargaining power of the B.M.A. He writes:

The medical profession has, by and large, prospered in its dealings with the Ministry of Health, 'We have the doctors: you want the doctors', one British Medical Association Chairman publicly told the Minister at an Annual Meeting of the Association. 'Crude pressure-group stuff' or 'political realities', the Minister could not ignore it and sought to gain peace by compromise.[63]

Surely in explaining the success of the B.M.A. mention should be made of the rate of substitution of doctors for other factors of production, such as nurses, technicians, the elasticity of demand for the product, and doctors' remuneration as a proportion of total N.H.S. costs. The precise influence of the institutional framework since 1912 is clearly a moot point, and as such the extent to which it influences membership recruitment remains uncertain.

Work environment

In discussing the influence of work environment on doctors' behaviour attention focuses on the extent to which their work has become bureaucratized. To what extent has the advent of the N.H.S. destroyed doctors' status as independent practitioners and bound them to a common code of behaviour? Have rules and regulations been established and standardized such that they have a greater collective awareness? It was standardization of working conditions in large-scale establishments that Lockwood used to explain the growth of clerical unions.[64]

It has already been argued that the unifying force that bureaucratization has engendered in the medical profession is a common revulsion of the concept. Clinical freedom is a concept that doctors prize, and hence standardization of their work by the imposition of rules and regulations, particularly by law administrators, is vehemently opposed. Indeed, the success of the doctors in resisting such influence from laymen leads one to doubt that the environment in which they work influences the likelihood that they would join associations.

M. W. Susser and M. Watson suggest that there is little evidence of a bureaucratic atmosphere within the medical profession. They refer to the profession as ' a company of peers in which the most junior may address the most senior as a colleague, and the professional and ethical obligations of the one to the other are fully reciprocal'.[65] Within hospitals 'consultants have been free largely to arrange their own work pattern',[66] and are hardly under strict bureaucratic control. Far from Hospital Management Committees exercising undue influence over them, it has been suggested that the reverse is the case.[67]

As for general practitioners, the N.H.S. has added very few conditions on the life of the G.P. In his contract with the executive council he agrees to render all services normally rendered by G.P.s, to keep adequate surgeries and medical record cards, to prescribe on health service prescription forms and to issue statutory certificates. Some constraints are placed on him, such as direction of location by the Medical Practices Bureau (M.P.B.), checks on excessive prescribing and limits on his list size (though not private practice), but these are hardly sufficient to describe his environment as rigidly bureaucratic.[68]

There is some evidence to suggest that doctors' views have been influenced by their work environment. For example, following the 1944 White Paper on the N.H.S. a questionnaire survey was pursued to discover doctors' reactions to the issues at hand. Strength of feeling on issues differed between service doctors, consultants, salaried doctors and G.P.s. The G.P.s showed markedly less enthusiasm on issues such as salaried service, health centres, free and complete hospital service, and larger areas for hospital administration. It was claimed that to a large extent familiarity of working within an organization accounted for the fact that consultants, salaried doctors, and service doctors were more willing to accept such proposals than G.P.s.[69] Even so, the existing data does not indicate that the work environment has influenced the decision to join the B.M.A. In 1948, for example, eight out of ten consultants were members of the B.M.A.[70] This was then typical of the 80 per cent membership of the profession. One might, therefore, hesitate to accept that existing data support the proposition that work environment plays a major part in determining B.M.A. membership.

Advertising and recruitment campaigns

Keith Hindell has suggested that advertising on the part of an association can be instrumental in increasing the size of its membership.[71] Such advertising could take place informally through individual persuasion by an existing member or branch official, or as a result of a particular co-ordinated advertisement drive. Hindell suggests that trade unions have tended to regard the first of these methods to be by far the most important.

There is considerable difficulty in estimating the importance of advertising in the growth of the B.M.A. If figures in the balance sheet showed the expenditure of the B.M.A. on this activity, or even if the B.M.J. ran pages of advertisements, then one might be able to suggest tentatively the importance of advertising on membership growth. The Organization Committee have made an inquiry into a recruiting effort they were carrying out.[72] This recruiting drive involved addressing letters to groups of non-members, and it appeared that some 10 per cent of doctors thus addressed joined the Association. Of course, factors other than the circular may have accounted for this increase in membership.

It would appear fair to suggest, however, that the B.M.A. finds personal persuasion an important part of any recruitment campaign. References in the B.M.J.s of the mid-1960s seem to confirm their faith in this approach. For example, in April 1967 the Chairman of the Organization Committee expressed his belief that personal contact through the local organizations was the best approach in recruiting new members.[73] In October 1968, Dr R. Gibson spoke of the need for more personal contact with non-members,[74] and the Annual Report of 1967 claimed that 'Experience in some divisions has shown clearly that the selective personal approach to non-members is by far the most effective means of recruiting'.[75]

Subscriptions

In looking to the effect of subscription rates on the membership of the B.M.A., one might suggest how many members were deterred by increases in the rate. Resignation figures are available in the B.M.J. from 1901 to 1966, and from 1919 the resignations withdrawn are also published. In looking to the effect of subscription rate increases it is possible to isolate seven years, 1903, 1913, 1920,

1950, 1953, 1960 and 1966. During these years it would appear that there was an 'announcement effect' of the rise in subscriptions during these years. With the exceptions of 1903 and 1960, resignations doubled as a result of the increase. However, the resignation figure is a very small percentage of the total membership figure. For the seven years quoted it was typically less than 3.5 per cent, and this leads one to discount any great importance in this observation.[76]

An assessment

The history of the B.M.A. represents an interesting and informative experiment in collective action. Pressure groups have been viewed as associations of individuals producing collective goods.[77] The output of the B.M.A , for example, in terms of improvement in wage and working conditions, is non-exclusive to non-members. In large groups individuals as such will not readily reveal preferences for a collective good.[78] The growth of membership of associations has been explained either by the imposition of closed-shop authority or by the existence of certain incentives, such as goods produced by the association and given only to members. In the case of the B.M.A. it has been argued that neither of these explanations is suitable.[79] Rather, from the preceding examination, it would appear that the existence of a well-defined group and a collective threat to that group are of importance in determining the likelihood that a member of that group will join the Association. A growing homogeneity and collective identity within the group and the presence of a collective threat by state intervention in the medical market appeared important to the growth of the B.M.A.

The stimulus of a collective threat to collective action has, of course, been referred to by Peacock and Wiseman.[80] In explaining why the ratio of public expenditure to gross national product grew, they began by viewing the individual in society as choosing to tax himself to provide public expenditure. His willingness to so do was arguably greater during periods of world wars and social depression. Their study is, therefore, similar, though not identical, to an examination of doctors' willingness to contribute to collective action. Doctors appear more ready to engage in this when faced with a collective threat.[81] As such, this asymmetric behaviour should perhaps have relevance to the question of the likelihood of the voluntary provision of collective goods.[82]

The second and more specific aspect of the study of the history of the B.M.A. is the light it casts on its present predicament. The homogeneity of the group and a collective threat to the group have aided its growth and enabled it to act as spokesman for the profession. Since 1948, however, differences within the profession have grown. The march of technology has been instrumental in this; 'since 1948, the gulf between hospital doctors and general practitioners has been widening so that today their respective roles and skills are quite distinct'.[83] Also, since the inception of the N.H.S. sections of the medical profession, G.P.s, junior hospital doctors and consultants, have become even more concerned that they do not fall behind in terms of remuneration and working conditions, *vis-à-vis* other sections. Thus, under a common paymaster the threat posed to doctors is that they are neglected relative to other sections of the profession, and the expression of this form of collective threat is the appearance of new 'Ginger Groups' to the B.M.A. Clearly, both these developments accentuate the difficulties of the B.M.A. On all but the more general issues the B.M.A. may experience increasing problems in presenting itself as *the* 'voice of the profession'.

Notes and References

1. First appeared as an article in *Social and Economic Administration*, Vol. 12, No. 1, Spring 1978.
2. P. R. Jones, 'The British Medical Association and the Closed Shop', *Industrial Relations*, Winter, Vol. 4, No. 4, 1974.
3. David L. Shapiro, 'Pressure Groups and Public Investment Decisions: A Note', *Public Choice*, Vol. X, 1971, pp. 103–108 notes that 'no model of public investment is complete without introducing the effects of the interaction between pressure groups and agency officials'.
4. E. M. Little, *History of the British Medical Association 1832–1932*, London, 1932.
5. J. Blondel, *Votes, Parties and Leaders*, Penguin, 1967, p. 169.
6. *British Medical Journal* (Supp.), Vol. 2, 12 April 1975, p. 101, puts the

membership of the Association in March 1975 at 64,032. Total current membership is 62,423 of whom 51,223 are in the United Kingdom (*British Medical Journal* (Supp.), Vol. 2, 29 July 1978, p. 374).

7. J. Dopson, *The Changing Scene in General Practice*, Christopher Johnson, London, 1971, p. 127.

8. P. Vaughan, *Doctors Commons: A Short History of the British Medical Association*, Heinemann, London, 1959, p. xiii.

9. This for example was employed by Harry Eckstein, *Pressure Group Politics: The Case of the British Medical Association*, George Allen and Unwin, London, 1960, p. 45, and G. Forsythe, *Doctors and State Medicine*, London, Pitman Medical, 1966, p. 8.

10. Annual Report of Council 1962–63, *British Medical Journal*, Supp., 11 May 1963, p. 197; Annual Report of Council 1967–68, *British Medical Journal*, Supp., 20 April 1968, p. 91.

11. R. Kessel, 'Price Discrimination Medicine', *Journal of Law and Economics*, October 1958, indicates the sorts of influence the American Medical Association can exert on doctors.

12. P. R. Jones, 'The British Medical Association and the Closed Shop', *op. cit.*

13. L. Wolman, *Ebb and Flow in Trade Unionism*, National Bureau of Economic Research, New York, 1936, links the prosperous period of business cycles with growth of unions.

14. H. B. Davis, 'The Theory of Union Growth', *Quarterly Journal of Economics*, Vol. 55, 1941, pp. 611–66; J. Shister, 'The Logic of Union Growth', *Journal of Political Economy*, 1953, claims 'worker "dissatisfaction", whether in absolute or in relative context has always been emphasised as a significant variable in inducing unionization, . . .'

15. See P. Vaughan, *Doctors Commons, op cit.*

16. See B. B. Gilbert, *The Evolution of National Insurance in Great Britain*, London, 1966.

17. J. Hogarth, *Payment of the General Practitioner*, Pergamon Press, London, 1963, p. 30.

18. R. Stevens, *Medical Practice in Modern England*, Yale University Press, 1966, p. 57.

19. *British Medical Journal*, Vol. II, 1937, p. 445, quoted in R. Stevens, *op. cit.*, p. 57.

20. See A. J. Willcocks, *The Creation of the National Health Service*, Routledge and Kegan Paul, London, 1967.

21. John Graham, 'What professional people earn', *The Scotsman*, Saturday, 13 February 1965.

22. Prof. D. S. Lees, 'Health Through Choice' in *Freedom or Free-for-All*,

R. Harris (ed.). The Institute of Economic Affairs, London, 1965, p. 62.

23. *British Medical Journal,* 5 July 1958, p. 20.
24. Ibid, p. 20.
25. *Royal Commission on Doctors' and Dentists' Remuneration,* 1960, Cmnd. 939, London, H.M.S.O.
26. *Report of the Review Body on Doctors' and Dentists' Remuneration,* Cmnd. 5010, 1972.
27. *Review Body on Doctors' and Dentists' Remuneration,* Seventh Report, Cmnd. 2992, 1966.
28. *Review Body on Doctors' and Dentists' Remuneration,* Twelfth Report, Cmnd. 4352, 1976.
29. *British Medical Journal,* Supp., 24 March 1973, p. 88.
30. *British Medical Journal,* Supp., 26 July 1975, p. 252.
31. *The Economist,* 6 December 1975, p. 18. The picture was now all too clear, As N. Parry and J. Parry, *The Rise of the Medical Profession,* Croom Helm, London, 1976, p. 232, point out, 'those who are poorly organized or apathetic have not been spontaneously rewarded . . .'.
32. Ibid., p. 233.
33. Mary Ann Elston, 'Medical Autonomy: Challenge and Response', in K. Barnard and K. Lee, *Conflicts in the National Health Service,* Croom Helm, London, 1977, p. 50.
34. R. A. Kessel, 'Price Discrimination in Medicine', *op. cit.*
35. G. Routh, *Occupation and Pay in Great Britain 1906–60,* Cambridge University Press, Cambridge, 1965, p. 63.
36. Rudolf Klein, *Complaints Against Doctors,* Charles Knight, London, 1973, pp. 60–1 writes 'At the beginning of the twentieth century the position of many general practitioners was professionally vulnerable and financially precarious. The myth of a golden age of medical practice, which contrasts with high social prestige and economic status of the doctor in his heyday as an independent professional man with his fallen state as an N.H.S. employee, tends to apply to the many what in fact was true only of the few. Certainly in economic terms, the position of the average doctor has improved – both relatively to other professions and absolutely – as the State has taken increasing responsibility for the provision of the health service.'
37. For example see Irving Bernstein, 'The Growth of American Unions', *American Economic Review,* Vol. LXL, 1964, p. 314; A. A. Blum, 'Why Unions Grow', *Labour History,* 1968, p. 57; and Guy Routh, 'Future Trade Union Membership', in *Industrial Relations: Contem-*

porary Problems and Perspectives, edited by B. C. Roberts, London, Methuen, 1962, pp. 62–82.

38. H. Merskey, 'Some Features of Medical Education in Great Britain During the First Half of the Nineteenth Century', *British Journal of Medical Education*, 1969, Vol. 3, pp. 118–121.

39. R. M. Titmuss, *Essays on 'The Welfare State'*, Unwin University Books, London, 1963, p. 162.

40. Ibid., p. 163.

41. *Report on an Inquiry into Applications for Admission to Universities*, R. K. Kelsall, 1957. The results of the Report are quoted in R. M. Titmuss Essays on 'The Welfare State', *op. cit.*, p. 162, and P. Elliot, *The Sociology of the Professions*, Macmillan, London, 1972, pp. 67–8.

42. *Report of the Royal Commission on Medical Education*, Cmnd. 3569, H.M.S.O., London, 1968, and quoted in J. Robson 'The N.H.S. Company Inc. The Social Consequence of the Professional Dominance in the National Health Service', *Journal of Health Services*, Vol. 3, 1973.

43. S. P. D. Donnan, 'British Medical Undergraduates in 1975: a student survey in 1975 compared with 1966', *Medical Education*, Vol. 10, 1976, pp. 341–7.

44. P. Elliot, *op. cit.*, p. 68.

45. Quoted in P. Elliot, *op. cit.*, p. 68.

46. R. K. Kelsall, 'Self-recruitment in Four Professions', in *Social Mobility in Britain*, edited by D. V. Glass, Routledge and Kegan Paul, 1954.

47. R. K. Kelsall, *Report on an Inquiry into Applications for Admission to Universities*, *op. cit.*

48. *Report of the Royal Commission on Medical Education*, Cmnd. 3569, Appendix 19.

49. S. P. B. Donnan, *op. cit.*, p. 342.

50. N. Parry and J. Parry, *The Rise of the Medical Profession*, *op. cit.*, p. 254. This factor may merit considerable importance since women are generally accepted to have a lower propensity to join associations and unions. For example, see J. Shister, 'The Logic of Union Growth', *Journal of Political Economy*, Vol. LXI, 1953, K. Hindell, *Trade Union Membership* (London: Political and Economic Planning 1962), B. C. Roberts, 'The Trends of Union Membership', *Trade Union Government and Administration in Great Britain* (London, Bell, 1956), H. A. Clegg, *The System of Industrial Relations in Great Britain*, Basil Blackwell, Oxford, 1970.

51. Jane Morton, 'Women Doctors', *New Society*, 28 February 1974, p. 511.
52. S. P. B. Donnan, *op. cit.*, p. 342.
53. K. A. Hill, 'Medical education at the crossroads', *British Medical Journal*, Vol. 1, 1966, pp. 970–3.
54. J. Robson, *op cit*, p. 415.
55. T. Johnson, 'The professions', printed in G. Hurd, *Human Societies*, Routledge and Kegan Paul, London, 1973, pp. 217–18, comments that the high development of colleagueship within the professions 'leaves the laymen with the feeling of a Kafkaesque hero; helpless in the fact of professional silence, solidarity and ritual'. George Bernard Shaw expressed this feeling well when he wrote in *The Doctor's Dilemma:* 'All the professions are conspirous against the laity.' Indeed the measure of solidarity within the profession in terms of similarity of class background is probably an inadequate index. There is of course some kind of esprit de corps within the profession. D. S. Lees, *The Economic Consequences of the Profession*, Institute of Economic Affairs, London, 1966, p. 31, refers to the difficulty, for example, for a plaintiff to get a doctor to testify against the defendant in cases of medical negligence.
56. G. S. Bain, *The Growth of White Collar Unionism*, Clarendon Press, Oxford, 1970. See also K. Prandy, Professional Organisation in Great Britai, *Industrial Relations*, Vol. V, October 1965, pp. 67–9.
57. H. Eckstein, *Pressure Group Politics, op. cit.*
58. A. Cox, *Among the Doctors, op. cit.*, p. 101.
59. R. Stevens, *op. cit.*, pp. 297–300.
60. Ibid., p. 294.
61. Mary Ann Elston, *op. cit.*, p. 40.
62. T. R. Marriot and D. Thomas, 'Doctors, Politics and Pay Disputes – "Pressure Group Politics" Revisited', *British Journal of Political Science*, Vol. 2, 1972, pp. 421–42.
63. A. J. Willcocks, *The Creation of the National Health Service, op cit.*, p. 105.
64. D. Lockwood, *The Blackcoated Worker*, Unwin, London, 1966.
65. M. W. Susser and M. Watson, *Sociology in Medicine*, Oxford University Press, 1962, p. 159.
66. G. Forsythe, *Doctors and State Medicine*, 2nd edition, Pitman Medical, 1973, p. 206.
67. See, for example, *Gillebaud Committee (1956) Report of the Committee of Enquiry into the Cost of the National Health Service*, London, H.M.S.O.; G. Forsythe, *Doctors and State Medicine*, 2nd edition,

Pitman Medical, 1973, p. 206; R. H. S. Crossman, *A Politician's View of Health Service Planning*, University of Glasgow, 1972.

68. R. Klein, 'National Health Service After Reorganisation', *Political Quarterly*, Vol. 22, p. 328, comments that general practitioners 'are not answerable to anyone (any more than consultants in hospitals) for what they do provided they do not over-prescribe too extravagantly'.
69. Harry H. Ecktein, *The English Health Service*, Oxford University Press, London, 1959.
70. R. Stevens, *Medical Practice in Modern England, op. cit.*, p. 89.
71. K. Hindell, *Trade Union Membership*, Political and Economic Planning, London, 1962, pp. 174–181.
72. *British Medical Journal* (Supp.), 1968, Vol. 1, p. 33.
73. *British Medical Journal* (Supp.), 28 April 1967, p. 28.
74. *British Medical Journal* (Supp.), 26 October 1968, p. 21.
75. *British Medical Journal* (Supp.), Annual Report, 6 May 1967, p. 68. It is worth noting that a personal approach to non-members has always appeared fairly effective. W. Gordon, 'Observations on the Organization of the Branches of the British Medical Association', *British Medical Journal*, 21 July 1900, p. 150, wrote of the problem of getting new members. 'The difficulty was apparently due to want of personal acquaintance with those whom I wished to secure. Men whom I knew personally rarely refused to join.'
76. John H. Pencavel, 'The Demand for Union Services: An exercise', *Industrial and Labour Relations Review*, Vol. 24, 1970–71, pp. 180–190, examined changes in registered Union membership in Britain between 1928 and 1966 and noted that the demand for union membership was relatively unrealistic with respect to the price of union membership.
77. M. Olson, Jr., *The Logic of Collective Action*, New York, 1968.
78. R. A. Musgrave, *The Theory of Public Finance*, McGraw-Hill, London, 1959.
79. P. R. Jones, 'Why Doctors Join the British Medical Association', *Social and Economic Administration*, 1973, Vol. 7, No. 3; P. R. Jones, 'The British Medical Association and the Closed Shop', *Industrial Relations*, Winter, Vol. 4, no. 4, 1974.
80. A. T. Peacock and J. Wiseman, *The Growth of Public Expenditure in the United Kingdom*, National Bureau of Economic Research, Princeton University Press, 1961.
81. One dimension of this threat of monopsonistic power of the State in the medical market is illustrated by Alan Maynard's comparison of expenditure on and efficiency of medical services in European countries. See

A. Maynard, *Health Care in the European Community*, Croom Helm, London, 1975.

82. A similar asymmetry has been noted in terms of voting, i.e. individuals are more ready to incur the costs of voting when they feel under collective threat. See Howard S. Bloom and H. Douglas Price, 'Voter Response to Short run Economic Conditions: The Asymmetric Effect of Poverty and Depression', *American Journal of Political Science*, December 1975.

83. M. H. Cooper and A. J. Culyer, 'An Economic Survey of the Nature and Intent of the British National Health Service', *Social Science and Medicine*, Vol. 5, No. 1, February 1971.

PART IV

Personal Social Services

CHAPTER TEN

Changes in Social Services for the Elderly[1]

ANDREW C. BEBINGTON

Townsend and Wedderburn's survey of the elderly living in the community was, in 1965, the first national account specifically devoted to the social needs and conditions of the elderly, following the substantial post-war legislation that provided the basis for many developments in domiciliary services for the aged. This survey was born of the recognition that social provision to the elderly was by no means as effective as had been commonly supposed. Thus, *The Aged in the Welfare State* (A.W.S.), the principal publication of this survey,[2] aimed to raise such general issues as the effectiveness of the existing range of social services in meeting the needs of the elderly; to quantify the extent of need and the degree to which these needs were being met; and to examine whether social change was creating new and possibly more complex needs. These issues have remained of central significance to social welfare policy throughout the 1960s and 1970s, and were remarkably little changed by 1978, when the next national survey of the social needs and conditions of the elderly was published, *The Elderly At Home*[3] (E.A.H.).

It is to review these issues and to investigate the nature and extent of progress between the two surveys that the present chapter is devoted.[4] We are going to present computations of the 'Elderly At

Home' survey as equivalent as possible to the earlier survey in order to examine these changes between the two survey years of 1962 and 1976. Some comparisons are also made with a third major survey of the elderly, Harris' *Social Welfare for the Elderly*[5] (S.W.E.), which took place in 1965. Although there is considerable continuity in the central issues during the time between these surveys, certain problems of comparability exist, both with regard to the conceptual basis of these surveys, reflecting current perceptions of social welfare, and in the technical compatibility of the data.[6]

First, there have been subtle ideational changes which in part must be considered due to the impact of Townsend's work on the elderly. Perhaps the most outstanding aspect is the increase of polarization between the social and medical aspects of the welfare of the elderly. This is reflected in the distinction between handicap and incapacity, about which we comment later. Townsend's work was also highly instrumental in bringing to light social aspects of deprivation of the elderly. Subsequent research has taken into account the change in social service policy and practice, and so the social conditions and resources of the elderly are even more fully explored in E.A.H.

There have been changes, secondly, in perspectives, and these are nowhere felt so much as in the measurement of need. In considering the extent of welfare shortfall in A.W.S., much use is made of 'felt need' for help with domestic and personal self-care. It has since been acknowledged that in the social services supply itself generates demand and 'felt need' is an unsatisfactory method of measuring welfare shortfall, since it is critically influenced by knowledge and expectations of service delivery. In 1965, S.W.E. attempted to determine the need for services by developing and applying normative judgements and definitions – a method that subsequently has received considerable research attention.

Third, some changes of issues have taken place. In the early 1960s, there was interest in the 'residualist' theory as to whether the role of the social services should diminish as national prosperity increased, and perhaps even prove to be a transitory feature of a developing society. By 1976, the concern had switched from 'role' to 'effectiveness' and, in particular, with the need to maintain standards of provision with fewer services.

Changes in biographic characteristics

In view of the phenomenal increase in numbers of the old, and in particular of the extremely old, Table 1 shows, perhaps surprisingly, that the average age of the elderly living in the community was unchanged between 1962 and 1976. The reason must be sought in terms of changes in the pattern of institutional provision. While there has been a very big increase in the number of places in old people's homes and in hospital beds for the elderly, the evidence suggests that most of this expansion has gone into increasing the provision for the over-eighties. For example, from the 1966 and 1971 Census reports, the elderly aged between sixty-five and seventy-nine living in private households in England and Wales increased by 11 per cent from 4,663,000 to 5,154,000 in this period, yet the numbers living in institutions remained almost constant at just under 160,000. At the same time, the numbers aged eighty plus

TABLE 1   *Sex and age composition of samples of old people from two surveys, and of the elderly population, 1962 and 1976.*

	1962		1976	
	A.W.S. *responding* *sample* *%*	*Population* *estimate*[a] *%*	*E.A.H.* *responding* *sample* *%*	*Population* *estimate*[b] *%*
Sex				
Male	39.8	38.4	39.8	38.9
Female	60.2	61.6	60.2	61.1
Age				
65–69 years	34.6	36.4	36.4	35.7
70–74 years	29.4	27.8	30.0	28.2
75–79 years	20.1	19.6	18.0	29.3
80–84 years	10.9	10.8	10.1	
85+ years	4.9	5.4	5.4	6.7
No answer	0.1	—	0.0	—
Total (number)	4,209	6,151,000	2,622	7,054,800

Notes
[a] Source: Registrar General's quarterly returns for England and Wales, and for Scotland, quarter ending 30 September, 1962.
[b] Population trends 10 (Winter, 1977) for England and Wales, mid-year 1976.

at home increased by 12 per cent from 861,000 to 965,000, while those in institutions jumped 40 per cent from 111,000 to 152,000.[7]

Although changes in the age and sex composition of the elderly in the community are slight, more significant social changes have taken place. The characteristics which are of particular interest – because they are widely recognized as the major conditions raising the need for social service intervention – are social isolation, functional incapacity, and condition of housing. The evidence is that there have been great changes in each of these between 1962 and 1976.

As Abrams[8] has recently stressed, one of the most striking changes has been in the number of elderly living alone, which has increased from 23 per cent in A.W.S. to 30 per cent in E.A.H. But it is among oldest that this expansion has entirely taken place. No fewer than 41 per cent of those aged eighty plus in 1976 were living alone compared with 25 per cent in 1962.[9] By contrast, only 2 per cent more of those aged between sixty-five and sixty-nine are now living alone. Abrams has shown how living alone is not only an important factor in social isolation, but also a major determinant of low life satisfaction among the elderly.

Townsend's studies did much to demonstrate the importance of the distinction between physical impairment and functional disability, and so to define the role of the personal social services for the elderly with respect to incapacity. While the proportion of elderly permanently bedfast and living at home has probably remained unchanged at about one in three hundred, in other respects there is evidence of a deterioration in functional ability. A range of essential personal self-care functions are compared in Table 2. Although the possibility exists that these are due to questionnaire differences, the A.W.S. figures are apparently confirmed by the S.W.E. survey, which has a very different format.

It is possible to investigate this further using a special measure of incapacity developed by Townsend.[10] This is a scale which registers whether the elderly person has the capacity to do six things without assistance, and runs from 0–12, higher scores indicating greater incapacity. Table 3 confirms the conclusion drawn from Table 2, that between A.W.S. and E.A.H. there has been virtually no change in the amount of severe incapacity in the elderly, but that there has

been a marked increase in the number moderately disabled, from
15 per cent to 21 per cent of the elderly population.

TABLE 2 *Proportions of persons having difficulty[d] in undertaking certain functions. (Includes those who cannot do them).*

Activity	A.W.S. (1962)[a]		S.W.E. (1965)[b]	E.A.H. (1976)[c]	
	All aged 65+ %	Aged 80+ %	All %	All aged 65+ %	Aged 80+ %
Go out of doors on own	19	41	18	24	50
Get around the house	9	20	7	11	25
Get in and out of bed	10	19	7	11	21
Bathing	17[e]	34[e]	17	26	54
Going up and down stairs	29	46	28	33	54
Cutting toenails	35	62	N.A.	39	65
Number on which based	4.067	N.A.	4,695	2,622	601

Notes
[a] From Townsend (1973), Table 3.
[b] From S.W.E., Table 19, averaged across ten areas of England and Wales.
[c] Not stated counts as ability (but affects results minimally).
[d] For A.W.S., categories were worded: can do without difficulty; only with
difficulty or assistance; not at all. For S.W.E., question wording was 'do you
usually have any difficulty: yes/no'. For E.A.H., categories were worded:
without any difficulty; with difficulty; only with help; not at all.
[e] Washing and bathing.

TABLE 3 *Townsend's personal incapacity scale for persons aged 65+ living at
home.*

	A.W.S. (1962)[a]			E.A.H. (1976)		
	Men %	Women %	Both %	Men %	Women %	Both %
None or slight (0–2)	83.5	71.2	76.1	77.1	65.1	69.9
Moderate (3–6)	10.9	17.4	14.8	17.5	22.6	20.6
Severe (7–12) and Bedfast	95.6	11.9	9.1	5.7	11.9	9.5
Number on which based	1,643[b]	2,486[b]	4,129	994	1,628	2,622

Notes
[a] From A.W.S., Table 4.
[b] Approximately.

What has happened to cause this? We can answer this question in part by considering the age distribution of the incapacitated. While certain incomparabilities exist in the figures of Table 4, one broad feature is striking; this is the steeper age gradient of incapacity, which is most prominent for the seventy-five to seventy-nine-years age band. In 1962, almost half of these people were fully functional; in 1976, only one-third. Among the 'eighty plus' living in the community, the modal group is now the moderately incapacitated: formerly it was the slightly incapacitated. For those under seventy-five, there has apparently been little change in capacity.

TABLE 4   *Townsend's personal incapacity score by age group, for persons aged 65+ living at home.*

	A.W.S. (1962)[a]				E.A.H. (1976)[b]			
	65–69 %	70–74 %	75–79 %	80+ %	65–69 %	70–74 %	75–79 %	80+ %
None (0)	71	55	47	27	67	53	33	21
Slight (1–2)	18	26	24	32	18	22	23	20
Moderate (3–6)	9	14	21	26	12	18	30	35
Severe (7+)	2	5	8	15	3	8	14	23
Number on which based	880	719	485	369	742	612	681	587

Notes
[a] From Shanas *et al.* (1966) Table II–10. Based on a partial sample of 2447 respondents only. It is important to note that these figures *exclude* the bedfast (and chairfast). This group comprises about 2 per cent of the total sample and would automatically be rated as severely handicapped.
[b] E.A.H. figures include the bedfast. Caution must be observed in making comparisons between the two surveys.

It is difficult to explain why there has been such an increase in disability among the very old, and this is a finding that has not been previously documented. Changes in expectations amongst the elderly cannot be ruled out.

By contrast, the housing conditions of the elderly have shown considerable improvement since the early sixties. At that time, the need for special housing was only just beginning to be realized, because for a long time after the war, priority had been given to the housing needs of young families. Forty-four per cent of the elderly were then living in sub-standard accommodation with the absence of certain basic amenities, such as a bath, kitchen, and indoor W.C. By 1976, this had reduced to 19 per cent of those living at home.

Use of welfare services

The ten-year plans collected by the Ministry of Health in the mid-1960s foresaw great expansion of both residential and community care for the elderly between 1965 and 1976. Table 5 indicates that very substantial increases have been achieved in the proportions of the elderly living at home who now receive regular visits from the home-help service, meals on wheels and the district nurse. Additionally, the coverage of day-care services has increased, particularly of social centres, which were visited by 12 per cent of the elderly at least once a week in 1976, compared with the 7 per cent of the A.W.S. sample who 'visited an old people's club last week'.[11] Also, warden-supervised sheltered housing schemes, novel in the early sixties, now house nearly 5 per cent of the elderly.

Although more of the elderly in the community are now receiving

TABLE 5   *Proportions of elderly persons receiving certain domiciliary services regularly.*

Welfare Service	A.W.S. (1962)[a] %	S.W.E. (1965) %	E.A.H. (1976) %
Home-help service	4.5	4.5	8.6[b]
Meals on wheels (at least once a week)	1.1	1.1[c]	2.4
District nurse regularly visits	N.A.	2.3[d]	5.5[e]
Health visitor regularly visits	N.A.	1.6[d]	1.7[e]
Number on which based	4,067	3,889	2,622

Notes
[a] From A.W.S., Table 2.
[b] At least once a fortnight.
[c] This is based on answers to the question: 'Who makes most of your meals?'
[d] The question is phrased: 'Does the . . . call on you now?'
[e] This relates to *regular* visits at least once every three months. Over 2 per cent more receive each of these services less regularly.

services, certain caveats remain. First, we should like to know to what extent services have changed the roles they perform. Changes in the availability of substitute services, and the way in which services 'interweave' in combining to provide care, complicate conclusions about overall standards of provision. Second, are the services reaching the right people? Have they become more efficient in locating the most needy clients? Third, what about the outputs from services? Have services become more effective in meeting the needs of their clients; has the quality of service improved?

The home-help service is easiest to compare with regard to quantity of service, role, and client composition. The tasks home helps do have changed very little, with floor and window-cleaning predominating along with shopping. Preparing meals and firelighting were less important in 1976 than in the mid-1960s. On the other hand, home helps visit considerably less often than they did. In both 1962 (A.W.S.) and 1965, about 64 per cent of those elderly receiving the home-help service did so more than once a week. In

TABLE 6   *Percentage of old people (i) receiving L.A. home help, (ii) not receiving L.A. home help, who had certain characteristics*[b]

	Those who receive an L.A. home help		Those who do not have an L.A. home help	
Characteristic	*A.W.S. (1962)*[a] *%*	*E.A.H. (1976)*[c] *%*	*A.W.S. (1962)*[a] *%*	*E.A.H. (1976) %*
Moderately or severely incapacitated	85	76	17[d]	26
Living alone	49	65	22	26
Childless	34	33	24	24
Social class V	12	9	12	11
Number on which based	172	279	3,834	2,343

Notes
[a] From A.W.S. Table 7.
[b] Note that the bedfast are excluded from this table.
[c] Those who have a home help at least fortnightly.
[d] The figure of 30 per cent given in A.W.S. is surely a misprint. This figure is estimated from textual remarks.

1976, this had been reduced to 42 per cent. (It should perhaps be added that there is a very considerable range of variation in this figure between different areas.) While less frequent visiting does not necessarily mean that a smaller amount of service is given, there is ancillary evidence to suggest that the number of hours of service given weekly now is, on average, only two-thirds of what it was in the mid-1960s.

Not only is the home-help service spread more thinly, but it is going to slightly different recipients. As is shown in Table 6, a much higher proportion of those receiving a home help live alone, a greater rise than can be accounted for by the rise in number living alone. Yet a *smaller* proportion of those receiving a home help are now moderately or severely incapacitated.

Community and other support systems

A major issue of the early sixties was the exact nature of the balance in meeting the welfare needs of the elderly between the roles of public and voluntary agencies on the one hand, and of the family and community on the other. While Townsend[2] speculated on the ideal form of this balance, we feel that in practice, in a world in which resources have been very limited, the domiciliary services have seen their task in terms of intervening to meet the needs of the elderly with which the family and community is unwilling or unable to cope, so as to diminish or postpone the need for instutional care. The key question is whether there have been changes in the extent to which families and the community support the elderly. In A.W.S., Townsend hypothesized that childlessness is one of the most important factors raising the need for institutionalization. In fact, the proportion of childless people is virtually unchanged at around 25 per cent. But despite this, the availability of relatives has considerably reduced since 1962: and as Hunt[12] says, 'often the first people to turn to in an emergency are relatives'. Not only are more of the elderly living alone, but for more there is no living relative (5 per cent in 1976 compared with 3 per cent in 1962).[13] Overall, the proportion of the elderly who see relatives regularly has dropped. Eight-four per cent of the A.W.S. sample 'had seen a relative in the last week' compared with 71 per cent of E.A.H. who 'saw a relative at least about once a week'.

Typical of the pattern of help received by old people in the form of personal care is bathing, which is compared between A.W.S. and E.A.H. in Table 7. Perhaps the most startling statistic shown in this table is that in 1976 as in 1962, almost half of those unable to bath themselves received no help. In A.W.S., Townsend speculates that this may be due not so much to the failure of support systems as to the desire of old people to preserve their independence at all costs. What certainly seems true is not only that now more of the elderly are unable to bath, but that most of the extra support has had to be found from outside the household. Although the domiciliary services now bath a slightly greater proportion of the elderly than they did, they have not, it seems, managed to keep pace with this big increase in need.

A quite different pattern of change emerges regarding support

TABLE 7   *Percentage of elderly persons unable to bath themselves without help, who received help from different sources.*

Source of help in bathing	Responding sample in A.W.S. (1962)[a] %	Responding sample in E.A.H. (1976) %
Person(s) in household	50	33
Relative(s) outside	7	9
Friend(s) outside	2	3
Social services	7	9
Other person outside	0	4
No-one	46	46
Total percentage[c]	112	104
Number on which based[b]	242	473

Notes
[a] From Table 12 of A.W.S.
[b] Excluding seven respondents from A.W.S. for whom source of help was not stated; and the bedfast.
[c] More than 100 per cent because of multiple responses. Reporting of multiple reponses is not strictly comparable between surveys; and it is consdiered probable that the 'persons in household' category of A.W.S. would drop to around 40 per cent if this is taken into account.

with household management, as is shown by Table 8, relating to housework and preparing meals. Here the evidence suggests that the immediate family is as important as ever in meeting needs. While the support from the social services has increased greatly, and possibly many fewer are without any kind of help, the elderly rely less on outsiders. The significant decrease in the amount of privately paid help is a factor of certain interest.

TABLE 8   *Percentage of elderly people having difficulty with household tasks, who receive help from different sources.*

	Heavy housework		Cooking	
Source of help	Have difficulty with heavy housework A.W.S. (1962)[a] %	Cannot manage washing floors E.A.H. (1976) %	Have difficulty preparing meals A.W.S. (1962)[a] %	Cannot manage to cook a main meal E.A.H. (1976) %
Other person(s) in household	51	53[b]	79	82[b]
Relative(s) outside	13	10	5	9
Friend(s) outside	3	1	4	1
Social services	8	21	4	9[d]
Paid help	11	7	2	0
Other(s) outside	6	11	0	0
None/not done	13	7	10	1
Total percentage[b]	104	110	104	102
Number on which based	1921	670	423	270
Proportion of total sample in this category	47.4	21.7	10.4	8.8

Notes

[a] From A.W.S. Tables 14 and 15.

[b] Includes those cases where in a joint interview the other partner could manage, regardless of whether other help was available.

[c] More than 100 per cent because of multiple responses. Reporting of multiple responses is not strictly comparable between surveys.

[d] Of which, meals on wheels account for 6 per cent. Nearly half of these also get help from another source.

The need for care

The final stage in the argument is to consider to what extent the great expansion of the domiciliary services in the fourteen years since A.W.S. have taken them towards meeting Townsend's major criticisms that:

> . . . substantially more old people than are receiving different services – sometimes double, treble or quadruple the existing number – feel a need and otherwise seem to qualify for them. . . . Many of those receiving services . . . are not getting all the help they might from the services in question; they need help more frequently . . . many people receiving only one service seem to need at least two or three services.

Townsend particularly showed shortfalls in the provision of the home-help service. The major point in his argument was that many of those feeling the need for services were in fact incapacitated or had needs similar to those who were receiving services. In all, on top of the 4.4 per cent of the elderly population of A.W.S. who were receiving the home-help service, Townsend found that 5.6 per cent of the elderly felt a need for such service, and a further 4.6 per cent, who had no help with housework, felt that they could not do for themselves. A three-fold expansion of the service was apparently required. Harris in the S.W.E. survey of 1965 adopted an objective, normative definition of need for home-help service instead of using felt need.[14] By this means, she determined that 9.3 per cent of the total population of retirement age in England and Wales needed a home help (S.W.E. Table 14), which would entail a doubling of the service. By 1976, 8.7 per cent received a home help. Does this then mean that the home-help services are now effectively meeting almost all need that falls within their domain? On the positive side, not only is the service close to Harris' target, but expansion in substitute services has meant that home helps no longer need be used for certain tasks such as cooking. On the negative side, however, increasing incapacity, social isolation and the decline of other, non-public support systems is expected to raise demand, while home-help services are now more thinly spread than they were typically in the mid-sixties. Moreover, Harris's definition is unquestionably stringent. Ideally, we should have liked to re-apply this definition to the E.A.H. survey, but regrettably the data base does not permit this to be done precisely. Instead, all individuals have been examined to see who were unable (or in the case of a joint interview, both were unable) to do any of a range of crucial domestic management tasks within the home, which it would be normal for a home help to be assigned to do.[15] It was found that, despite the increase in home-help provision, there remained a residual 1.3 per cent of the total elderly population who could not do (or in the case of a joint interview, neither could do) at least one of these tasks, and for whom there was no one, either in the household or outside it, who provided help. In some cases, the task was managed jointly by an elderly couple working at it together. In other cases, one had to assume that failure to get such tasks done implied an appallingly low quality of life. The needs of this group are very high. And, of course, this by no means necessarily represents the extent of unmet need for the home-help service. Judging by those who were receiving home helps, the service was often provided when the above conditions did not hold. There are a further 6 per cent of the elderly population who, although not necessarily urgently in need of home-help services, must be considered as high risk. These are people who rely for essential domestic help exclusively from people outside the household (other than those in sheltered housing, currently receiving a home help, or employing a domestic help). Either they are unable (or in the case of a joint interview, both are unable) to do one of the listed tasks or they live alone and are unable to get out unassisted. Table 9 shows that it is the oldest whose needs are greatest.

In A.W.S. it was found that as many as 5.9 per cent of the elderly population would like to receive the mobile meals service, as compared with 1.1 per cent who were actually receiving it. Harris, in S.W.E. (Table 41) estimated that 1.2 per cent were receiving meals, but a further 2.9 per cent could not get a daily cooked meal without difficulty; a total need level of 4.1 per cent of the elderly living at home. In 1976, 2.4 per cent of the elderly received meals. In contrast to the home-help service, a more intensive provision of meals was made in 1976, with nine recipients out of ten getting

TABLE 9   *Percentage of old persons (by age) who are in need, or at risk of needing, the home-help service. (E.A.H., 1976).*

Age	65–69 %	70–74 %	75–79 %	80–84 %	85+ %	All %
In need[a]	1.3	0.4	0.7	3.3	2.9	1.2
At risk[b]	2.0	4.2	8.9	13.8	16.7	5.9
Other	96.7	95.4	90.4	82.9	80.4	92.9
Number on which based	708	603	646	337	193	2487

Notes

[a] An individual is defined as in need if he/she is known to be unable to do one of the tasks for which a home help might be supplied; or in the case of a joint interview, both are unable to do one of them, and no help is available from any source.

[b] An individual is defined as at risk if he/she is in the above condition except that he/she is dependent for help on someone *outside* the household, other than the social services or paid help. Those in sheltered accommodation are excluded.

more than one meal per week (compared with four out of five in 1962).[16]

Sheltered housing was novel in the early 1960s. Although some schemes had been started, less than 1 per cent of the elderly population were living in sheltered housing. Townsend estimated that, judging by the proportion of the elderly who lived alone, had no children within ten minutes' journey, and were moderately or severely incapacitated, 5.1 per cent of those living in the community ought, in time, live in sheltered accommodation. By 1976, 4.7 per cent of the elderly in the community were living in a warden-supervised old person's flat or bungalow (while a further 3 per cent lived in other forms of old people's accommodation).

Again the question must be asked, does this imply that the need for sheltered accommodation has nearly been met? One problem in answering this is that it is difficult to assess how many in 1976 were in sheltered accommodation, who in 1962 would have been in a residential home.[17] Even so, Townsend's estimate proved to be a somewhat misleading guide since subsequently, substandard housing was to be the main reason for rehousing the elderly,[18] and it is assumed that many of those living in sheltered accommodation in 1976 were allocated this accommodation for this reason. Certainly, only 14 per cent of those in sheltered accommodation in the E.A.H. survey lived alone, were moderately or severely disabled, and had relatives visit less than once a week. This compares with 3.6 per cent with similar conditions in the rest of the E.A.H. sample. We conclude, therefore, that if, as Townsend thought, sheltered housing does have a role to play in combating the needs of those who are both incapacitated and socially isolated, then it has only just begun to meet that need.

Conclusions

This broad pattern of results has suggested an enormous expansion in domiciliary welfare provision, leading to very real increases in the volume of services received by the elderly. About twice as many elderly people received home help, meals on wheels and domestic nursing it seems, comparing E.A.H. with A.W.S. The proportion attending day centres (at least weekly) has likewise apparently almost doubled. Warden-supervised sheltered accommodation in 1976 housed nearly 5 per cent of the elderly, compared with less than 1 per cent in 1962. It is particularly to the very elderly that these extra services have gone, with 30 per cent of those over eighty receiving a home help compared with 22 per cent in 1962. Though it has proved difficult to provide exact comparisons, our evidence has suggested that there is probably a smaller proportion of the elderly not receiving some assistance with basic household management. For example, we have estimated that there are only 1.3 per cent of the elderly obtaining no help with essential houshold tasks, compared with the estimate by S.W.E. in 1965 of 4.8 per cent urgently needing home helps to cope with such tasks. In 1962, very few of the elderly were receiving more than one domiciliary service: a situation which Townsend[19] hinted might imply poor co-ordination among the services. By 1976, one in three of the elderly receiving services received more than one of home helps, meals on wheels and district nurse.

But the real gains made had not increased to the same degree as the *per capita* expansion in services might appear to suggest, primarily because of the rising tide of social isolation, as well as of increasing incapacity, which has chiefly affected the very elderly living in the community. Of those aged eighty plus, 58 per cent in E.A.H. were moderately or severely incapacitated, compared with about 46 per cent in A.W.S.; and 41 per cent are living alone compared with 25 per cent in A.W.S. This has happened despite the increased institutional care absorbing a greater proportion of the very elderly than it had fourteen years before. A different interpretation of the figures of Table 6 (page 212) is that the proportion of the moderately and severely incapacitated elderly population in the community who received the home-help service remained almost unchanged at about 20 per cent between 1962 and 1976 although of those living alone, the proportion receiving it has doubled. These are two of the main conditions with which receipt of domiciliary services is associated. There is evidence, too, that more people receiving services may be at the expense of the amount of service received by each. In E.A.H., only 42 per cent have home helps more than weekly compared with 64 per cent in A.W.S. Finally, some evidence suggests that in part the increase in provision has not been entirely an additional supplementary source of help to the elderly, but has partly been absorbed in plugging gaps left by the loss of other sources of assistance from the community.

Notes and References

1. First appeared as an article in *Social Policy and Administration*, Vol. 13, No. 2, Summer 1979.
   I should like to thank Audrey Hunt of O.P.C.S. for generously making the data available to us: also Bleddyn Davies of the University of Kent for help in the formation of these ideas.
2. P. Townsend and D. Wedderburn, *The Aged in the Welfare State*, London: G. Bell and Sons, 1965. The results of this survey have been presented in a number of other publications: E. Shanas, P. Townsend, D. Wedderburn, H. Friis, P. Milhoj and J. Stehouwer, *Old People in Three Industrial Societies*, London: Routledge and Kegan Paul, 1968. Also, J. Turnstall, *Old and Alone*, London: Routledge and Kegan Paul, 1966. Also, P. Townsend, *The needs of the elderly and the planning of hospitals.* Chapter 6 of R. W. Canvin, and N. G. Pearson, *Needs of the Elderly*, University of Exeter, 1973.

3. A. Hunt, *The Elderly At Home*, London: H.M.S.O., 1978.
4. Consideration of the medical and financial needs and conditions of the elderly are excluded.
5. A. I. Harris, *Social Welfare for the Elderly*, London: H.M.S.O., 1968.
6. The principal technical differences are those of sampling and of question wording. *The Aged in the Welfare State* survey considered all over the age of sixty-five in Great Britain and used a multi-stage design in eighty chosen areas, data being gathered in two sweeps in 1962. *The Elderly At Home* survey differs in excluding Scotland, and using a multi-stage design in ninety areas. The sampling fraction was halved for those aged under seventy-five and though the statistics presented in the tables are weighted to allow for this, the numbers of cases are unweighted. Response rates were similar for the two surveys. *Social Welfare for the Elderly* drew a sample of all people of retirement age in nine areas of Engalnd and Wales. (The other parts of this survey have been ignored.) Changes in question wording create the possibility that quite innocuous seeming differences may actually produce unexpected results. We have attempted to detail major differences beneath each table though some are dealt with in the text.
7. Excluding those in hotels, boarding houses and prisons.
8. M. Abrams, *Beyond Three-Score and Ten*, London: Age Concern, 1978.
9. Quoted by Tunstall, *op. cit.*, p. 49.
10. The index of incapacity used in A.W.S. was based on answers to the following questions: can the respondent walk outdoors, walk indoors, negotiate stairs, wash down or bath, dress, and cut toenails. If a particular function could not be carried out at all without help, a score of 2 was assigned, if only with difficulty, a score of 1. This is a simpler version of the index described in P. Townsend, *The Last Refuge*, London: R.K.P., 1963. As dressing was not included in the E.A.H. survey, it was replaced with 'getting in and out of bed'. It is not believed this will cause any appreciable discrepancy – see A. C. Bebbington, *Scaling Indices of Disablement*, B. J. Prev. & Soc. Med., 31, pp. 122–6, 1977.
11. Quoted by Tunstall, *op. cit.*, p. 218.
12. A. Hunt, *op. cit.*, p. 94.
13. From Table IX–1 of Shanas *et al.*, *op cit*.
14. Harris' definition of need for the home help service is given in section 4.15 of *Social Welfare for the Elderly*. Roughly speaking, individuals were considered in need by reason of immobility, of difficulty with housework, shopping or cooking, except when someone

else was reasonably available to do these duties, or there were other ways of overcoming the problem.

15. The tasks identified as being with in the normal provision of a home help's work-load were: opening screw-top bottles and little sewing jobs (considered typical of light household duties); using a frying pan; making a cup of tea; cooking a main meal; sweeping floors; washing floors; and making the fire, where necessary. Jobs involving climbing and cleaning windows were excluded.

16. Given by *Aged in the Welfare State*, p. 51.

17. The distinction between those in need of sheltered accommodation by Townsend's definition and those who might preferably enter an old people's home is difficult to make with survey data. Isaacs and Neville, in *The Measurement of Need in Old People*, Scottish Health Studies paper 34, 1975, Chapter 18, consider the distinction should be made on the basis of the *frequency* of attention required by the condition of the elderly person combined with the degree of strain that is being placed on the caring system, or if, indeed, basic maintenance needs are being met properly. W. R. Bytheway, in *The Rationale for Sheltered Housing* (read to the Social Services Research Group, King's Fund Centre, November 1976), is of interest with regard to actual role sheltered accommodation has fulfilled. He has argued that rather than simply providing a more suitable form of housing for the elderly, they are in general small institutions.

18 This was recognised by Harris, *op. cit.*, sections 5.5–5.7.

19. See *Aged in the Welfare State*, p. 69.

CHAPTER ELEVEN

Towards a Theory of Rationing[1]

ELLIE SCRIVENS

For the past thirty years the British public have been able to receive, free of charge or at very reduced prices, services such as health, education and personal social services. Expenditure on these services has increased over this period and has been accompanied by parallel increases in consumption and apparent demand which has mostly exceeded the resources available. The effect of demand increasing at a faster rate than available resources has led to concern about the ways in which the resources are allocated among the demands, and concern about how decisions are made to exclude some demands altogether. The methods by which these objectives are achieved have become known as 'rationing processes'. Thus the phenomenon of rationing has, in recent times, become associated with the provision of those services, which, facing severe resource constraints, have been forced to look at the processes by which their resources are allocated. This chapter offers some ideas as to why such processes exist, and develops a number of ideas on the nature of rationing at the client-worker interface. This form of rationing is referred to as 'service rationing' as opposed to 'financial rationing', which discusses the processes by which cash resources are allocated between agencies and public bodies. Ken Judge's recent contribution to the rationing field has given some very useful ideas on the nature and format of the allocation of financial resources, especially from central Government to local authorities. Judge devoted little time to service rationing, his reasons being:

> Service rationing is probably one of the most important functions of Social Services departments, but our understanding of what actually happens is very limited. It is not so much that there is a shortage of literature but that what research and analysis has been reported has been patchy in coverage and variable in quality and relevance.[2]

Though there has been little specific research into rationing, a number of ideas have been put forward about the processes that are involved. These are discussed at the end of the chapter, together with some of the author's own ideas on rationing. The first part is concerned with the reasons why rationing at the client-worker interface exists.

The services discussed here are for the most part those of health and the personal social services. Social security is only mentioned in passing because although rationing processes (considered later) are applicable to certain aspects of this provision, especially to the area of supplementary benefits, this service does not suffer from the problems of short-term supply restrictions. Financial aid is guaranteed to all those who require it. Education and housing are dealt with later in the paper.

Rationing is essentially that process by which a limited resource is divided between various competing bodies. Probably the best known instance of rationing occurred during the Second World War, when the supply of most goods was restricted. Government policy was to suspend the price mechanism, which in the free market serves to equalize demand with supply on the basis of ability to pay. Financial advantage causes inequality of consumption and prevents those in need from obtaining the commodities they require. The removal of the price mechanism necessitated government intervention in deciding how much would-be buyers could obtain. The solution chosen was to allocate by exchange of tokens, that is, ration books. The universal supply of ration books made equal access to the resources available to everyone.

The services of health, education, housing and the personal social services present a similar picture today. The growth of egalitarian ideals required universal provision of these services free of charge or at very reduced prices. As with war-time goods, the price mechanism was suspended and tokens of exchange were considered unnecessary. Provision was requested and made on the basis of need. Certain economists of the day felt they were able to abandon neo-classical theory in relation to these services because of their beliefs about the nature of the services.

Of all the social services, education was the easiest to reconcile with free allocation of resources. For example, Dalton in 1922 claimed that:

The policy of free or very cheap supply is suited best to commodities and services with inelastic demand at low prices. Therefore free education would be more economical than free transport or clothing.[3]

In 1943 Pigou expressed a similar view. He felt that the limitation of aggregate resources implied a certain restriction in the supply of every service, as against the amount people would use if they were allowed to have as much as they desired at zero cost. According to Pigou no restriction would lead to social waste. However, if the demand for the service were inelastic, then provision free at the point of consumption would cause only a small amount of wasted resources. Conversely, if the demand were elastic, the social wastage would be large. Pigou selected as services suitable for free provision education, water, and interestingly, health. The reason given for free education was that elementary education has inelastic demand because people who want it will purchase it at any price. He reasoned similarly that 'medical attendance has a highly inelastic demand, because when people are well they do not want doctoring at any price'.[4] This argument, based on observations of the sick insurance clubs, led Pigou to conclude that if a set price was paid weekly in the form of an insurance contribution, then the use of a doctor's services was not dictated by the price. This view was also held by many others involved with the provision of these services, such as the Webbs and indeed the founders of the National Health Service. However, they would appear to have been mistaken in this assumption, because evidence indicates that sickness rates in fact increase with the introduction of insurance schemes.[5] Experience of the free health service has forced us to conclude, as Buchanan[6] has demonstrated, that though emergency and acute services may well have inelastic demand, the demand for G.P. and other services appears to be highly elastic at low prices to the consumer.

It is a mistake to assume that the education teaching service (as distinguished from other services provided by the local education authorities) is comparable with the other social services. In this respect, it is necessary to distinguish between the provision of compulsory education and voluntary post-compulsory education. The former has very different properties of supply and demand. For a selected age group consumption is compulsory, and in consequence free provision must be made. Arguments of elasticity are irrelevant for determining the demand that will be made on the free service. On the other hand, contracts with the health, housing and personal social services, and also post-compulsory education, are for the most part voluntary, and consequently elasticities become important. The demand for post-compulsory education shows a very high elasticity of demand at low prices, as was strikingly demonstrated in the 1960s. Of course, general practitioners and social workers do have certain powers to compel individuals to 'consume' resources – for example, patients of psychiatric hospitals who are admitted under the Mental Health Act, 1959.

Education has additional fundamental differences. Because of the particular methods used to teach children, that is, one teacher giving information to a number of children, education possesses, to a certain extent, the properties of, to use the Public Finance term, divisibility. This means, that it is possible for one extra person to consume the same service without detriment to existing consumers. Thus, as demand for education increases due to more children in a certain age group, it is possible to make the classes larger, because the pupils consume the same output at the same time. Education obviously does not possess complete divisibility because a certain amount of one-to-one contact between teacher and pupil is considered necessary, and an increase in class size would lessen the time available for this. The education service also provides other facilities such as clothing, free school meals and grants. The provision of these is very similar to the material provision of the personal social services and may be treated in the same light.

The health and personal social services do not, however, possess the property of divisibility. This is obvious for material provisions, because, for example, only one person can occupy a hospital bed or a place in a residential home at one time. This is not so obvious in the provision of services in which the output comprises the skill of a professional worker. Yet, only one individual, or possibly in certain cases, one household, can consume the output of a doctor, social worker or a home help at any one time. As Judge[7] points out, it is possible to divide the time available between increasing numbers of clients by decreasing the amount of time spent with each individual client. Thus, the services provided may be said to be in a sense 'time divisible', though not wholly so. Workers can work only for a maximum number of hours a day. Workers are physically restricted from giving an infinite amount of service to an infinite number of consumers. Also, the extent to which the total number of available time units can be divided between patients or clients in a meaningful way is dependent upon the benefit received from the service. Figure 1 illustrates the short run situation for social service intervention. Consider the case of the home-help service provided for a short period of time to, for example, an expectant mother. It would appear that to provide amount OA of the service would not be cost-effective because the marginal cost exceeds the marginal benefit of one extra unit of home-help time. Of course, it may be that the marginal benefit curve in fact resembeles Figure 2 and that the benefit derived from receiving OA is negative. The home help may be in the client's home for such a short time that disappointment and feelings of rejection may occur, and the home help has not time to do anything for the client. After point C the marginal cost may again exceed marginal benefit.

The marginal cost may be constant as MC_1, providing that the increased number of home helps all gave the same service to the same, maximum number of clients. If the employment of an extra home help provided the same or less service to fewer clients, then the marginal costs of home help provision would increase as in MC_2. So if a home help can provide a service to twenty clients a week at maximum capacity and at maximum benefit to clients, and the

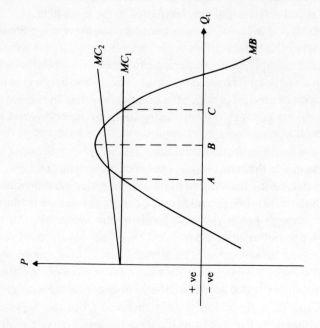

FIGURE 2

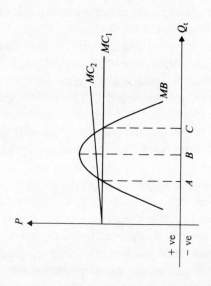

FIGURE 1

department has twenty more clients in need of home help, then the marginal cost of employing an extra home help will be constant. On the other hand, if ten clients are in need of home-help provision then another full-time home help may be employed, but under conditions of increasing marginal cost.

Similarly, these diagrams may explain social work intervention. The problems faced in allocating social-work time, as with all services of this nature, are due to the fact that we do not know the exact location of point *B*. Nor is there any means of assessing the time scale over which the curves span, or the ways these would differ for each social worker's approach to the client. Services also possess the added dimension of quality of provision. Unless we can determine the quality of output, it is not productive to look for measures of length of time of input.

With the exception, for the reasons explained above, of the education teaching services, the social services are generally facing the same problems of demand exceeding limited resources available, with no methods to assess the effectiveness of distribution of resources. This, combined with indivisibility of provision, necessitates the institution of some means by which the equilibrating effects of the free market price mechanism are replaced, to choke off or hold back demand. To do this the social services use procedures which can be classified under the general heading of rationing.

In the few theoretical discussions of service rationing that have taken place a number of different approaches have been made. These basically can be classified under four main headings:

(1) The rationing base, or that part of the system upon which the rationing processes act
(2) Taxonomy of the rationing processes
(3) Properties of the rationing process
(4) The specific aims of the rationing process

The rationing base

The first method of examining rationing processes is to view them as again falling into two categories: those that act to reduce demand and those that act to reduce supply.

DEMAND INHIBITERS

These processes act upon the consumer before he ever asks for a service. There are a multitude of reasons why people may choose to not use a particular service. To visit a G.P. involves not only the expense of actually getting to his surgery, but also the opportunity cost of the money and time foregone which could have been spent on other acitivites, plus the wages the prospective patient may be losing by not working. A mother may fear that a doctor's diagnosis may lead to her being admitted to hospital which could result in problems of care of her children. There are many experiments which support these views.

Those processes which deter demand are important to services concerned with the low take-up of their provisions. Among these Supplementary Benefits (S.B.) faces the dual problems of consumer ignorance of benefits and the stigma felt by the potential claimants about the service. The nature and appearance of the building which clients must enter to claim a service may also act to deter them. This was an important concern of the Seebohm Committee[8] which claimed that: 'Some of the buildings occupied by the personal social services are forbidding and the reception arrangements are often not such as to encourage anyone let alone anyone in distress to approach them'. These factors actually deter individuals from expressing demands to the services, so that when they arrive at the counter they may be put off by the reception encountered there.

SUPPLY INHIBITORS

When the demand has actually been expressed at the counter, the client having overcome the various emotional and psychological barriers, there are no reasons to prevent the individual from consuming anything that is provided, apart from his own decision to refuse. A set of processes acting upon the supply of resources then comes into play. These take the form of eligibility criteria, need assessment by the professionals, and so on. Basically the process followed is:

(1) Professional assessment
(2) Decision on whether to treat or turn away
(3) Decision on whether to move the client further into the provision system or to treat at the initial contact point

This is the process followed by the G.P., social worker, intake team, or housing manager who are responsible for deciding how resources should be allocated. In fact, the social work intake team, in particular, offers a very good illustration of a supply rationing process at work. Loewenstein[9] defines intake as 'the process which occurs between the initial contact of a client with a social service department whether by letter, telephone or personal application, through the assessment of the problem to the allocation of the case to a social worker'. From this definition Gosteck identifies a number of functions of the intake team.

(i) Filtering: inappropriate applications can be filtered off to agencies more capable of providing assistance.
(ii) Assessment: a full assessment of the applicant's needs should be made during the applicant's initial contact with the agency.
(iii) Clarification: especially of the resources the agency has available and how these match applicant needs.
(vi) Decision: decisions regarding agency resources in relation to applicant needs (in which Gosteck includes 'the operalization of agency priorities over scarce resources').

Thus, the functions of the intake team are essentially concerned with the rationing of the supply of available resources to clients.

Taxonomy of the rationing processes

In 1967 Roy Parker[11] made the very first contribution to rationing theory when he identified three strategies for rationing which Judge[2] has usefully summarized.

RESTRICTIVE

This involves the use of either explicit or implicit deterrence of consumption of the social services. The oldest of these was the principle of less eligibility embodied in the Poor Law Amendment Act of 1834. This principle was used to make those who received a service feel less eligible than those who did not. Though the principle was gradually abandoned as deliberate policy during the twentieth century, the ideas still remain today, in that certain groups of people are reluctant to apply for certain services because they feel that they will be stigmatized or considered less worthy members of society. Thus, an explicit policy has become implicit in the receipt of a service. A classic example of rationing at the beginning of this century is to be found in the Education (Provision of School Meals Act) of 1906. Gilbert[12] describes the policy of education authorities to provide food of the plainest variety, and only between the hours of 8.15 and 8.45 in the morning. He indicates that this was essentially to prevent the abuse of the school feeding programme, and in fact was referred to as the 'food test'.

Pricing is another explicit deterrent, because many people who could receive free services may think twice about demanding them if any charges are made. Also, as Hunt[13] found in the H.M.S.O. survey of home helps, charges may deter those who would benefit from such provision because they do not have the resources to purchase it. Eligibility criteria are explicit and often define precisely the limits of the service. In this category Parker also includes delay, which essentially performs two functions. First it may act as a deterrent, in that delay, once experienced, may prevent further demands being made on the service. Second, delay experienced in the form of waiting lists and queues actually works to control the flow of demand, relative to the supply of the service.

DILUTANT

This requires reductions in the level of service provided to individual clients, as above in the discussion on home helps. The amount of time devoted to a client and the quality of the provision may be reduced. A poor substitute for a service may be provided – for example, the allocation of an unqualified, inexperienced social worker to a particularly difficult case which requires qualified and experienced treatment.

PREMATURE TERMINATION

In some cases provision may be terminated sooner than is desirable. This form of rationing is limited in its application to services, and is dependent upon the nature of the provision. For example, it would be neither ethical nor practicable to stop a surgical operation before it was completed. But for certain long-term services such as a spell in hospital following an operation or a period of casework, the service may not be carried on for as long as would be desired by the practitioner. However, it is difficult to determine the optimum amount of such provision as this is dependent upon the opinions of the individual practitioners. Effectiveness criteria for these cases have not yet been developed, and may be undesirable to pursue, as each client or patient presents a unique problem for treatment.

Stevens[14] followed Parker's approach in developing a taxonomy of rationing, though Stevens has separated the forms of rationing into more well-defined groups, numbering seven in total. The first six are in fact all facets of Parker's restrictive category:

(i) Denial: a combination of not recognizing needs and allowing ignorance about the social service to continue among the general public.

(ii) Referral: while recognizing that a client's needs are the concern of the service approached, referring them to other agencies.

(iii) Deflection: because many clients do not understand the organization of local government and the responsibilities of different departments, one department may not provide for a client or client groups in the knowledge that, though such provision is its responsibility, another department can make alternative provision. Stevens gives the example of children's committees being forced to take children into care because the family could not be housed, although they were homeless. Essentially, it would appear that this argument depends upon the availability of substitutes to certain provisions. Deflection may be better described as one department sending clients whom they could help to other agencies who provide a perfect substitute service. This means the same type of service, as for example, when housing authorities sent homeless families to Shelter.

(iv) Deterrence: again the result of feelings of stigma and rooted in the concept of less eligibility as identified by Parker.

(v) Eligibility: according to Stevens, the only reasonable and democratically acceptable form of control over needs.

(vi) Delay: seen by Stevens as the product of the five rationing processes listed above. He distinguished between organized and unplanned delay. Examples of the former are queues and waiting lists, while the latter, and the more serious, refers to delays due to the inability of the service to cope with the demands upon it. In practice, however, the two types may not be mutually exclusive. When Stevens cites the example of people dying from kidney failure because of the lack of kidney machines, it would appear that he has identified an example of rationing, but has attributed the wrong reasons to it. These delays are in the most part not unplanned,[15] but carefully considered ways of using and distributing resources. The health service does not have enough resources within its limited budget so that opportunity cost considerations of the resources available results in more kidney machines being lower on the list of priorities than some people would like.

(vii) Dilution: this means that more has to be done with the same resources, and hence that fewer resources are ascribed to each individual case. Stevens identifies the same rationing process as Parker, but unlike Parker he sees it as a product of the rationing processes listed above rather than as a separate form of rationing.

Properties of the rationing process

1. Rees[16] has looked at various forms of rationing, but has been more concerned with the identification of the processes themselves than with developing a typology. He did, however distinguish between overt and covert rationing, and proposed these as a basis for a continuum of rationing, along which different forms of rationing could be placed. At the overt end he placed rationing by pricing, followed by queueing and waiting lists, and then priority classes of need. At the covert end of the scale he placed rationing by personal predilection, restrictions on time allocated to cases (Steven's and Parker's dilution effects), rationing by ignorance and by providing deterrent levels of service. This brief selection of Rees' examples shows that this is very different from the taxonomy approach. Parker's restrictive categories cover the types of rationing which Rees identifies as lying at the two most extreme ends of his overt-covert continuum.

2. It is also possible to examine rationing as formal and informal processes. Formal rationing processes take the form of official rules, regulations and procedures concerning access to the services. These must be distinguished from Rees' overt processes in certain cases. Assessment by the social services professional of a client's needs is a formally accepted procedure. This is obvious and open, but it also possesses a covert nature. Recent evidence[17] has shown that individual professionals vary in their assessment, and the clients who receive a service are by no means equal in their needs. In a study of treatment allocation in a renal dialysis unit eight clinicians were asked to classify the suitability of one hundred theoretical cases for treatment. The ways in which they classified the patients differed considerably, with only six cases being placed in the same category by all eight clinicians. This is an example of formal rationing in that it is a formally accepted process necessary to the functioning of the service, but at the same time the differences in the results of assessment are neither open nor acknowledged. For those social services professionals who feel that this is a slight on their abilities, some consolation may be derived from the information that a study of chartered accountants demonstrated that if they were given

exactly the same figures from which to calculate a profit figure for a certain company, the chances of their arriving at the same figure were very remote.

Hall's[18] study (pre-Seebohm) of receptionists in Children's Departments demonstrates rationing of an informal nature. In this study Hall examined the reception facilities of four agencies in different local authorities, making systematic observations of activities in the reception office and carrying out informal interviews with the reception staff. He found that receptionists, when dealing with new applicants, had to listen to the client's problems and make a decision as to whether the client was approaching the right agency. The receptionist could then decide whether or not to pass the case on to the social work staff. If the case was passed on, then the extent to which the receptionist acted as an advocate on the client's behalf in ensuring that contact was made with a social worker depended upon the receptionist's assessment of the client's situation and also her personal liking of the client. Similarly, if the receptionist was not prepared to pursue a client's case, delay in contacting social workers could inhibit the take-up of the case by the agency.

The specific aims of the rationing process

The final approach is to examine rationing in terms of its aims. The various rationing processes and the forms that they can take ultimately perform one of two functions:

(1) turning away expressed demands which the service feels are not suitable for their treatment, or which do not fall within their definition of need;
(2) holding off those needs which are accepted and recognized until resources become available to meet those needs.

The former may be termed primary rationing and the latter secondary rationing. Thus, these processes which deter clients from approaching the services, the assessments which fail to identify need, and the eligibility criteria which clients fail to fulfil are all examples of primary rationing. The intake team described above can deflect clients to other agencies, can decide that the applicant is not suitable for their services, or can discourage further use of the services. All these functions result in the client's either not receiving a service or not returning for further provision, and are therefore primary rationing mechanisms.

The secondary rationing processes come into operation after the client or patient has surmounted the primary barriers, that is, when the number of recognized and accepted needs exceed the supply available. An example of this is when G.P. referrals of patients to hospital exceed the number of beds available. So it is necessary to institute waiting lists and the like. Sometimes, more selective rationing processes are required to select the most needy cases for immediate treatment from the total pool of patients; an example of this is the priority waiting list. It is also possible for those processes, which are designed to be secondary in nature, to become, in practice, primary. For example, if a hospital waiting list is very long, and the referral rate remains constant, or even increases over time, then a priority waiting list, used in conjunction with the normal list, causes the latter to stop, hold off supply, and assume the function of containing demands that will never be met, simply because the resources will never be available to meet them.

Secondary rationing may also have effects on the allocation of resources in other parts of the system. For example, those awaiting hospital admission may require the help of supportive services to maintain them until beds become available. So the patient with an arthritic hip, waiting for a hip replacement operation, will require G.P. services at least for the provision of pain killers.

Finally a thought on the value of rationing. G.P.s and social workers act as 'gatekeepers'[19, 20] to the expensive resources of the health and personal social services respectively. Here their function is to filter out from the cases of expressed demand not only those who require treatment by the professionals themselves, but also those who require access to the limited resources of, for example, the hospital and specialist services of the N.H.S., or places in residential homes. The cost of providing these facilities is greater than the rest of the total expenditure on the health and personal social services. Therefore, the outer layers of the service possess the characteristic of universality, but the inner sanctums of the health and personal social services function on a purely selective basis. It is apparent that, owing to limited supply, and professionally-judged needs exceeding supply this selectivity is necessary and consequently would seem to refute the idea that the principle of universality can never be applied. Consequently, rationing processes would seem to be the best solution to Titmuss' statement about the social services.[21]

> The real challenge resides in the question: what particular infrastructure of universalist services is needed in order to provide a framework of values and opportunity bases within and around which can be developed acceptable selective services.

As ·Parker[22] points out, waiting lists accomplish this by allowing universal access while accounting for the realities of the supply situation. But waiting lists or secondary rationing mechanisms are only one aspect of this. All rationing processes work as selective processes behind a cover of universal provision. Their evolution within the social services has made it possible to offer socially acceptable selective services within a universalist framework. However, these processes have evolved slowly and consequently, have never been questioned, and their effect on the efficiency and effectiveness of the provisions has never been evaluated. It is not that we should wish to do away with rationing, nor that we ever could, for it is the only solution to excess demand for free provision, but that some of the forms it can take would be better replaced by others. Random processes of 'losing' clients as they pass through the services or before they even reach them, may be efficient in terms of saving money, but are not effective in reaching those individuals for whom the service was originally intended. In 1972 Stevens[23] wrote, 'The word rationing has yet to break into the consciousness of most of us, as expressing one of the fundamental concepts upon which our social service society is based'. It would be safe to say that it has now broken in, and having recognized it, we must now begin to understand it.

The concern must be not whether but how services ration; which of the forms of rationing mentioned above are intolerable and which are acceptable. Open and formalized rationing methods involving universally accepted and utilized criteria as a basis for allocation necessitate the development of explicit principles of allocation. This is fundamental to the most taxing tasks of those responsible for welfare services, that of choosing priorities. To preserve the universalist framework of our welfare provision within the selectivist situation that the shortage of resources leaves us with, we must determine, by research and value judgement, where resources should be diverted. Failing this, there exists the strong possibility that universalism will vanish from our services altogether, or at least we will continue with the situation described by Pinker:[24]

'. . . in a range of social services suddenly committed to provide the best possible standards of provision the main consequence of this basic lack of research has been to bring universalism into disrepute.'

Notes and References

1. First appeared as an article in *Social Policy and Administration*, Vol. 13, No. 1, Spring 1979.
2. Ken Judge, *Rationing Social Services*, Heinemann, London, 1978, p. 142.
3. H. Dalton, *Principles of Public Finance*, Routledge and Kegan Paul, London, 1922 – reprinted 1964, p. 159.
4. A. C. Pigou, *Public Finance*, London, Macmillan, 1947, p. 25.
5. Kaim Caudle, *Comparative Social Policy*, Martin Robertson, 1973, p. 105.
6. J. M. Buchanan, *The Inconsistencies of the N.H.S.*, London, Institute of Economic Affairs, Occasional Paper 7, 1965.
7. Ken Judge, *op. cit.*, p. 133.
8. *Report of the Committee on Local Authority and Allied Personal Social Services*, Cmnd. 3703, July 1965.
9. Loewenstein, 'An Intake Room in Action in a Social Services Department'. *British Journal of Social Work*, Vol. 4, No. 2, pp. 115–41.
10. C. Gostick, 'The Intake Phenomenon'. *Social Work Today*, Vol. 8, No. 10, 7.12, 1976.

11. R. A. Parker, 'Social Administration and Scarcity', *Social Work Today*, April 1967.

12. B. Gilbert; *The Evolution of National Insurance in Great Britain*, Michael Joseph, p. 114.

13. A. Hunt, 'The Home Help Service in England and Wales'. H.M.S.O., 1970.

14. A. G. Stevens, 'Rationing in the Social Services', *The Welfare Offices*, 1972.

15. Cooper quotes from the D.H.S.S. 'We actually set aside a sum of money which we told the Hospital Boards should be spent on dialysis and we determined where it should be spent and how much should be spent'. M. Cooper, *Rationing Health Care*. Croom Helm, London, p. 92.

16. A. Rees, 'Access to the Personal Health and Welfare Services', *Social and Economic Administration*, January 1972.

17. T. R. Taylor, J. Aitchison, L. S. Parker and M. F. Moore, 'Individual Differences in Selecting Patients for Regular Haemodialysis', *British Medical Journal*, 17 May 1975.

18. A. Hall, *The Point of Entry*, Allen and Unwin, 1975.

19. R. G. S. Brown, *The Management of Welfare*, Fontana Public Administration, 1975, p. 129.

20. M. Cooper, *op. cit.*, p. 46.

21. R. Titmuss, *Commitment to Welfare*, George Allen and Unwin Ltd, London, 1968, p. 122.

22. R. Parker, *op. cit.*

23. Stevens, *op. cit.*

24. Pinker, *Social Theory and Social Policy*, Heinemann Educational Books Ltd, 1971, p. 188.

Notes on contributors

R. A. B. Leaper is Professor of Social Administration at the University of Exeter and Editor of *Social Policy and Administration* (formerly *Social and Economic Administration*). Author of *Community Work*, and of several international social policy studies.

Brian Showler is Lecturer in Social Administration, University of Hull. Director, youth and job entry research project for the Department of Employment. Editor, *International Journal of Social Economics*, and author of several publications on unemployment and policy including *The Public Employment Service*, Routledge, 1976.

David C. Stafford is a lecturer in Economics at the University of Exeter and is the Assistant Editor of *Social Policy and Administration*. He has published in various journals, mainly on public sector economies and financial institutions, and is author of *The Economics of Housing Policy*, Croom-Helm, 1978.

Michael H. Cooper is Professor of Economics at the University of Otago, New Zealand. Formerly Reader in Social Economics at the University of Exeter. Editor of *Social and Economic Administration*, 1967–73.

Michael Ryan Ph.D. holds the post of Lecturer in Social Policy at University College of Swansea. He has published articles on various aspects of medical care in Britain and the Soviet Union and is the author of two books: *The Work of the Welsh Hospital Board 1948–1974* and *The Organization of Soviet Medical Care*.

241

Alan Maynard is Senior Lecturer in Economics and Director of the Graduate Programme in Health Economics at the University of York.

Philip R. Jones, formerly a lecturer at Hull University, is at present Lecturer in Economics at Bath University. His research interests in the economic analysis of collective behaviour, for which the BMA stood as a case study, began at Leicester University where he was awarded a Ph.D. degree. He has also published articles within this general field of interest in the *Industrial Relations Journal* and the *British Journal of Political Science.*

A. C. Bebbington is a Research Fellow in the Statistics of the Personal Social Services, Personal Social Services Research Unit, University of Kent at Canterbury. He is currently collaborating in a research programme developing and examining the implications of indicators of need for the personal social services.

Ellie Scrivens is a graduate in Social Administration of the University of Exeter, since when she has worked as Tutorial Fellow at the University College of Cardiff. She is currently lecturer and research worker at the Community Medicine Department, St. Thomas's Hospital Medical School, University of London.

David Donnison is Professor of Town and Regional Planning at the University of Glasgow. He was chairman of the Supplementary Benefits Commission from 1975 to 1980. He was formerly Professor of Social Administration, London School of Economics.

Index

This index should be used in conjunction with the List of Contents. Where a whole chapter covers a particular topic it has not been thought necessary to give a reference to it in the index.